The key to social dynamics that Marx found in wealth and Freud in sex, Bertrand Russell finds, convincingly, in power. This brilliant study brings a new order of comprehension into the problems of human government. Russell analyses the forms that power can take, the limits and interactions of its different organs, the effectiveness of ideas and moral codes in buttressing or undermining power, and, finally, how power can, and must, be tamed today.

'Extremely penetrating analysis of human nature in politics.'

Sunday Times

'An acute and learned study of the ways in which men seek power.'

The Economist

BY BERTRAND RUSSELL

Power
A New Social Analysis

BERTRAND RUSSELL

LONDON

First published in Great Britain by George Allen & Unwin 1938
Reprinted six times
First published in paperback 1960
Reprinted five times
First published in Unwin® Paperbacks, an imprint of
Unwin Hyman Limited, 1975
Re-issued 1983
Reprinted 1985, 1988
Reprinted in 1992 by
Routledge
11 New Fetter Lane, London EC4P 4EE

A CIP record is available from the British Library

ISBN 0-415-09456-9

Printed in Great Britain in 9pt Plantin
by Cox & Wyman Ltd, Reading

Contents

Chapter 1

The Impulse
to Power

Between man and other animals there are various differences, some intellectual, some emotional. One of the chief emotional differences is that some human desires, unlike those of animals, are essentially boundless and incapable of complete satisfaction. The boa constrictor, when he has had his meal, sleeps until appetite revives; if other animals do not do likewise, it is because their meals are less adequate or because they fear enemies. The activities of animals, with few exceptions, are inspired by the primary needs of survival and reproduction, and do not exceed what these needs make imperative.

With men, the matter is different. A large proportion of the human race, it is true, is obliged to work so hard in obtaining necessaries that little energy is left over for other purposes; but those whose livelihood is assured do not, on that account, cease to be active. Xerxes had no lack of food or raiment or wives at the time when he embarked upon the Athenian expedition. Newton was certain of material comfort from the moment when he became a Fellow of Trinity, but it was after this that he wrote the *Principia*. St Francis and Ignatius Loyola had no need to found Orders to escape from want. These were eminent men, but the same characteristic, in varying degrees, is to be found in all but a small exceptionally sluggish minority. Mrs A, who is quite sure of her husband's success in business, and has no fear of the workhouse, likes to be better dressed than Mrs B, although she could escape the danger of pneumonia at much less expense. Both she and Mr A are pleased if he is knighted or elected to Parliament. In day-dreams there is no limit to imagined triumphs, and if they are regarded as possible, efforts will be made to achieve them.

Imagination is the goad that forces human beings into restless exertion after their primary needs have been satisfied. Most of us have known very few moments when we could have said:

> If it were now to die,
> 'Twere now to be most happy, for I fear
> My soul hath her content so absolute
> That not another comfort like to this
> Succeeds in unknown fate.

And in our rare moments of perfect happiness, it is natural, like Othello, to wish for death, since we know that contentment cannot last. What we need for lasting happiness is impossible for human beings: only God can have complete bliss, for His is 'the kingdom and the power and the glory'. Earthly kingdoms are limited by other kingdoms; earthly power is cut short by death; earthly glory, though we build pyramids or be 'married to immortal verse', fades with the passing of centuries. To those who have but little of power and glory, it may seem that a little more would satisfy them, but in this they are mistaken: these desires are insatiable and infinite, and only in the infinitude of God could they find repose.

While animals are content with existence and reproduction, men desire also to expand, and their desires in this respect are limited only by what imagination suggests as possible. Every man would like to be God, if it were possible; some few find it difficult to admit the impossibility. These are the men framed after the model of Milton's Satan, combining, like him, nobility with impiety. By 'impiety' I mean something not dependent upon theological beliefs: I mean refusal to admit the limitations of individual human power. This Titanic combination of nobility with impiety is most notable in the great conquerors, but some element of it is to be found in all men. It is this that makes social cooperation difficult, for each of us would like to conceive of it after the pattern of the cooperation between God and His worshippers, with ourself in the place of God. Hence competition, the need of compromise and government, the impulse to rebellion, with instability and periodic violence. And hence the need of morality to restrain anarchic self-assertion.

Of the infinite desires of man, the chief are the desires for power and glory. These are not identical, though closely allied: the Prime Minister has more power than glory, the King has more glory than power. As a rule, however, the easiest way to obtain glory is to obtain power; this is especially the case as regards the men who are active in relation to public events. The desire for glory, therefore, prompts, in the main, the same actions as are prompted by the desire for power, and the two motives may, for most practical purposes, be regarded as one.

The orthodox economists, as well as Marx, who in this respect agreed with them, were mistaken in supposing that economic self-interest could be taken as the fundamental motive in the social sciences. The desire for commodities, when separated from power and glory, is finite, and can be fully satisfied by a moderate competence. The really expensive desires are not dictated by a love of material comfort. Such commodities as a legislature rendered subservient by corruption, or a private picture gallery of Old Masters selected by experts, are sought for the sake of power or glory, not as affording comfortable places in which to sit. When a moderate degree of comfort is assured, both individuals and communities will pursue power rather than wealth: they may seek wealth as a means to power, or they may forgo an increase of wealth in order to secure an increase of power, but in the former case as in the latter their fundamental motive is not economic.

This error in orthodox and Marxist economics is not merely theoretical, but is of the greatest practical importance, and has caused some of the principal events of recent times to be misunderstood. It is only by realising that love of power is the cause of the activities that are important in social affairs that history, whether ancient or modern, can be rightly interpreted.

In the course of this book I shall be concerned to prove that the fundamental concept in social science is Power, in the same sense in which Energy is the fundamental concept in physics. Like energy, power has many forms, such as wealth, armaments, civil authority, influence on opinion. No one of these can be regarded as subordinate to any other, and there is no one form from which the others are derivative. The attempt to treat one form of power, say wealth, in isolation, can only be partially successful, just as the study of one form of energy will be defective at certain points, unless other forms are taken into account. Wealth may result from military power or from influence over opinion, just as either of these may result from wealth. The laws of social dynamics are laws which can only be stated in terms of power, not in terms of this or that form of power. In former times, military power was isolated, with the consequence that victory or defeat appeared to depend upon the accidental qualities of commanders. In our day, it is common to treat economic power as the source from which all other kinds are derived; this, I shall contend, is just as great an error as that of the purely military historians whom it has caused to seem out of date. Again, there are those who regard propaganda as the fundamental form of power. This is by no means a new opinion; it is embodied in such traditional sayings as *magna est veritas et prevalebit* and 'the blood of the martyrs is the seed of the Church'. It has about the same measure of truth and falsehood as the military view or the economic view. Propaganda, if it can create an almost unanimous opinion, can generate an irresistible power; but those who have military or economic control can, if they choose, use it for the purpose of propaganda. To revert to the analogy of physics: power, like energy, must be regarded as continually passing from any one of its forms into any other, and it should be the business of social science to seek the laws of such transformations. The attempt to isolate any one form of power, more especially, in our day, the economic form, has been, and still is, a source of errors of great practical importance.

There are many ways in which different societies differ in relation to power. They differ, to begin with, in the degree of power possessed by individuals or organisations; it is obvious, for example, that, owing to increase of organisation, the State has more power now than in former times. They differ, again, as regards the kind of organisation that is most influential: a military despotism, a theocracy, a plutocracy, are very dissimilar types. They differ, thirdly, through diversity in the ways of acquiring power: hereditary kingship produces one kind of eminent man, the qualities required of a great ecclesiastic produce another kind, democracy produces a third kind, and war a fourth.

Where no social institution, such as aristocracy or hereditary monarchy, exists to limit the number of men to whom power is possible, those who most desire power are, broadly speaking, those most likely to acquire it. It follows that, in a social system in which power is open to all, the posts which confer power will, as a rule, be occupied by men who differ from the average in being exceptionally power-loving. Love of power, though one of the strongest of human motives, is very unevenly distributed, and is limited by various other motives, such as love of ease, love of pleasure, and sometimes love of approval. It is disguised, among the more timid, as an impulse of submission to leadership, which increases the scope of the power-impulses of bold men. Those whose love of power is not strong are unlikely to have much influence on the course of events. The men who cause social changes are, as a rule, men who strongly desire to do so. Love of power, therefore, is a characteristic of the men who are causally important. We should, of course, be mistaken if we regarded it as the sole human motive, but this mistake would not lead us so much astray as might be expected in the search for causal laws in social science, since love of power is the chief motive producing the changes which social science has to study.

The laws of social dynamics are – so I shall contend – only capable of being stated in terms of power in its various forms. In order to discover these laws, it is necessary first to classify the forms of power, and then to review various important historical examples of the ways in which organisations and individuals have acquired control over men's lives.

I shall have, throughout, the twofold purpose of suggesting what I believe to be a more adequate analysis of social changes in general than that which has been taught by economists, and of making the present and the probable near future more intelligible than it can be to those whose imaginations are dominated by the eighteenth and nineteenth centuries. Those centuries were in many ways exceptional, and we seem to be now returning, in a number of respects, to forms of life and thought which were prevalent in earlier ages. To understand our own time and its needs, history, both ancient and mediaeval, is indispensable, for only so can we arrive at a form of possible progress not unduly dominated by the axioms of the nineteenth century.

Chapter 2

Leaders and Followers

The power impulse has two forms: explicit, in leaders; implicit, in their followers. When men willingly follow a leader, they do so with a view to the acquisition of power by the group which he commands, and they feel that his triumphs are theirs. Most men do not feel in themselves the competence required for leading their group to victory, and therefore seek out a captain who appears to possess the courage and sagacity necessary for the achievement of supremacy. Even in religion this impulse appears. Nietzsche accused Christianity of inculcating a slave-morality, but ultimate triumph was always the goal. 'Blessed are the meek, *for they shall inherit the earth.*' Or as a well-known hymn more explicitly states it:

> The Son of God goes forth to war,
>   A kingly crown to gain.
> His blood-red banner streams afar.
>   Who follows in His train?
>
> Who best can drink his cup of woe,
>   Triumphant over pain,
> Who patient bears his cross below,
>   He follows in His train.

If this is a slave-morality, then every soldier of fortune who endures the rigours of a campaign, and every rank-and-file politician who works hard at electioneering, is to be accounted a slave. But in fact, in every genuinely cooperative enterprise, the follower is psychologically no more a slave than the leader.

It is this that makes endurable the inequalities of power which organisation makes inevitable, and which tend to increase rather than diminish as society grows more organic.

Inequality in the distribution of power has always existed in human communities, as far back as our knowledge extends. This is due partly to external necessity, partly to causes which are to be found in human nature. Most collective enterprises are only possible if they are directed by some governing body. If a house is to be built, someone must decide on the plans; if the trains are to run on a railway, the timetable cannot be left to the caprices of engine-drivers; if a new road is to be constructed, someone must decide where it is to go. Even a democratically elected government is still a government, and therefore, on grounds that have nothing to do with psychology, there must, if collective enterprises are to succeed, be some men who give orders and others who obey them. But the fact that this is possible, and still more the fact that the actual inequalities of power exceed what is made necessary by technical causes, can only be explained in terms of individual psychology and physiology. Some men's characters lead them always to command, others always to obey; between these extremes lie the mass of average human beings, who like to command in some situations, but in others prefer to be subject to a leader.

Alder, in his book on *Understanding Human Nature*, distinguishes a submissive type and an imperious type. 'The servile individual', he says, 'lives by the rules and laws of others, and this type seeks out a servile position almost compulsively.' On the other hand, he continues, the imperious type, who asks: 'How can I be superior to everyone?' is found whenever a director is needed, and rises to the top in revolutions. Adler regards both types as undesirable, at any rate in their extreme forms, and he considers both as products of education. 'The greatest disadvantage of an authoritative education,' he says, 'lies in the fact that it gives the child an ideal of power, and shows him the pleasures which are connected with the possession of power.' Authoritative education, we may add, produces the slave type as well as the despotic type, since it leads to the feeling that the only possible relation between two human beings who cooperate is that in which one issues orders and the other obeys them.

Love of power, in various limited forms, is almost universal, but in its absolute form it is rare. A woman who enjoys power in the management of her house is likely to shrink from the sort of political power enjoyed by a Prime Minister; Abraham Lincoln, on the contrary, while not afraid to govern the United States, could not face civil war in the home. Perhaps Napoleon, if the *Bellerophon* had suffered shipwreck, would have tamely obeyed the orders of British officers as to escaping in boats. Men like power so long as they believe in their own competence to handle the business in question, but when they know themselves incompetent they prefer to follow a leader.

The impulse of submission, which is just as real and just as common as the impulse to command, has its roots in fear. The most unruly gang of children ever imagined will become completely amenable to the orders of a competent adult in an alarming situation, such as a fire; when the War came, the Pankhursts made their peace with Lloyd George. Whenever there is acute danger, the impulse of most people is to seek out Authority and submit to it; at such moments, few would dream of revolution. When war breaks out, people have similar feelings towards the Government.

Organisations may not be designed for the purpose of meeting dangers. Economic organisations in some cases, such as coal mines, involve dangers, but these are incidental, and if they were eliminated the organisations would flourish all the better. In general, meeting dangers is no part of the essential purpose of economic organisations, or of governmental organisations concerned with internal affairs. But lifeboats and fire-brigades, like armies and navies, are constructed for the purpose of meeting dangers. In a certain less immediate sense, this is also true of religious bodies, which exist in part to allay the metaphysical fears that are buried deep in our nature. If anyone feels inclined to question this, let him think of such hymns as:

> Rock of Ages, cleft for me,
> Let me hide myself in thee;

> Jesu, lover of my soul,
> Let me to thy bosom fly,
> While the gathering waters roll,
> While the tempest still is high.

In submission to the Divine Will there is a sense of ultimate safety, which has led to religious abasement in many monarchs who could not submit to any merely earthly being. All submissiveness is rooted in fear, whether the leader to whom we submit be human or divine.

It has become a commonplace that aggressiveness also often

has its roots in fear. I am inclined to think that this theory has been pushed too far. It is true of a certain kind of aggressiveness, for instance, that of D. H. Lawrence. But I greatly doubt whether the men who become pirate chiefs are those who are filled with retrospective terror of their fathers, or whether Napoleon, at Austerlitz, really felt that he was getting even with Madame Mère. I know nothing of the mother of Attila, but I rather suspect that she spoilt the little darling, who subsequently found the world irritating because it sometimes resisted his whims. The type of aggressiveness that is the outcome of timidity is not, I think, that which inspires great leaders; the great leaders, I should say, have an exceptional self-confidence which is not only on the surface, but penetrates deep into the subconscious.

The self-confidence necessary to a leader may be caused in various ways. Historically, one of the commonest has been a hereditary position of command. Read, for example, the speeches of Queen Elizabeth in moments of crisis: you will see the monarch over-riding the woman, convincing her and through her the nation, that she knows what must be done, as no mere commoner can hope to do. In her case, the interests of the nation and the sovereign were in harmony; that is why she was 'Good Queen Bess'. She could even praise her father without arousing indignation. There is no doubt that the habit of command makes it easier to bear responsibilities and to take quick decisions. A clan which follows its hereditary chief probably does better than if it chose its chief by lot. On the other hand, a body like the mediaeval church, which chose its chief on account of conspicuous merits, and usually after he had had considerable experience of important administrative posts, secured, on the average, considerably better results than were secured, in the same period, in hereditary monarchies.

Some of the ablest leaders known to history have arisen in revolutionary situations. Let us consider, for a moment, the qualities which brought success to Cromwell, Napoleon, and Lenin. All three, in difficult times, dominated their respective countries, and secured the willing service of able men who were not by nature submissive. All three had boundless courage and self-confidence, combined with what their colleagues considered sound judgement at difficult moments. Of the three, however, Cromwell and Lenin belonged to one type, and Napoleon to another. Cromwell and Lenin were men of profound religious faith, believing themselves to be the appointed ministers of a non-human purpose. Their power-impulses thus seemed to themselves indubitably righteous, and they cared little for those rewards of power – such as luxury and ease – which could not be harmonised with their identification with the cosmic purpose. This is specially true of Lenin, for Cromwell, in his last years, was conscious of falling into sin. Nevertheless, in both cases it was the combination of faith with great ability that gave them courage, and enabled them to inspire their followers with confidence in their leadership.

Napoleon, as opposed to Cromwell and Lenin, is the supreme example of the soldier of fortune. The Revolution suited him, since it made his opportunity, but otherwise he was indifferent to it. Though he gratified French patriotism and depended upon it, France, like the Revolution, was to him merely an opportunity; he had even, in his youth, toyed with the idea of fighting for Corsica against France. His success was due, not so much to any exceptional qualities of character, as to his technical skill in war: when other men would have been defeated, he was victorious. At crucial moments, such as the 18 Brumaire and Marengo, he depended upon others for success; but he had the spectacular gifts that enabled him to annex the achievements of his coadjutors. The French army was full of ambitious young men; it was Napoleon's cleverness, not his psychology, that gave him the power to succeed where the others failed. His belief in his star, which finally led to his downfall, was the effect of his victories, not their cause.

To come to our own day, Hitler must be classed, psychologically, with Cromwell and Lenin, Mussolini with Napoleon.

The soldier of fortune, or pirate chief, is a type of more importance in history than is thought by 'scientific' historians. Sometimes, like Napoleon, he succeeds in making himself the leader of bodies of men who have purposes that are in part impersonal: the French revolutionary armies conceived of themselves as the liberators of Europe, and were so regarded in Italy as well as by many in Western Germany, but Napoleon himself never brought any more liberation than seemed useful for his own career. Very often there is no pretence of impersonal aims. Alexander may have set to work to hellenise the East, but it is doubtful whether his Macedonians were much interested in this aspect of his campaigns. Roman generals, during the last hundred years of the Republic, were mainly out for cash, and secured their soldiers' loyalty by distributions of land and treasure. Cecil

Rhodes professed a mystical belief in the British Empire, but the belief yielded good dividends, and the troopers whom he engaged for the conquest of Matabeleland were offered nakedly pecuniary inducements. Organised greed, with little or no disguise, has played a very large part in the world's wars.

The ordinary quiet citizen, we said, is led largely by fear when he submits to a leader. But this can hardly be true of a gang of pirates, unless no more peaceable profession was open to them. When once the leader's authority is established, he may inspire fear in mutinous individuals; but until he is a leader, and is recognised as such by the majority, he is not in a position to inspire fear. To acquire the position of leader, he must excel in the qualities that confer authority: self-confidence, quick decision, and skill in deciding upon the right measures. Leadership is relative: Caesar could make Antony obey him, but no one else could. Most people feel that politics is difficult, and that they had better follow a leader – they feel this instinctively and unconsciously, as dogs do with their masters. If this were not the case, collective political action would scarcely be possible.

Thus love of power, as a motive, is limited by timidity, which also limits the desire for self-direction. Since power enables us to realise more of our desires than would otherwise be possible, and since it secures deference from others, it is natural to desire power except in so far as timidity interferes. This sort of timidity is lessened by the habit of responsibility, and accordingly responsibilities tend to increase the desire for power. Experience of cruelty and unfriendliness may operate in either direction: with those who are easily frightened it produces the wish to escape observation, while bolder spirits are stimulated to seek positions in which they can inflict cruelties rather than suffer them.

After anarchy, the natural first step is despotism, because this is facilitated by the instinctive mechanisms of domination and submission; this has been illustrated in the family, in the State, and in business. Equal cooperation is much more difficult than despotism, and much less in line with instinct. When men attempt equal cooperation, it is natural for each to strive for complete mastery, since the submissive impulses are not brought into play. It is almost necessary that all the parties concerned should acknowledge a common loyalty to something outside all of them. In China, family businesses often succeed because of Confucian loyalty to the family; but impersonal joint-stock companies are apt to prove unworkable, because no one has any compelling motive for honesty towards the other shareholders. Where there is government by deliberation, there must, for success, be a general respect for the law, or for the nation, or for some principle which all parties respect. The Society of Friends, when any doubtful matter has to be decided, do not take a vote and abide by the majority: they discuss until they arrive at 'the sense of the meeting', which used to be regarded as prompted by the Holy Spirit. In their case we are concerned with an unusually homogeneous community, but without some degree of homogeneity government by discussion is unworkable.

A sense of solidarity sufficient to make government by discussion possible can be generated without much difficulty in a family, such as the Fuggers or Rothschilds, in a small religious body such as the Quakers, in a barbarous tribe, or in a nation at war or in danger of war. But outside pressure is all but indispensable: the members of a group hang together for fear of hanging separately. A common peril is much the easiest way of producing homogeneity. This, however, affords no solution of the problem of power in the world as a whole. We wish to prevent the perils - e.g. war – which at present cause cohesion, but we do not wish to destroy social cooperation. This problem is difficult psychologically as well as politically, and if we may judge by analogy, it is likely to be solved, if at all, by an initial despotism of some one nation. Free cooperation among nations, accustomed as they are to the *liberum veto*, is as difficult as among the Polish aristocracy before the Partition. Extinction, in this case as in that, is likely to be thought preferable to common sense. Mankind need government, but in regions where anarchy has prevailed they will, at first, submit only to despotism. We must therefore seek first to secure government, even though despotic, and only when government has become habitual can we hope successfully to make it democratic. 'Absolute power is useful in building the organisation. More slow, but equally sure, is the development of social pressure demanding that the power shall be used for the benefit of all concerned. This pressure, constant in ecclesiastical and political history, is already making its appearance in the economic field.'[1]

I have spoken hitherto of those who command and those who obey, but there is a third type, namely, those who withdraw.

[1] A. A. Berle and G. C. Means, *The Modern Corporation and Private Property*, p. 353. They are speaking of industrial corporations.

There are men who have the courage to refuse submission without having the imperiousness that causes the wish to command. Such men do not fit readily into the social structure, and in one way or another they seek a refuge where they can enjoy a more or less solitary freedom. At times, men with this temperament have been of great historical importance; the early Christians and the American pioneers represent two species of the genus. Sometimes the refuge is mental, sometimes physical; sometimes it demands the complete solitude of a hermitage, sometimes the social solitude of a monastery. Among mental refugees are those who belong to obscure sects, those whose interests are absorbed by innocent fads, and those who occupy themselves with recondite and unimportant forms of erudition. Among physical refugees are men who seek the frontier of civilisation, and such explorers as Bates, the 'naturalist on the Amazon', who lived happily for fifteen years without other society than the Indians. Something of the hermit's temper is an essential element in many forms of excellence, since it enables men to resist the lure of popularity, to pursue important work in spite of general indifference or hostility, and to arrive at opinions which are opposed to prevalent errors.

Of those who withdraw, some are not genuinely indifferent to power, but only unable to obtain it by the usual methods. Such men may become saints or heresiarchs, founders of monastic orders or of new schools in art or literature. They attach to themselves as disciples people who combine a love of submission with an impulse to revolt; the latter prevents orthodoxy, while the former leads to uncritical adoption of the new tenets. Tolstoy and his followers illustrate this pattern. The genuine solitary is quite different. A perfect example of this type is the melancholy Jacques, who shares exile with the good Duke because it is exile; and afterwards remains in the forest with the bad Duke rather than return to Court. Many American pioneers, after suffering long hardship and privation, sold their farms and moved further West as soon as civilisation caught up with them. For men of this temperament, the world affords fewer and fewer opportunities. Some drift into crime, some into a morose and anti-social philosophy. Too much contact with their fellow-men produces misanthropy, which, when solitude is unattainable, turns naturally towards violence.

Among the timid, organisation is promoted, not only by submission to a leader, but by the reassurance which is felt in being

one of a crowd who all feel alike. In an enthusiastic public meeting, with whose purpose one is in sympathy, there is a sense of
exaltation, combined with warmth and safety: the emotion which
is shared grows more and more intense until it crowds out all
other feelings except an exultant sense of power produced by the
multiplication of the *ego*. Collective excitement is a delicious
intoxication, in which sanity, humanity, and even self-preservation are easily forgotten, and in which atrocious massacres
and heroic martyrdom are equally possible. This kind of intoxication, like others, is hard to resist when its delights have once
been experienced, but leads in the end to apathy and weariness,
and to the need for a stronger and stronger stimulus if the former
fervour is to be reproduced.

Although a leader is not essential to this emotion, which can be
produced by music, and by some exciting event which is seen by
a crowd, the words of an orator are the easiest and most usual
method of inducing it. The pleasure of collective excitement is,
therefore, an important element in the power of leaders. The
leader need not share in the feelings which he arouses; he may
say to himself, like Shakespeare's Antony:

> Now let it work: mischief, thou art afoot,
> Take thou what course thou wilt!

But the leader is hardly likely to be successful unless he enjoys
his power over his followers. He will therefore be led to a prefer-
ence for the kind of situation, and the kind of mob, that makes
his success easy. The best situation is one in which there is a
danger sufficiently serious to make men feel brave in combating
it, but not so terrifying as to make fear predominant – such a
situation, for example, as the outbreak of war against an enemy
who is thought formidable but not invincible. A skilful orator,
when he wishes to stimulate warlike feeling, produces in his audi-
ence two layers of belief: a superficial layer, in which the power
of the enemy is magnified so as to make great courage seem
necessary, and a deeper layer, in which there is a firm conviction
of victory. Both are embodied in such a slogan as 'right will
prevail over might'.

The kind of mob that the orator will desire is one more given
to emotion than to reflection, one filled with fears and consequent hatreds, one impatient of slow and gradual methods, and
at once exasperated and hopeful. The orator, if he is not a complete cynic, will acquire a set of beliefs that justify his activities.

He will think that feeling is a better guide than reason, that our opinions should be formed with the blood rather than the brain, that the best elements in human life are collective rather than individual. If he controls education, he will make it consist of an alternation of drill and collective intoxication, while knowledge and judgement will be left to the cold devotees of inhuman science.

Power-loving individuals, however, are not all of the orator type. There are men of quite a different kind, whose love of power has been fed by control over mechanism. Take, for example, Bruno Mussolini's account of his exploits from the air in the Abyssinian war:

'We had to set fire to the wooded hills, to the fields and little villages. ... It was all most diverting. ... The bombs hardly touched the earth before they burst out into white smoke and an enormous flame and the dry grass began to burn. I thought of the animals: God, how they ran ... After the bomb-racks were emptied I began throwing bombs by hand. ... It was most amusing: a big Zariba surrounded by tall trees was not easy to hit. I had to aim carefully at the straw roof and only succeeded at the third shot. The wretches who were inside, seeing their roof burning, jumped out and ran off like mad.

'Surrounded by a circle of fire about five thousand Abyssinians came to a sticky end. It was like hell.'

While the orator needs much intuitive psychology for his success, the aviator of Bruno Mussolini's type can get his pleasure with no more psychology than is involved in knowing that it is unpleasant to burn to death. The orator is an ancient type; the man whose power is based on mechanism is modern. Not wholly: read, for example, how Carthaginian elephants were used, at the end of the first Punic War, to trample mutinous mercenaries to death, where the psychology, though not the science, is the same as Bruno Mussolini's.[1] But speaking comparatively, mechanical power is more characteristic of our age than of any previous time.

The psychology of the oligarch who depends upon mechanical power is not, as yet, anywhere fully developed. It is, however, an imminent possibility, and quantitatively, though not qualitatively, quite new. It would now be feasible for a technically

[1] Diodorus Siculus, Bk. XXV (fragment). See Flaubert's *Salammbo*.

trained oligarchy, by controlling aeroplanes, navies, power stations, motor transport, and so on, to establish a dictatorship demanding almost no conciliation of subjects. The empire of Laputa was maintained by its power of interposing itself between the sun and a rebellious province; something almost equally drastic would be possible for a union of scientific technologists. They could starve a recalcitrant region, and deprive it of light and heat and electrical power after encouraging dependence on these sources of comfort; they could flood it with poison gas or with bacteria. Resistance would be utterly hopeless. And the men in control, having been trained on mechanism, would view human material as they had learnt to view their own machines, as something unfeeling governed by laws which the manipulator can operate to his advantage. Such a régime would be characterised by a cold inhumanity surpassing anything known in previous tyrannies.

Power over men, not power over matter, is my theme in this book; but it is possible to establish a technicological power over men which is based upon power over matter. Those who have the habit of controlling powerful mechanisms, and through this control have acquired power over human beings, may be expected to have an imaginative outlook towards their subjects which will be completely different from that of men who depend upon persuasion, however dishonest. Most of us have, at some time, wantonly disturbed an ants' nest, and watched with mild amusement the scurrying confusion that resulted. Looking down from the top of a sky-scraper on the traffic of New York, the human beings below cease to seem human, and acquire a faint absurdity. If one were armed, like Jove, with a thunderbolt, there would be a temptation to hurl it into the crowd, from the same motive as in the case of the ants' nest. This was evidently Bruno Mussolini's feeling, as he looked down upon the Abyssinians from his aeroplane. Imagine a scientific government which, from fear of assassination, lives always in aeroplanes, except for occasional descents on to landing stages on the summits of high towers or rafts on the sea. Is it likely that such a government will have any profound concern for the happiness of its subjects? Is it not, on the contrary, practically certain that it will view them, when all goes well, in the impersonal manner in which it views its machines, but that, when anything happens to suggest that after all they are not machines, it will feel the cold rage of men whose axioms are questioned by underlings, and will exterminate resistance in whatever manner involves least trouble?

All this, the reader may think, is mere unnecessary nightmare. I wish I could share this view. Mechanical power, I am convinced, tends to generate a new mentality, which makes it more important than in any former age to find ways of controlling governments. Democracy may have become more difficult owing to technical developments, but it has also become more important. The man who has vast mechanical power at his command is likely, if uncontrolled, to feel himself a god – not a Christian God of Love, but a pagan Thor or Vulcan.

Leopardi describes what volcanic action has achieved on the slopes of Vesuvius:

> These lands that now are strewn
> With sterilising cinders, and embossed
> With lava frozen to stone,
> That echoes to the lonely pilgrim's foot;
> Where nestling in the sun the snake lies coiled,
> And where in some cleft
> In cavernous rocks the rabbit hurries home –
> Here once were happy farms,
> And tilth, and yellowing harvests, and the sound
> Of lowing herds; here too
> Gardens and palaces:
> Retreats dear to the leisure
> Of powerful lords; and here were famous towns,
> Which the implacable mountain, thundering forth
> Molten streams from its fiery mouth, destroyed
> With all their habitants. Now all around
> Lies crushed 'neath one vast ruin.[1]

These results can now be achieved by men. They have been achieved at Guernica; perhaps before long they will be achieved where as yet London stands. What good is to be expected of an oligarchy which will have climbed to dominion through such destruction? And if it were Berlin and Rome, not London and Paris, that were destroyed by the thunderbolts of the new gods, could any humanity survive in the destroyers after such a deed?

[1] Questi campi cosparsi
Di ceneri infeconde, e ricoperti
Dall' impietrata lava,
Che sotto i passi al peregrin risona;
Dove s'annida e si contorce al sole
La serpe, e dove al noto

Would not those who had human feelings to begin with be driven mad by suppressed pity, and become even worse than those who had no need of suppressing their compassion?

In former days, men sold themselves to the Devil to acquire magical powers. Nowadays they acquire these powers from science, and find themselves compelled to become devils. There is no hope for the world unless power can be tamed, and brought into the service, not of this or that group of fanatical tyrants, but of the whole human race, white and yellow and black, fascist and communist and democrat; for science has made it inevitable that all must live or all must die.

> Cavernoso covil torna il coniglio;
> Fur liete ville e colti,
> E biondeggiàr di spiche, e risonaro
> Di muggito d'armenti;
> Fur giardini e palagi,
> Agli ozi de' potenti
> Gradito ospizio, e fur città famose,
> Che coi torrenti suoi l' altero monte
> Dall' ignea bocco fulminando oppresse
> Con gli abitanti insieme. Or tutto intorno
> Una ruina involve.

I owe the above translation to the kindness of my friend, Mr R. C. Trevelyan.

Chapter 3

The Forms of Power

Power may be defined as the production of intended effects. It is thus a quantitative concept: given two men with similar desires, if one achieves all the desires that the other achieves, and also others, he has more power than the other. But there is no exact means of comparing the power of two men of whom one can achieve one group of desires, and another another; e.g. given two artists of whom each wishes to paint good pictures and become rich, and of whom one succeeds in painting good pictures and the other in becoming rich, there is no way of estimating which has the more power. Nevertheless, it is easy to say, roughly, that A has more power than B, if A achieves many intended effects and B only a few.

There are various ways of classifying the forms of power, each of which has its utility. In the first place, there is power over human beings and power over dead matter or non-human forms of life. I shall be concerned mainly with power over human beings, but it will be necessary to remember that the chief cause of change in the modern world is the increased power over matter that we owe to science.

Power over human beings may be classified by the manner of influencing individuals, or by the type of organisation involved.

An individual may be influenced: A. By direct physical power over his body, e.g. when he is imprisoned or killed; B. By rewards and punishments as inducements, e.g. in giving or withholding employment; C. By influence on opinion, i.e. propaganda in its broadest sense. Under this last head I should include the opportunity for creating desired habits in others, e.g. by military drill, the only difference being that in such cases action follows without any such mental intermediary as could be called opinion.

These forms of power are most nakedly and simply displayed in our dealings with animals, where disguises and pretences are not thought necessary. When a pig with a rope round its middle is hoisted squealing into a ship, it is subject to direct physical power over its body. On the other hand, when the proverbial donkey follows the proverbial carrot, we induce him to act as we wish by persuading him that it is to his interest to do so. Intermediate between these two cases is that of performing animals, in whom habits have been formed by rewards and punishments; also, in a different way, that of sheep induced to embark on a ship, when the leader has to be dragged across the gangway by force, and the rest then follow willingly.

All these forms of power are exemplified among human beings.

The case of the pig illustrates military and police power.

The donkey with the carrot typifies the power of propaganda.

Performing animals show the power of 'education'.

The sheep following their unwilling leader are illustrative of party politics, whenever, as is usual, a revered leader is in bondage to a clique or to party bosses.

Let us apply these Aesopian analogies to the rise of Hitler. The carrot was the Nazi programme (involving, e.g. the abolition of interest); the donkey was the lower middle class. The sheep and their leader were the Social Democrats and Hindenburg. The pigs (only so far as their misfortunes are concerned) were the victims in concentration camps, and the performing animals are the millions who make the Nazi salute.

The most important organisations are approximately distinguishable by the kind of power that they exert. The army and the police exercise coërcive power over the body; economic organisations, in the main, use rewards and punishments as incentives and deterrents; schools, churches, and political parties aim at influencing opinion. But these distinctions are not very clearcut, since every organisation uses other forms of power in addition to the one which is most characteristic.

The power of the Law will illustrate these complexities. The ultimate power of the Law is the coercive power of the State. It is the characteristic of civilised communities that direct physical coercion is (with some limitations) the prerogative of the State, and the Law is a set of rules according to which the State exercises this prerogative in dealing with its own citizens. But the Law uses punishment, not only for the purpose of making undesired actions physically impossible, but also as an inducement; a fine, for example, does not make an action impossible, but only unattractive. Moreover – and this is a much more important matter – the Law is almost powerless when it is not supported by public sentiment, as might be seen in the United States during Prohibition, or in Ireland in the eighties, when moonlighters had the sympathy of a majority of the population. Law, therefore, as an effective force, depends upon opinion and sentiment even more than upon the powers of the police. The degree of feeling in favour of Law is one of the most important characteristics of a community.

This brings us to a very necessary distinction, between traditional power and newly acquired power. Traditional power has on its side the force of habit; it does not have to justify itself at every moment, nor to prove continually that no opposition is strong enough to overthrow it. Moreover it is almost invariably associated with religious or quasi-religious beliefs purporting to show that resistance is wicked. It can, accordingly, rely upon public opinion to a much greater degree than is possible for revolutionary or usurped power. This has two more or less opposite consequences: on the one hand, traditional power, since it feels secure, is not on the look-out for traitors, and is likely to avoid much active political tyranny; on the other hand, where ancient institutions persist, the injustices to which holders of power are always prone have the sanction of immemorial custom, and can therefore be more glaring than would be possible under a new form of government which hoped to win popular support. The reign of terror in France illustrates the revolutionary kind of tyranny, the *corvée* the traditional kind.

Power not based on tradition or assent I call 'naked' power. Its characteristics differ greatly from those of traditional power. And where traditional power persists, the character of the régime depends, to an almost unlimited extent, upon its feeling of security or insecurity.

Naked power is usually military, and may take the form either of internal tyranny or of foreign conquest. Its importance, especially in the latter form, is very great indeed – greater, I think, than many modern 'scientific' historians are willing to admit. Alexander the Great and Julius Caesar altered the whole course of history by their battles. But for the former, the Gospels would not have been written in Greek, and Christianity could not have been preached throughout the Roman Empire. But for the latter, the French would not speak a language derived from Latin, and the Catholic Church could scarcely have existed. The military superiority of the white man to the American Indian is an even more undeniable example of the power of the sword. Conquest by force of arms has had more to do with the spread of civilisation than any other single agency. Nevertheless, military power is, in most cases, based upon some other form of power, such as wealth, or technical knowledge, or fanaticism. I do not suggest that this is always the case; for example, in the War of the Spanish Succession Marlborough's genius was essential to the result. But this is to be regarded as an exception to the general rule.

When a traditional form of power comes to an end, it may be succeeded, not by naked power, but by a revolutionary authority commanding the willing assent of the majority or a large minority of the population. So it was, for example, in America in the War of Independence. Washington's authority had none of the characteristics of naked power. Similarly, in the Reformation, new Churches were established to take the place of the Catholic Church, and their success was due much more to assent than to force. A revolutionary authority, if it is to succeed in establishing itself without much use of naked power, requires much more vigorous and active popular support than is needed by a traditional authority. When the Chinese Republic was proclaimed in 1911, the men of foreign education decreed a parliamentary Constitution, but the public was apathetic, and the régime quickly became one of naked power under warring Tuchuns (military governors). Such unity as was afterwards achieved by the Kuo-Min-Tang depended on nationalism, not parliamentarianism. The same sort of thing has happened frequently in Latin America. In all these cases, the authority of Parliament, if it had had sufficient popular support to succeed, would have been revolutionary; but the purely military power which was in fact victorious was naked.

The distinction between traditional, revolutionary, and naked power is psychological. I do not call power traditional merely because it has ancient forms: it must also command respect which is partly due to custom. As this respect decays, traditional power gradually passes over into naked power. The process was to be seen in Russia in the gradual growth of the revolutionary movement up to the moment of its victory in 1917.

I call power revolutionary when it depends upon a large group united by a new creed, programme, or sentiment, such as Protestantism, Communism, or desire for national independence. I call power naked when it results merely from the power-loving impulses of individuals or groups, and wins from its subjects only submission through fear, not active cooperation. It will be seen that the nakedness of power is a matter of degree. In a democratic country, the power of the government is not naked in relation to opposing political parties, but is naked in relation to a convinced anarchist. Similarly, where persecution exists, the power of the Church is naked in relation to heretics, but not in relation to orthodox sinners.

Another division of our subject is between the power of organisations and the power of individuals. The way in which an organisation acquires power is one thing, and the way in which an individual acquires power within an organisation is quite another. The two are, of course, interrelated: if you wish to be Prime Minister, you must acquire power in your Party, and your Party must acquire power in the nation. But if you had lived before the decay of the hereditary principle, you would have had to be the heir of a king in order to acquire political control of a nation; this would, however, not have enabled you to conquer other nations, for which you would have needed qualities that kings' sons often lack. In the present age, a similar situation still exists in the economic sphere, where the plutocracy is largely hereditary. Consider the two hundred plutocratic families in France against whom French Socialists agitate. But dynasties among the plutocracy have not the same degree of permanence as they formerly had on thrones, because they have failed to cause the widespread acceptance of the doctrine of Divine Right. No one thinks it impious for a rising financial magnate to impoverish one who is the son of his father, provided it is done according to the rules and without introducing subversive innovations.

Different types of organisation bring different types of individuals to the top, and so do different states of society. An age appears in history through its prominent individuals, and derives its apparent character from the character of these men. As the qualities required for achieving prominence change, so the prominent men change. It is to be presumed that there were men like Lenin in the twelfth century, and that there are men like Richard Coeur de Lion at the present time; but history does not know of them. Let us consider for a moment the kinds of individuals produced by different types of power.

Hereditary power has given rise to our notion of a 'gentleman'. This is a somewhat degenerate form of a conception which has a long history, from magic properties of chiefs, through the divinity of kings, to knightly chivalry and the blue-blooded aristocrat. The qualities which are admired, where power is hereditary, are such as result from leisure and unquestioned superiority. Where power is aristocratic rather than monarchical, the best manners include courteous behaviour towards equals as an addition to bland self-assertion in dealing with inferiors. But whatever the prevalent conception of manners may be, it is only where power is (or lately was) hereditary that men will be judged by their manners. The *bourgeois gentilhomme* is only laughable when he intrudes into a society of men and women who have never had anything better to do than study social niceties. What survives in the way of admiration of the 'gentleman' depends upon inherited wealth, and must rapidly disappear if economic as well as political power ceases to pass from father to son.

A very different type of character comes to the fore where power is achieved through learning or wisdom, real or supposed. The two most important examples of this form of power are traditional China and the Catholic Church. There is less of it in the modern world than there has been at most times in the past; apart from the Church, in England, very little of this type of power remains. Oddly enough, the power of what passes for learning is greatest in the most savage communities, and steadily decreases as civilisation advances. When I say 'learning' I include, of course, reputed learning, such as that of magicians and medicine men. Twenty years of study are required in order to obtain a Doctor's Degree at the University of Lhasa, which is necessary for all the higher posts except that of Dalai Lama. This position is much what it was in Europe in the year 1000, when Pope Silvester II was reputed a magician because he read books, and was consequently able to increase the power of the Church by inspiring metaphysical terrors.

The intellectual, as we know him, is a spiritual descendant of the priest; but the spread of education has robbed him of power. The power of the intellectual depends upon superstition: reverence for a traditional incantation or a sacred book. Of these, something survives in English-speaking countries, as is seen in the English attitude to the Coronation Service and the American reverence for the Constitution: accordingly, the Archbishop of Canterbury and the Supreme Court Judges still have some of the traditional power of learned men. But this is only a pale ghost of the power of Egyptian priests or Chinese Confucian scholars.

While the typical virtue of the gentleman is honour, that of the man who achieves power through learning is wisdom. To gain a reputation for wisdom a man must seem to have a store of recondite knowledge, a mastery over his passions, and a long experience of the ways of men. Age alone is thought to give something of these qualities; hence 'presbyter', 'seigneur', 'alderman', and 'elder' are terms of respect. A Chinese beggar addresses passersby as 'great old sire'. But where the power of wise men is organised, there is a corporation of priests or literati, among whom all wisdom is held to be concentrated. The sage is a very different type of character from the knightly warrior, and produces, where he rules, a very different society. China and Japan illustrate the contrast.

We have already noted the curious fact that, although knowledge plays a larger part in civilisation now than at any former time, there has not been any corresponding growth of power among those who possess the new knowledge. Although the electrician and the telephone man do strange things that minister to our comfort (or discomfort), we do not regard them as medicinemen, or imagine that they can cause thunderstorms if we annoy them. The reason for this is that scientific knowledge, though difficult, is not mysterious, but open to all who care to take the necessary trouble. The modern intellectual, therefore, inspires no awe, but remains a mere employee; except in a few cases, such as the Archbishop of Canterbury, he has failed to inherit the glamour which gave power to his predecessors.

The truth is that the respect accorded to men of learning was never bestowed for genuine knowledge, but for the supposed possession of magical powers. Science, in giving some real acquaintance with natural processes, has destroyed the belief in magic, and therefore the respect for the intellectual. Thus it has come about that, while men of science are the fundamental cause of the features which distinguish our time from former ages, and have, through their discoveries and inventions, an immeasurable influence upon the course of events, they have not, as individuals, as great a reputation for wisdom as may be enjoyed in India by a naked fakir or in Melanesia by a medicine-man. The intellectuals, finding their prestige slipping from them as a result of their own activities, become dissatisfied with the modern world. Those in whom the dissatisfaction is least take to Communism; those in whom it goes deeper shut themselves up in their ivory tower.

The growth of large economic organisations has produced a

new type of powerful individual: the 'executive', as he is called in America. The typical 'executive' impresses others as a man of rapid decisions, quick insight into character, and iron will; he must have a firm jaw, tightly closed lips, and a habit of brief and incisive speech. He must be able to inspire respect in equals, and confidence in subordinates who are by no means nonentities. He must combine the qualities of a great general and a great diplomatist: ruthlessness in battle, but a capacity for skilful concession in negotiation. It is by such qualities that men acquire control of important economic organisations.

Political power, in a democracy, tends to belong to men of a type which differs considerably from the three that we have considered hitherto. A politician, if he is to succeed, must be able to win the confidence of his machine, and then to arouse some degree of enthusiasm in a majority of the electorate. The qualities required for these two stages on the road to power are by no means identical, and many men possess the one without the other. Candidates for the Presidency in the United States are not infrequently men who cannot stir the imagination of the general public, though they possess the art of ingratiating themselves with party managers. Such men are, as a rule, defeated, but the party managers do not foresee their defeat. Sometimes, however, the machine is able to secure the victory of a man without 'magnetism'; in such cases, it dominates him after his election, and he never achieves real power. Sometimes, on the contrary, a man is able to create his own machine; Napoleon III, Mussolini, and Hitler are examples of this. More commonly, a really successful politician, though he uses an already existing machine, is able ultimately to dominate it and make it subservient to his will.

The qualities which make a successful politician in a democracy vary according to the character of the times; they are not the same in quiet times as they are during war or revolution. In quiet times, a man may succeed by giving an impression of solidity and sound judgement, but in times of excitement something more is needed. At such times, it is necessary to be an impressive speaker – not necessarily eloquent in the conventional sense, for Robespierre and Lenin were not eloquent, but determined, passionate, and bold. The passion may be cold and controlled, but must exist and be felt. In excited times, a politician needs no power of reasoning, no apprehension of impersonal facts, and no shred of wisdom. What he must have is the capacity of persuading the multitude that what they passionately desire is attainable, and that he, through his ruthless determination, is the man to attain it.

The most successful democratic politicians are those who succeed in abolishing democracy and becoming dictators. This, of course, is only possible in certain circumstances; no one could have achieved it in nineteenth-century England. But when it is possible, it requires only a high degree of the same qualities as are required by democratic politicians in general, at any rate in excited times. Lenin, Mussolini, and Hitler owed their rise to democracy.

When once a dictatorship has been established, the qualities by which a man succeeds a dead dictator are totally different from those by which the dictatorship was originally created. Wire-pulling, intrigue, and Court favour are the most important methods when heredity is discarded. For this reason, a dictatorship is sure to change its character very considerably after the death of its founder. And since the qualities by which a man succeeds to a dictatorship are less generally impressive than those by which the régime was created, there is a likelihood of instability, palace revolutions, and ultimate reversion to some different system. It is hoped, however, that modern methods of propaganda may successfully counteract this tendency, by creating popularity for the Head of the State without the need for any display of popular qualities on his part. How far such methods can succeed it is as yet impossible to say.

There is one form of the power of individuals which we have not yet considered, namely, power behind the scenes: the power of courtiers, intriguers, spies, and wire-pullers. In every large organisation, where the men in control have considerable power, there are other less prominent men (or women) who acquire influence over the leaders by personal methods. Wire-pullers and party bosses belong to the same type, though their technique is different. They put their friends, quietly, into key positions, and so, in time, control the organisation. In a dictatorship which is not hereditary, such men may hope to succeed to the dictator when he dies; but in general they prefer not to take the front of the stage. They are men who love power more than glory; often they are socially timid. Sometimes, like eunuchs in Oriental monarchies, or kings' mistresses elsewhere, they are, for one reason or another, debarred from titular leadership. Their influence is greatest where nominal power is hereditary, and least where it is the reward of personal skill and energy. Such men, however, even in the most modern forms of government, inevitably have considerable power in those departments which average men consider mysterious. Of these the most important, in our time, are currency and foreign policy. In the time of the Kaiser William II, Baron Holstein (permanent Head of the German Foreign Office) had immense power, although he made no public appearances. How great is the power of the permanent officials in the British Foreign Office at the present day, it is impossible for us to know; the necessary documents may become known to our children. The qualities required for power behind the scenes are very different from those required for all other kinds, and as a rule, though not always, they are undesirable qualities. A system which accords much power to the courtier or the wire-puller is, therefore, in general not a system likely to promote the general welfare.

Chapter 4

Priestly Power

In this chapter and the next I propose to consider the two forms of traditional power which have had most importance in past times, namely, priestly amd kingly authority. Both are now somewhat in eclipse, and, although it would be rash to assume that neither will revive, their decline, whether permanent or temporary, makes it possible to study both institutions with a completeness which is not attainable where still vigorous forms of power are concerned.

Priests and kings, though in a rudimentary form, exist among the most primitive societies known to anthropologists. Sometimes one person combines the functions of both. This occurs not only among savages, but in highly civilised States. Augustus, in Rome, was Pontifex Maximus, and in the provinces was a god. The Caliph was the head of the Mohammedan religion as well as of the State. The Mikado, at the present day, has a similar position in the Shinto religion. There has been a strong tendency for kings to lose their secular functions owing to their sacredness, and thus to develop into priests. Nevertheless, at most times and places, the distinction between priest and king has been obvious and definite.

The most primitive form of priest is the medicine-man, whose powers are of two kinds, which anthropologists distinguish as religious and magical. Religious powers depend upon the assistance of superhuman beings, while magical powers are supposed to be natural. For our purposes, however, this distinction is not important. What is important is that the medicine-man, whether by magic or by religion, is thought to be able to do good or harm to other people, and that his powers are not shared by all and sundry. A certain amount of magic, it is thought, may be practised by the laity, but the medicine-man's magic is stronger. When a man falls ill or meets with an accident, it is usually due to the malevolent magic of an enemy, but the medicine-man knows of ways by which the evil spell can be removed. Thus in

Duke of York Island the medicine-man, after discovering by divination the source of the patient's illness, takes a packet of lime and recites a magical formula:

'Lime of exorcism. I banish the octopus; I banish the *teo* snake; I banish the spirit of the *Ingiet* (a secret society); I banish the crab; I banish the water snake; I banish the *balivo* snake; I banish the python; I banish the *kaia* dog. Lime of exorcism. I banish the slimy fluid; I banish the *kete* creeping plant; I banish *To Pilana*; I banish *To Wuwu-Tawur*; I banish *Tumbal*. One has sunk them right down deep in the sea. Vapour shall arise to hold them afar; clouds shall arise to hold them afar; darkness shall reign to hold them afar; they shall betake themselves to the depths of the sea.'[1]

It must not be supposed that this formula is usually ineffective. Savages are much more subject to suggestion than civilised men, and therefore their diseases can very often be both caused and cured by this agency.

In most parts of Melanesia, according to Rivers, the man who cures diseases is the sorcerer or priest. There is not apparently, in these regions, a very clear differentiation between medicine-men and others, and some of the simpler remedies may be used by anyone. But

'Those who combine the practice of medicine with that of magical or religious rites usually acquire their art by a special process, either of initiation or instruction, and in Melanesia such knowledge has always to be purchased. The most complete instruction in any branch of medico-magical or medico-religious art is of no avail to the pupil unless money has passed from himself to his instructor.'[2]

From such beginnings it is easy to imagine the development of a definite priestly caste, with a monopoly of the more important magical and religious powers, and consequently with great authority over the community. In Egypt and Babylonia their power proved itself greater that that of the king when the two came into conflict. They defeated the 'atheist' Pharaoh Ikhnaton,[3] and they seem to have treacherously helped Cyrus to

[1] W. H. R. Rivers, *Medicine, Magic, and Religion*, p. 16.
[2] Ibid., p. 44.
[3] Or Akhnaton.

conquer Babylon because their native king showed a tendency to anti-clericalism.

Greece and Rome were peculiar in antiquity owing to their almost complete freedom from priestly power. In Greece, such religious power as existed was chiefly concentrated in the oracles, especially Delphi, where the Pythoness was supposed to fall into a trance and give answers inspired by Apollo. It was, however, well known by the time of Herodotus that the oracle could be bribed. Both Herodotus and Aristotle relate that the Alcmaeonidae, an important Athenian family exiled by Peisistratus (died 527 B.C.), corruptly procured the support of Delphi against his sons. What Herodotus says is curious: the Alcmaeonidae, he tells us, 'if we may believe the Athenians, persuaded the Pythoness by a bribe to tell the Spartans, whenever any of them came to consult the oracle, either on their own private affairs or on the business of the State, that they must free Athens (from the tyranny of the Peisistratidae). So the Lacedaemonians, when they found no answer ever returned to them but this, sent at last Anchimolius, the son of Aster – a man of note among their citizens – at the head of an army against Athens, with orders to drive out the Peisistratidae, albeit they were bound to them by the closest ties of friendship. For they esteemed the things of heaven more highly than the things of men'.[1]

Though Anchimolius was defeated, a subsequent larger expedition was successful, the Alcmaeonidae and the other exiles recovered power, and Athens again enjoyed what was called 'freedom'.

There are several remarkable features in this narrative. Herodotus is a pious man, completely devoid of cynicism, and he thinks well of the Spartans for listening to the oracle. But he prefers Athens to Sparta, and in Athenian affairs he is against the Peisistratidae. Nevertheless it is the Athenians whom he cites as authorities for the bribery, and no punishment befell the successful party or the Pythoness for their impiety.[2] The Alcmaeonidae were still prominent in the days of Herodotus; in fact the most famous of them was his contemporary Pericles.

Aristotle, in his book on the Constitution of Athens, represents the transaction in an even more discreditable light. The temple at Delphi had been destroyed by fire in 548 B.C., and funds for the

[1] Bk. V, Ch. 63. Rawlinson's translation.
[2] Herodotus gives another instance of corruption of the Pythoness, Bk. VI, Ch. 66.

purpose of rebuilding it were collected throughout Greece by the Alcmaeonidae. They – so Aristotle avers – used part of the funds to bribe the Pythoness, and made the expenditure of the rest conditional on the overthrow of Hippias, son of Peisistratus, by which means Apollo was won over to their side.

In spite of such scandals, control of the oracle at Delphi remained a matter of such political importance as to be the cause of a serious war, called, on account of its connection with religion, the 'Sacred' War. But in the long run the open recognition of the fact that the oracle was open to political control must have encouraged the spread of free thought, which ultimately made it possible for the Romans, without incurring the odium of sacrilege, to rob Greek temples of most of their wealth and all of their authority. It is the fate of most religious institutions, sooner or later, to be used by bold men for secular purposes, and thereby to forfeit the reverence upon which their power depends. In the Graeco-Roman world this happened more smoothly and with less upheaval than elsewhere, because religion had never the same strength as in Asia and Africa and mediaeval Europe. The only country analogous to Greece and Rome in this respect is China.

Hitherto we have been concerned only with religions which have come down from immemorial antiquity, without any known historical origin. But these have been superseded, almost everywhere, by religions derived from founders; the only important exceptions are Shinto and Brahmanism. The origins of the older religions, as of those found by anthropologists among present-day savages, are completely obscure. Among the most primitive savages, as we have seen, there is not a clearly differentiated priestly caste; it would seem that, at first, priestly functions are a prerogative of the older men, and presumably especially of such as produce an impression of wisdom, or sometimes of pre-eminence in malignant magic.[1]

With advancing civilisation, in most countries, priests become increasingly separate from the rest of the population and increasingly powerful. But as the guardians of an ancient tradition they are conservative, and as possessors of wealth and power they tend to become hostile or indifferent to personal religion. Sooner or later, their whole system is overthrown by the followers of a revolutionary prophet. Buddha, Christ, and Mohammed are the historically most important examples. The power of their fol-

[1] W. H. R. Rivers, *Social Organization*, p. 167.

lowers was at first revolutionary, and only gradually became traditional. In the process they usually absorbed much of the old tradition which they had nominally overthrown.

Both religious and secular innovators – at any rate those who have had most lasting success – have appealed, as far as they could, to tradition, and have done whatever lay in their power to minimise the elements of novelty in their system. The usual plan is to invent a more or less fictitious past and pretend to be restoring its institutions. In 2 Kings xxii we are told how the priests 'found' the Book of the Law, and the King caused a 'return' to observance of its precepts. The New Testament appealed to the authority of the Prophets; the Anabaptists appealed to the New Testament; the English Puritans, in secular matters, appealed to the supposed institutions of England before the Conquest. The Japanese, in A.D. 645, 'restored' the power of the Mikado; in 1868, they 'restored' the constitution of A.D. 645. A whole series of rebels, throughout the Middle Ages and down to the 18 Brumaire, 'restored' the republican institutions of Rome. Napoleon 'restored' the empire of Charlemagne, but this was felt to be a trifle too theatrical, and failed to impress even that rhetorically minded age. These are only a few illustrations, selected at random, of the respect which even the greatest innovators have shown for the power of tradition.

The most powerful and important of all priestly organisations known to history has been the Catholic Church. I am concerned in this chapter with the power of priests only in so far as it is traditional; I will not, therefore, at present, consider the early period when the power of the Church was revolutionary. After the fall of the Roman Empire, the Church had the good fortune to represent *two* traditions: in addition to that of Christianity, it also embodied that of Rome. The barbarians had the power of the sword, but the Church had a higher level of civilisation and education, a consistent impersonal purpose, the means of appealing to religious hopes and superstitious fears, and, above all, the sole organisation that extended throughout Western Europe. The Greek Church, which had to deal with the comparatively stable empires of Constantinople and Moscow, became completely subordinate to the State; but in the West the struggle continued, with varying fortunes, until the Reformation, and to this day is not ended in Germany and Mexico and Spain.

For the first six centuries after the barbarian invasion the Western Church was unable to contend on equal terms with the turbulent and passionate Germanic kings and barons who ruled in England and France, in North Italy and in Christian Spain. For this there were several reasons. Justinian's conquests in Italy had for a time made the Papacy a Byzantine institution, and had greatly diminished its influence in the West. The higher clergy were drawn, with few exceptions, from the feudal aristocracies, with whom they felt more at one than with a distant and alien Pope whose interferences were resented. The lower clergy were ignorant and mostly married, with the result that they were more anxious to transmit their benefices to their sons than to fight the battles of the Church. Travel was so difficult that Roman authority could not be exerted in distant kingdoms. The first effective government over a large area was not that of the Pope, but that of Charlemagne, whom all his contemporaries regarded as unquestionably the Pope's superior.

After the year 1000, when it was found that the expected end of the world had not taken place, there was a rapid advance in civilisation. Contact with the Moors in Spain and Sicily hastened the rise of the scholastic philosophy. The Normans, after being for centuries a mere piratical scourge, acquired, in France and Sicily, whatever the contemporary world had to teach, and became a force for order and religion instead of for disorder; moreover they found papal authority useful for the purpose of legitimising their conquests. By them, for the first time, ecclesiastical England was brought completely under the domination of Rome. Meanwhile, both the Emperor and the King of France were having the greatest difficulty in controlling their vassals. It was in these circumstances that the statesmanship and ruthless energy of Gregory VII (Hildebrand) inaugurated the increase of the papal power which continued throughout the next two centuries. As this period affords the supreme example of priestly power, I shall consider it in some detail.

The great days of the Papacy, which begin with the accession of Gregory VII (1073), extend to Clement V's establishment of the Papacy at Avignon (1306). Its victories during this period were won by what are called 'spiritual' weapons, i.e. by superstition, not by force of arms. Throughout the whole period, the Popes were outwardly at the mercy of the Roman mob, led by the turbulent nobles of the City – for, whatever the rest of Christendom might think, Rome never had any reverence for its Pontiff. The great Hildebrand himself died in exile; yet he acquired and transmitted the power to humble even the greatest monarchs.

Canossa, though its immediate political consequences were convenient for the Emperor Heny IV, became a symbol for subsequent ages. Bismarck, during the Kulturkampf, said 'we will not go to Canossa'; but he boasted prematurely. Henry IV, who had been excommunicated, needed absolution to further his schemes, and Gregory, though he could not refuse absolution to a penitent, exacted humiliation as the price of reconciliation with the Church. As politicians, men might rail against the Pope, but only heretics questioned the power of the keys, and heresy was not countenanced even by the Emperor Frederick II at the height of his struggle with the Papacy.

Gregory VII's pontificate was the culmination of an important period of ecclesiastical reform. Until his day, the Emperor had been definitely above the Pope, and had claimed, not infrequently, a decisive voice in his election. Henry III, father of Henry IV, had deposed Gregory VI for simony, and had made a German Pope, Clement II. Yet Henry II was not in conflict with the Church; on the contrary, he was a saintly man, allied with all the most zealous ecclesiastics of his time. The reform movement which he supported, and which Gregory VII carried to triumph, was directed essentially against the tendency of the Church to become infected with feudalism. Kings and nobles appointed Archbishops and Bishops, who themselves, as a rule, belonged to the feudal aristocracy, and took a very secular view of their own position. In the Empire, the greatest men under the Emperor had been originally officials, who held their lands in virtue of their official position; but by the end of the eleventh century they had become hereditary nobles, whose possessions passed by inheritance. There was a danger of something similar in the Church, particularly in the lower ranks of the secular clergy. The reforming party in the Church attacked the cognate evils of simony and 'concubinage' (as they called the marriage of priests). In their campaign they showed zeal, courage, devotion, and much worldly wisdom; by their holiness they secured the support of the laity, and by their eloquence they won over assemblies originally hostile. At Milan in 1058, for example, St Peter Damian summoned the clergy to obedience to the reforming decrees of Rome; at first he provoked so much anger that his life was in danger, but at last he prevailed, and it was found that every single priest among the Milanese, from the Archbishop downward, had been guilty of simony. All confessed, and promised obedience for the future; on these terms, they were not dispossessed, but it was made clear that future offences would be punished without mercy.

Clerical celibacy was one of Hildebrand's preoccupations; in enforcing it, he enlisted the laity, who were frequently guilty of gross cruelty towards priests and their wives. The campaign was not, of course, completely successful – to this day it has not succeeded in Spain – but one of its main objects was achieved by the decree that sons of priests could not be ordained, which prevented the local priesthood from becoming hereditary.

One of the most important triumphs of the reform movement was the fixing of the method of Papal election by the decree of 1059. Before this decree, the Emperor and the Roman populace had certain ill-defined rights, which made schisms and disputed elections frequent. The new decree succeeded – though not immediately and not without a struggle – in confining the right of election to the Cardinals.

This reform movement, which filled the latter half of the eleventh century, succeeded, to a great extent, in separating Abbots, Bishops, and Archbishops from the feudal nobility, and in giving the Pope a voice in their appointment – for when he had been given no voice he could usually find a taint of simony. It impressed the laity and greatly increased their reverence for the Church. When it succeeded in imposing celibacy, it made priests more markedly separate from the rest of the world, and no doubt stimulated their power impulses, as asceticism does in most cases. It inspired leading ecclesiastics with moral enthusiasm for a cause in which every one believed except those who profited by the traditional corruption, and as the chief means of furthering this cause it involved a great increase of Papal power.

Power dependent upon propaganda usually demands, as in this case, exceptional courage and self-sacrifice at the start; but when respect has been won by these qualities, they can be discarded, and the respect can be used as a means to worldly advancement. Then, in time, the respect decays, and the advantages which it had secured are lost. Sometimes the process takes a few years, sometimes thousands of years, but in essence it is always the same.

Gregory VII was no pacifist. He favourite text was: 'Cursed be the man that keepeth back his sword from blood'. But he explained this as prohibiting keeping back the word of preaching from carnal men, which shows the justice of his views on the power of propaganda.

Nicholas Breakspear, the only Englishman who ever occupied the Papal Chair (1154–59), shows the theological power of the Pope in a somewhat different connection. Arnold of Brescia, a pupil of Abélard, preached the doctrine that 'clerks who have estates, bishops who hold fiefs, monks who possess property, cannot be saved'. This doctrine, of course, was not orthodox. St Bernard said of him: 'A man who neither eats nor drinks, he only, like the Devil, hungers and thirsts for the blood of souls.' St Bernard none the less admitted his exemplary piety, which made him a useful ally for the Romans in their conflict with the Pope and Cardinals, whom, in the year 1143, they had succeeded in driving into exile. He supported the revived Roman Republic, which sought moral sanction in his doctrine. But Adrian IV (Breakspear), taking advantage of the murder of a Cardinal, placed Rome under an interdict during Holy Week. As Good Friday approached, theological terrors seized upon the Senate, which made abject submission. By the help of the Emperor Frederick Barbarossa, Arnold was captured; he was hanged, his body was burnt, and his ashes were thrown into the Tiber. Thus it was proved that priests have a right to be rich. The Pope, to reward the Emperor, crowned him in St Peter's. The Emperor's troops had been useful, but not so useful as the Catholic Faith, to which, much more than to secular support, the Church owed both its power and its wealth.

The doctrines of Arnold of Brescia were such as to reconcile Pope and Emperor to each other; for each recognized that both were necessary to the established order. But when Arnold was disposed of, the inevitable quarrel soon broke out afresh. In the long war that ensued, the Pope had a new ally, namely the Lombard League. The cities of Lombardy, especially Milan, were rich and commercial; they were at that time in the forefront of economic development, a fact which is commemorated for Englishmen in the name 'Lombard Street'. The Emperor stood for feudalism, to which bourgeois capitalism was already hostile. Although the Church prohibited 'usury', the Pope was a borrower, and found the capital of North Italian bankers so useful that theological rigour had to be softened. The conflict of Barbarossa with the Papacy, which lasted for about twenty years, ended in a draw, and it was chiefly owing to the Lombard Cities that the Emperor was not victorious.

In the long contest between the Papacy and the Emperor Frederick II, the ultimate victory of the Pope was due, in the main, to two causes: the opposition of the commercially minded cities of North Italy, Tuscany as well as Lombardy, to the feudal system, and the pious enthusiasm aroused by the Franciscans. St Francis preached apostolic poverty and universal love; but within a few years of his death his followers were acting as recruiting sergeants in a fierce war to defend the property of the Church. The Emperor was defeated largely because he was unable to clothe his cause in a garb of piety or morality.

At the same time, the war measures adopted by the Popes during this struggle made many men critical of the Papacy on moral grounds. Of Innocent IV, the Pope with whom Frederick was contending at the time of his death, the *Cambridge Medieval History* (Vol. VI, p. 176) says:

'His conception of the Papacy was more secular than any other Pope's before him. He viewed his weakness as political and his remedies were political. He used his spiritual powers constantly to raise money, buy friends, injure foes, and by his unscrupulousness he roused a disrespectful hostility to the Papacy everywhere. His dispensations were a scandal. In contempt of his spiritual duties and of local rights, he used the endowments of the Church as papal revenue and means of political rewards: there would be four papal nominees waiting one after another for a benefice. Bad appointments were a natural consequence of such a system; and, further, legates chosen for war and diplomacy would more likely than not be thoroughly worldly in character ... Of the loss of prestige and spiritual influence occasioned by him Innocent was unconscious. He had good intentions, but not good principles. Endowed with courage, with invincible resolution, with astuteness, his cold equanimity was seldom shaken by disaster or good-fortune, and he patiently pursued his ends with a cunning faithlessness which lowered the standards of the Church. His influence on events was enormous. He wrecked the Empire; he started the Papacy on its decline; he moulded the destinies of Italy.'

The death of Innocent IV produced no change in papal policy. His successor Urban IV carried on the struggle, with complete success, against Frederick's son Manfred, and won the support of the still rising capitalism of Italy, wherever it was wavering, by an interesting use of his authority in matters of morals, which affords a classic example of the transformation of propaganda power into economic power. Most of the bankers, owing to their large transactions in collecting the papal revenue, were already on the side of the Pope, but in some cities, for instance Siena, Ghibelline feeling was so strong that the bankers, at first, sided with Manfred. Wherever this happened, the Pope informed the Banks' debtors that it was their Christian duty not to pay their debts, a pronouncement which the debtors readily accepted as authoritative. Siena, as a result, lost the English trade. Throughout Italy, the bankers who escaped ruin were compelled by this papal manoeuvre to become Guelphs.[1]

But such means, though they could win the political support of the bankers, could hardly increase their respect for the Pope's claims to divine authority.

The whole of the period from the fall of the Western Empire to the end of the sixteenth century may be viewed as a contest between two traditions: that of imperial Rome, and that of Teutonic aristocracy, the former embodied in the Church, the latter in the State. The Holy Roman Emperors made an attempt to annex the tradition of imperial Rome, but failed. They themselves, with the exception of Frederick II, were too ignorant to understand the Roman tradition, while the political institution of feudalism, with which they were familiar, was Germanic. The language of educated men – including those who served the Emperors – was pedantically derived from antiquity; law was Roman, philosophy was Greek, but the customs, which were Teutonic in origin, were not such as could be mentioned in polite speech. There was the same sort of difficulty as a classical scholar of the present day would find in describing in Latin the processes of modern industry. It was not until the Reformation and the adoption of modern languages in place of Latin that the Teutonic element in the civilisation of Western Europe found adequate literary and intellectual expression.

After the fall of the Hohenstaufen, the Church seemed, for a few decades, to have re-established the rule of Italy over the Western world. Judged by money standards, this rule was at least as firm as in the days of the Antonines – the revenue that flowed from England and Germany to Rome far exceeded what the Roman legions had been able to extract. But it was extorted by means of the reverence felt for the Papacy, not by force of arms.

As soon as the Popes moved to Avignon, however, they began

[1] Cf. *Cambridge Medieval History*, Vol. VII, p. 182.

to lose the respect which they had won during the three preceding centuries. This was due not only to their complete subservience to the King of France, but also to their participation in vast atrocities, such as the suppression of the Templars. King Philip IV, being in financial difficulties, coveted the lands of this order. It was decided to accuse them, quite groundlessly, of heresy. With the help of the Pope, those who were in France were seized, tortured until they confessed that they had paid homage to Satan and spat upon the crucifix, etc., and then burnt in large numbers, while the King disposed of their property, not without pickings for the Pope. Such deeds began the moral degeneration of the Papacy.

The Great Schism made it still more difficult to reverence the Pope, since no one knew which of the claimants was the legitimate one, and each claimant anathematised the other. Throughout the Great Schism, each of the two rivals showed an unedifying tenacity of power, extending to repudiation of the most solemn oaths. In various countries, the State and the local Church, in unison, withdrew obedience from both Popes. At length it became clear that only a general council could end the trouble. The Council of Pisa, misguidedly, merely created a third Pope without successfully getting rid of the other two, although it pronounced their deposition as heretics; the Council of Constance at last succeeded in removing all three and restoring unity. But the struggle had destroyed the traditional reverence for the Papacy. At the end of this period of confusion, it had become possible for Wyclif to say of the Papacy:

'To get rid of such a demon would not harm the Church, but would be useful to it; in working for his destruction, the Church would be working solicitously for the cause of God.'

The fifteenth-century Papacy, while it suited Italy, was too worldly and secular, as well as too openly immoral, to satisfy the piety of Northern countries. At last, in Teutonic countries, the moral revolt became strong enough to allow free play to economic motives: there was a general refusal to pay tribute to Rome, and princes and nobles seized the lands of the Church. But this would not have been possible without the doctrinal revolt of Protestantism, which could never have taken place but for the Great Schism and the scandals of the Renaissance Papacy. If the moral force of the Church had not been weakened from within, its assailants could not have had moral force on their side, and would have been defeated as Frederick II was defeated.

It is interesting in this connection to observe what Machiavelli has to say on the subject of ecclesiastical principalities in Chapter XI of *The Prince*:

'It only remains now to speak of ecclesiastical principalities, touching which all difficulties are prior to getting possession, because they are acquired either by capacity or good fortune, and they can be held without either; for they are sustained by the ancient ordinances of religion, which are so all-powerful, and of such a character, that the principalities may be held no matter how their princes behave and live. These princes alone have states and do not defend them, they have subjects and do not rule them; and the states, though unguarded, are not taken from them, and the subjects, though not ruled, do not care, and they have neither the desire nor the ability to alienate themselves. Such principalities only are secure and happy. But being upheld by power to which the human mind cannot reach, I shall speak no more of them, because, being exalted and maintained by God, it would be the act of a presumptuous and rash man to discuss them.'

These words were written during the pontificate of Leo X, which was that in which the Reformation began. To pious Germans, it gradually became impossible to believe that the ruthless nepotism of Alexander VI, or the financial rapacity of Leo, could be 'exalted and maintained by God'. Luther, a 'presumptuous and rash man', was quite willing to enter upon the discussion of the papal power, from which Machiavelli shrank. And as soon as there existed moral and theological support for opposition to the Church, motives of self-interest caused the opposition to spread with great rapidity. Since the power of the Church had been based upon the power of the keys, it was natural that opposition should be associated with a new doctrine of Justification. Luther's theology made it possible for lay princes to despoil the Church without fear of damnation, and without incurring moral condemnation from their own subjects.

While economic motives contributed greatly to the spread of the Reformation, they are obviously not sufficient to account for it, since they had been operative for centuries. Many Emperors tried to resist the Pope; so did sovereigns elsewhere, e.g. Henry II and King John in England. But their attempts were thought wicked, and therefore failed. It was only after the Papacy had, for a long time, so abused its traditional powers as to cause a moral revolt, that successful resistance became possible.

The rise and decline of papal power are worthy of study by anyone who wishes to understand the winning of power by propaganda. It is not enough to say that men were superstitious and believed in the power of the keys. Throughout the Middle Ages there were heresies, which would have spread, as Protestantism spread, if the Popes had not, on the whole, deserved respect. And without heresy secular rulers made vigorous attempts to keep the Church in subordination to the State, which failed in the West though they succeeded in the East. For this there were various reasons.

First, the Papacy was not hereditary, and was therefore not troubled with long minorities, as secular kingdoms were. A man could not easily rise to eminence in the Church except by piety, learning or statesmanship; consequently most Popes were men considerably above the average in one or more respects. Secular sovereigns might happen to be able, but were often quite the reverse; moreover they had not the training in controlling their passions that ecclesiastics had. Repeatedly, kings got into difficulties from desire for divorce, which, being a matter for the Church, placed them at the mercy of the Pope. Sometimes they tried Henry VIII's way of dealing with this difficulty, but their subjects were shocked, their vassals were liberated from their oath of allegiance, and in the end they had to submit or fall.

Another great strength of the Papacy was its impersonal continuity. In the contest with Frederick II, it is astonishing how little difference is made by the death of a Pope. There was a body of doctrine, and a tradition of statecraft, to which kings could oppose nothing equally solid. It was only with the rise of nationalism that secular governments acquired any comparable continuity or tenacity of purpose.

In the eleventh, twelfth, and thirteenth centuries, kings, as a rule, were ignorant, while most Popes were both learned and well-informed. Moreover Kings were bound up with the feudal system, which was cumbrous, in constant danger of anarchy, and hostile to the newer economic forces. On the whole, during those centuries, the Church represented a higher civilisation than that represented by the State.

But by far the greatest strength of the Church was the moral respect which it inspired. It inherited, as a kind of moral capital, the glory of the persecutions in ancient times. Its victories, as we have seen, were associated with the enforcement of celibacy, and the mediaeval mind found celibacy very impressive. Very many ecclesiastics, including not a few Popes, suffered great hardships rather than yield on a point of principle. It was clear to ordinary men that, in a world of uncontrolled rapacity, licentiousness, and self-seeking, eminent dignitaries of the Church not infrequently lived for impersonal aims, to which they willingly subordinated their private fortune. In successive centuries, men of impressive holiness – Hildebrand, St Bernard, St Francis – dazzled public opinion, and prevented the moral discredit that would otherwise have come from the misdeeds of others.

But to an organisation which has ideal ends, and therefore an excuse for love of power, a reputation for superior virtue is dangerous, and is sure, in the long run, to produce a superiority only in unscrupulous ruthlessness. The Church preached contempt for the things of this world, and in doing so acquired dominion over monarchs. The Friars took a vow of poverty, which so impressed the world that it increased the already enormous wealth of the Church. St Francis, by preaching brotherly love, generated the enthusiasm required for the victorious prosecution of a long and atrocious war. In the end, the Renaissance Church lost all the moral purpose to which it owed its wealth and power, and the shock of the Reformation was necessary to produce regeneration.

All this is inevitable whenever superior virtue is used as a means of winning tyrannical power for an organisation.

Except when due to foreign conquest, the collapse of traditional power is always the result of its abuse by men who believe, as Machiavelli believed, that its hold on men's minds is too firm to be shaken even by the grossest crimes.

In the United States at the present day, the reverence which the Greeks gave to oracles and the Middle Ages to the Pope is given to the Supreme Court. Those who have studied the working of the American Constitution know that the Supreme Court is part of the forces engaged in the protection of the plutocracy. But of the men who know this, some are on the side of the plutocracy, and therefore do nothing to weaken the traditional reverence for the Supreme Court, while others are discredited in the eyes of ordinary quiet citizens by being said to be subversive and Bolshevik. A considerable further career of obvious partisanship will be necessary before a Luther will be able to attack successfully the authority of the official interpreters of the Constitution.

Theological power is much less affected by defeat in war than secular power. It is true that Russia and Turkey, after the Great War, suffered a theological as well as a political revolution, but in both countries the traditional religion was very intimately connected with the State. The most important instance of theological survival in spite of defeat in war is the victory of the Church over the barbarians in the fifth century. St Augustine, in the *City of God,* which was inspired by the sack of Rome, explained that temporal power was not what was promised to the true believer, and was therefore not to be expected as the result of orthodoxy. The surviving pagans within the Empire argued that Rome was vanquished as a punishment for abandoning the gods, but in spite of the plausibility of this contention it failed to win any general support; among the invaders, the superior civilisation of the vanquished prevailed, and the victors adopted the Christian faith. Thus through the medium of the Church the influence of Rome survived among the barbarians, of whom none before Hitler succeeded in shaking off the tradition of ancient culture.

Chapter 5

Kingly Power

The origin of kings, like that of priests, is prehistoric, and the early stages in the evolution of kingship can only be conjectured from what still exists among the most backward savages. When the institution is fully developed, but has not yet begun to decline, the king is a man who leads his tribe or nation in war, who decides when to make war and when to make peace; often, though not always, he makes the laws and controls the administration of justice. His title to the throne is usually in a greater or less degree hereditary. He is, moreover, a sacred person: if not himself a god, he is at least the Lord's anointed.

But kingship of this sort presupposes a long evolution of government, and a community much more highly organised than those of savages. Even the savage chief, as most Europeans imagine him, is not to be found in really primitive societies. The man whom we regard as a chief may have only religious and ceremonial functions to perform; sometimes, like the Lord Mayor, he is only expected to give banquets. Sometimes he declares war, but takes no part in the fighting, because he is too sacred. Sometimes his *mana* is such that no subject may look upon him; this effectually prevents him from taking much part in public business. He cannot make the laws, since they are decided by custom; he is not needed for their administration, since, in a small community, punishment can be spontaneously administered by neighbours. Some savage communities have two chiefs, one secular and one religious, like the Shogun and the Mikado in old Japan – not like the Emperor and the Pope, since the religious chief has, as a rule, only ceremonial power. Among primitive savages generally, so much is decided by custom, and so little by formal government, that the prominent men whom Europeans call chiefs have only faint beginnings of kingly power.[1]

[1] On this subject, see Rivers, *Social Organization.*

Migration and foreign invasion are powerful forces in the destruction of custom, and therefore in creating the need of government. At the lowest level of civilization at which there are rulers worthy to be called kings, the royal family is sometimes of alien origin, and has won respect, initially, by some definite superiority. But whether this is a common or uncommon stage in the evolution of monarchy is a controversial question among anthropologists.

It is clear that war must have played a great part in increasing the power of kings, since in war the need of a unified command is obvious. To make the monarchy hereditary is the easiest way of avoiding the evils of a disputed succession; even if the king has the power of appointing his successor, he is pretty sure to choose one of his family. But dynasties do not last for ever, and every royal family begins with a usurper or foreign conqueror. Usually religion legitimises the new family by means of some traditional ceremony. Priestly power profits by these occasions, since it comes to be an essential support of the royal prestige. 'No Bishop, no King,' said Charles I, and the analogue of this maxim has been true in all ages in which kings have existed. The position of king appears to ambitious people such a desirable one that only powerful religious sanctions will make them renounce the hope of acquiring it themselves.

Whatever may have been the stages by which the primitive chief developed into the historical king, the process was already completed in Egypt and Babylonia at the earliest period of which records exist. The Great Pyramid is considered to have been built before 3000 B.C., and its construction would only have been possible for a monarch possessed of immense power over his subjects. Babylonia, at this period, had a number of kings, none having a territory comparable to that of Egypt; but they were very completely rulers in their respective areas. Before the end of the third millennium B.C. we reach the great king Hammurabi (2123–2081 B.C.), who did all the things that a king should do. He is best known by his code of laws, which was given to him by the sun-god, and shows that he succeeded in achieving what mediaeval monarchs never could do, namely, subordinating ecclesiastical to civil courts. But he was also distinguished as a soldier and as an engineer. Patriotic poets sang the praises of his conquests:

> For all time he his mighty strength hath shown,
> The mighty warrior, Hammurabi, king,

Who smote the foe, a very storm in battle.
Sweeping the lands of foemen, bringing war to nought,
Giving rebellion surcease, and destroying,
Like dolls of clay, malignants, hath laid open
The steeps of the impenetrable hills.

He recorded himself his exploits in irrigation: 'When Anu and Enlil [a god and goddess] gave me the lands of Sumer and Akkad to rule, and entrusted their sceptre to me, I dug the canal *Hammurabi-the-abundance-of-the-people* which bringeth water for the lands of Sumer and Akkad. The scattered people of Sumer and Akkad I gathered, with pasturage and watering I provided them; I pastured them with plenty and abundance, and settled them in peaceful dwellings.'

Kingship as an institution had reached its utmost limits of development in Egypt at the time of the Great Pyramid and in Babylonia at the time of Hammurabi. Later kings have had larger territories, but none have had more complete rule over their kingdoms. The power of Egyptian and Babylonian kings was ended only by foreign conquest, not by internal rebellion. They could not, it is true, afford to quarrel with the priesthood, since the submission of their subjects depended upon the religious significance of the monarchy; but except in this respect their authority was unlimited.

The Greeks, in most cities, got rid of their kings, as political rulers, at or before the beginning of the historical period. The Roman kings are prehistoric, and the Romans retained, throughout their history, an unconquerable aversion to the name of king. The Roman Emperor, in the West, was never a monarch in the full sense of the word. His origin was extra-legal, and he depended always upon the army. To civilians, he might declare himself a god, but to the soldiers he remained merely a general who gave, or did not give, adequate donatives. Except occasionally for short periods, the Empire was not hereditary. The real power was always the army, and the Emperor was merely its nominee for the time being.

The barbarian invasion reintroduced monarchy, but with a difference. The new kings were the chiefs of Germanic tribes, and their power was not absolute, but depended always upon the cooperation of some Council of Elders or kindred body. When a Germanic tribe conquered a Roman province, its chief became king, but his most important companions became nobles with a certain measure of independence. Hence arose the feudal system, which left all the monarchs of Western Europe at the mercy of turbulent Barons.

Monarchy consequently remained weak until it had got the better of both the Church and the feudal nobility. The causes of the weakening of the Church we have already considered. The nobility was worsted in the struggle with the king, in England and France, because it was an obstacle to orderly government. In Germany its leaders developed into petty kings, with the result that Germany was at the mercy of France. In Poland, aristocratic anarchy continued until the partition. In England and France, after the Hundred Years War and the Wars of the Roses, ordinary citizens were compelled to put their faith in a strong king. Edward IV became victorious by the help of the City of London, from which he even chose his Queen. Louis XI, the enemy of the feudal aristocracy, was the friend of the higher bourgeoisie, who helped him against the nobles while he helped them against the artisans. 'He ruled like a great capitalist', is the official verdict of the *Encyclopaedia Britannica.*

The renaissance monarchies had one great advantage, as compared with earlier kings in their conflicts with the Church, namely that education was no longer a monopoly of ecclesiastics. The help of lay lawyers was invaluable in the establishment of the new monarchy.

The new monarchies, in England, France, and Spain, were above the Church and above the aristocracy. Their power depended upon the support of two growing forces, nationalism and commerce: so long as they were felt to be useful to these two, they were strong, but when they failed in these respects there was revolution. The Tudors were faultless in both respects, but the Stuarts hampered trade by monopolies granted to courtiers, and allowed England to be dragged at the chariot wheels of Spain first, and then France. The French monarchy favoured commerce and enhanced national power until the end of Colbert's régime. After that time, the Revocation of the Edict of Nantes, a series of increasingly disastrous wars, crushing taxation, and the exemption of clergy and nobles from financial burdens, turned both commerce and nationalism against the king, and in the end brought about the Revolution. Spain was deflected by the conquest of the New World; but the Spanish New World itself, when it rebelled, did so chiefly in order to be able to trade with England and the United States.

Commerce, though it supported kings against feudal anarchy,

has always been republican when it has felt sufficiently strong. It was so in antiquity, in the North Italian and Hanseatic cities of the Middle Ages, and in Holland during its greatest days. The alliance between kings and commerce was therefore an uneasy one. Kings appealed to 'divine right', and sought, as far as possible, to make their power traditional and quasi-religious. In this they were partially successful: the execution of Charles I was felt to be an impiety, not merely an ordinary crime. In France, St Louis was erected into a legendary figure, some of whose piety descended as a cloak even to Louis XV, who was still 'the most Christian King'. Having created a new Court aristocracy, kings tended to prefer it to the bourgeoisie. In England, the higher aristocracy and the bourgeoisie combined, and installed a king with a merely parliamentary title, who had none of the old magic properties of majesty: George I, for instance, could not cure the king's evil, though Queen Anne could. In France, the king won over the aristocracy, and his and their heads fell together under the guillotine.

The alliance of commerce and nationalism, which began with the Lombard League in the time of Frederick Barbarossa gradually spread over Europe, achieving its last and briefest triumph in the Russian February Revolution. Wherever it won power, it turned against hereditary power based on land, at first in alliance with the monarchy, and then in opposition to it. In the end, kings everywhere disappeared or were reduced to figure-heads. Now, at least, nationalism and commerce have parted company; in Italy, Germany, and Russia it is nationalism that has triumphed. The Liberal movement, begun in Milan in the twelfth century, has run its course.

Traditional power, when not destroyed from without, runs, almost always, through a certain development. Emboldened by the respect which it inspires, it becomes careless as regards the general approval, which it believes that it cannot ever lose. By sloth, folly, or cruelty it gradually forces men to become sceptical of its claims to divine authority. Since these claims have no better source than habit, criticism, once aroused, easily disposes of them. Some new creed, useful to the rebels, takes the place of the old one; or sometimes, as in the case of Haiti when it won freedom from the French, mere chaos succeeds. As a rule, a long period of very flagrant misgovernment is necessary before mental rebellion becomes widespread; and in many cases the rebels succeed in transferring to themselves part or the whole of the old authority. So Augustus absorbed into himself the traditional dignity of the Senate; Protestants retained the reverence for the Bible, while rejecting reverence for the Catholic Church; the British Parliament gradually acquired the power of the king, without destroying the respect for monarchy.

All these, however, were limited revolutions; those which were more thoroughgoing involved greater difficulties. The substitution of the republican form of government for hereditary monarchy, where it has been sudden, has usually led to various kinds of trouble, since a new constitution has no hold over men's mental habits, and will only be respected, broadly speaking, in so far as it accords with self-interest. Ambitious men, therefore, will seek to become dictators, and will only desist after a considerable period of failure. If there is no such period, a republican constitution will fail to acquire that hold over men's thoughts that is necessary for stability. The United States is almost the only example of a new republic which has been stable from the beginning.

The chief revolutionary movement of our time is the attack of Socialism and Communism upon the economic power of private persons. We may expect to find here the common characteristics of such movements, as exemplified, for example, in the rise of Christianity, of Protestantism, and of political democracy. But on this subject I shall have more to say at a later stage.

Chapter 6

Naked Power

As the beliefs and habits which have upheld traditional power decay, it gradually gives way either to power based upon some new belief, or to 'naked' power, i.e. to the kind that involves no acquiescence on the part of the subject. Such is the power of the butcher over the sheep, of an invading army over a vanquished nation, and of the police over detected conspirators. The power of the Catholic Church over Catholics is traditional, but its power over heretics who are persecuted is naked. The power of the State over loyal citizens is traditional, but its power over rebels is naked. Organisations that have a long career of power pass, as a rule, through three phases: first, that of fanatical but not traditional belief, leading to conquest; then, that of general acquiescence in the new power, which rapidly becomes traditional; and finally that in which power, being now used against those who reject tradition, has again become naked. The character of an organisation changes very greatly as it passes through these stages.

The power conferred by military conquest oftentceases, after a longer or shorter period of time, to be merely military. All the provinces conquered by the Romans, except Judea, soon became loyal subjects of the Empire, and ceased to feel any desire for independence. In Asia and Africa the Christian countries conquered by the Mohammedans submitted with little reluctance to their new rulers. Wales gradually acquiesced in English rule, though Ireland did not. After the Albigensian heretics had been overcome by military force, their descendants submitted inwardly as well as outwardly to the authority of the Church. The Norman Conquest produced, in England, a royal family which, after a time, was thought to possess a Divine Right to the throne. Military conquest is stable only when it is followed by psychological conquest, but the cases in which this has occurred are very numerous.

Naked power, in the internal government of a community not

lately submitted to foreign conquest, arises in two different sets of circumstances: first, where two or more fanatical creeds are contending for mastery; secondly, where all traditional beliefs have decayed, without being succeeded by new ones, so that there are no limitations to personal ambition. The former kind of case is not pure, since the adherents of the dominant creed are not subject to naked power. I shall consider it in the next chapter, under the head of revolutionary power. For the present I shall confine myself to the second kind of case.

The definition of naked power is psychological, and a government may be naked in relation to some of its subjects but not in relation to others. The most complete examples known to me, apart from foreign conquest, are the later Greek tyrannies and some of the States of Renaissance Italy.

Greek history affords, as in a laboratory, a large number of small-scale experiments of great interest to the student of political power. The hereditary kingship of the Homeric age came to an end before the beginning of historical records, and was succeeded by a hereditary aristocracy. At the point where reliable history of Greek cities begins, there was a contest between aristocracy and tyranny. Except in Sparta, tyranny was everywhere victorious for a time, but was succeeded either by democracy or by a restoration of aristocracy, sometimes in the form of plutocracy. This first age of tyranny covered the greater part of the seventh and sixth centuries B.C. It was not an age of naked power, as was the later period with which I shall be specially concerned; nevertheless, it prepared the way for the lawlessness and violence of later times.

The word 'tyrant' did not, originally, imply any bad qualities in the ruler, but only an absence of legal or traditional title. Many of the early tyrants governed wisely, and with the consent of the majority of their subjects. Their only implacable enemies, as a rule, were the aristocrats. Most of the early tyrants were very rich men, who bought their way to power, and maintained themselves more by economic than by military means. They are to be compared rather with the Medici than with the dictators of our day.

The first age of tyranny was that in which coinage first came into use, and this had the same kind of effect in increasing the power of rich men as credit and paper money have had in recent times. It has been maintained[1] – with what truth I am not com-

[1] See P. N. Ure, *The Origin of Tyranny*.

petent to judge – that the introduction of currency was connected with the rise of tyranny; certainly the possession of silver mines was a help to any man who aimed at becoming a tyrant. The use of money, when it is new, profoundly disturbs ancient customs, as may be seen in the parts of Africa which have not been long under European control. In the seventh and sixth centuries B.C., the effect was to increase the power of commerce, and to diminish that of territorial aristocracies. Until the Persians acquired Asia Minor, wars in the Greek world were few and unimportant, and not much of the work of production was performed by slaves. The circumstances were ideal for economic power, which weakened the hold of tradition in much the same way as industrialism did in the nineteenth century.

So long as it was possible for everybody to be prosperous, the weakening of tradition did more good than harm. It led, among the Greeks, to the most rapid advance in civilisation that has ever occurred – with the possible exception of the last four centuries. The freedom of Greek art and science and philosophy is that of a prosperous age unhampered by superstition. But the social structure had not the toughness required to resist misfortune, and individuals had not the moral standards necessary for the avoidance of disastrous crimes when virtue could no longer bring success. A long series of wars diminished the free population and increased the number of slaves. Greece proper finally fell under the dominion of Macedonia, while Hellenic Sicily, in spite of increasingly violent revolutions, civil wars, and tyrannies, continued to struggle against the power of Carthage, and then of Rome. The Syracusan tyrannies deserve our attention, both because they afford one of the most perfect examples of naked power, and because they influenced Plato, who quarrelled with the elder Dionysius and endeavoured to make a pupil of the younger. The views of later Greeks, and of all subsequent ages, on Greek tyrants in general, were largely influenced by the unfortunate contacts of the philosophers with Dionysius the elder and his successors in Syracusan misgovernment.

'The machinery of fraud,' says Grote, 'whereby the people were to be cheated into a temporary submission as a prelude to the machinery of force whereby such submission was to be perpetuated against their consent – was the stock in trade of Grecian usurpers.' How far the earlier tyrannies were perpetuated without popular consent may be doubted, but of the later tyrannies, which were military rather than economic, this is certainly true. Take, for example, Grote's description, based on Diodorus, of the crucial moment in the rise of Dionysius the elder. The arms of Syracuse had suffered defeat and disgrace under a more or less democratic régime, and Dionysius, the chosen leader of the champions of vigorous war, was demanding the punishment of the defeated generals.

'Amidst the silence and disquietude which reigned in the Syracusan assembly, Dionysius was the first who rose to address them. He enlarged upon a topic suitable alike to the temper of his auditors and to his own views. He vehemently denounced the generals as having betrayed the security of Syracuse to the Carthaginians – and as the persons to whom the ruin of Agrigentum, together with the impending peril of every man around, was owing. He set forth their misdeeds, real and alleged, not merely with fulness and acrimony, but with a ferocious violence outstripping all the limits of legitimate debate, and intended to bring upon them a lawless murder, like the death of the generals recently at Agrigentum. "There they sit, the Traitors! Do not wait for legal trial or verdict, but lay hands upon them at once, and inflict upon them summary justice." Such a brutal exhortation ... was an offence against law as well as against parliamentary order. The presiding magistrates reproved Dionysius as a disturber of order, and fined him, as they were empowered by law. But his partisans were loud in his support. Philistus not only paid down the fine for him on the spot, but publicly proclaimed that he would go on for the whole day paying all similar fines which might be imposed – and incited Dionysius to persist in such language as he thought proper. That which had begun as illegality, was now aggravated into open defiance of the law. Yet so enfeebled was the authority of the magistrates, and so vehement the cry against them, in the actual position of the city that they were unable either to punish or repress the speaker. Dionysius pursued his harangue in a tone yet more inflammatory, not only accusing the generals of having corruptly betrayed Agrigentum, but also denouncing the conspicuous and wealthy citizens generally, as oligarchs who had tyrannical sway – who treated the many with scorn, and made their own profit out of the misfortunes of the city. Syracuse (he contended) could never be saved, unless men of a totally different character were invested with authority; men, not chosen from wealth or station, but of humble birth, belonging to the people by position, and kind in their deportment from consciousness of their own weakness.'[1]

And so he became tyrant; but history does not relate any consequent advantage to the poor and humble. True, he confiscated the estates of the rich, but it was to his bodyguard that he gave them. His popularity soon waned, but not his power. A few pages further on we find Grote saying:

'Feeling more than ever that his dominion was repugnant to the Syracusans, and rested only on naked force, he thus surrounded himself with precautions probably stronger than any other Grecian despot had ever accumulated.'

Greek history is peculiar in the fact that, except in Sparta, the influence of tradition was extraordinarily weak in Greece; moreover there was almost no political morality. Herodotus states that no Spartan could resist a bribe. Throughout Greece, it was useless to object to a politician on the ground that he took bribes from the King of Persia, because his opponents also did so if they became sufficiently powerful to be worth buying. The result was a universal scramble for personal power, conducted by corruption, street fighting, and assassination. In this business, the friends of Socrates and Plato were among the most unscrupulous. The final outcome, as might have been foreseen, was subjugation by foreign Powers.

It used to be customary to lament the loss of Greek independence, and to think of the Greeks as all Solons and Socrateses. How little reason there was to deplore the victory of Rome may be seen from the history of Hellenic Sicily. I know no better illustration of naked power than the career of Agathocles, a contemporary of Alexander the Great, who lived from 361 to 289 B.C., and was tyrant of Syracuse during the last twenty-eight years of his life.

Syracuse was the largest of Greek cities, perhaps the largest city in the Mediterranean. Its only rival was Carthage, with which there was always war except for a short time after a serious defeat of either party. The other Greek cities in Sicily sided sometimes with Syracuse, sometimes with Carthage, according to the turns of party politics. In every city, the rich favoured oligarchy and the poor favoured democracy; when the partisans of

[1] G. Grote, *History of Greece*, Ch. LXXXI.

democracy were victorious, their leader usually succeeded in making himself a tyrant. Many of the beaten party became exiles, and joined the armies of those cities in which their party was in power. But the bulk of the armed forces consisted of mercenaries, largely non-Hellenic.

Agathocles[1] was a man of humble origin, the son of a potter. Owing to his beauty he became the favourite of a rich Sycracusan named Demas, who left him all his money, and whose widow he married. Having distinguished himself in war, he was thought to be aspiring to the tyranny; he was accordingly exiled, and orders were given that he should be murdered on his journey. But he, having foreseen this, changed clothes with a poor man, who was murdered in error by the hired assassins. He then raised an army in the interior of Sicily, which so terrified the Sycracusans that they made a treaty with him: he was readmitted, and swore in the temple of Ceres that he would do nothing to the prejudice of the democracy.

The government of Syracuse at this time seems to have been a mixture of democracy and oligarchy. There was a council of six hundred, consisting of the richest men. Agathocles espoused the cause of the poor against these oligarchs. In the course of a conference with forty of them, he roused the soldiers and had all the forty murdered, saying there was a plot against him. He then led the army into the city, telling them to plunder all the six hundred; they did so, and massacred citizens who came out of their houses to see what was happening; in the end, large numbers were murdered for booty. As Diodorus says: 'Nay, there was no safety even to them that fled to the temples under the shelter of the gods; but piety towards the gods was crushed and borne down by the cruelty of men: and these things Greeks against Greeks in their own country, and kindred against kindred in a time of peace, without any regard either to the laws of nature, or leagues, or reverence to the gods, dared thus audaciously to commit: upon which account not only friends, but even enemies themselves, and every sober man, could not but pity the miserable condition of these distressed people.'

Those of Agathocles's party spent the day-time slaughtering the men, and at nightfall turned their attention to the women.

[1] What follows rests on the authority of Diodorus Siculus. Some modern authorities say that he was biased, and that Agathocles was an admirable ruler. But it is difficult to believe that Diodorus is not correct as to the main facts.

After two days' massacre, Agathocles brought forth the prisoners and killed all but his friend Dinocrates. He then called the assembly, accused the oligarchs, and said he would purge the city of all friends of monarchy, and himself would live a private life. So he stripped off his uniform and dressed in mufti. But those who had robbed under his leadership wanted him in power, and he was voted sole general. 'Many of the poorer sort, of those that were in debt, were much pleased with this revolution,' for Agathocles promised remission of debts and sharing out of lands to the poor. Then he was mild for a time.

In war, Agathocles was resourceful and brave, but rash. There came a moment when it seemed as if the Carthaginans must be completely victorious; they were besieging Syracuse, and their navy occupied the harbour. But Agathocles, with a large army, sailed to Africa, where he burnt his ships to prevent then from falling into the hands of the Carthaginians. For fear of revolt in his absence, he took children as hostages; and after a time his brother, who was representing him in Syracuse, exiled eight thousand political opponents, whom the Carthaginians befriended. In Africa he was at first amazingly successful; he captured Tunis, and besieged Carthage, where the government became alarmed, and set to work to propitiate Moloch. It was found that aristocrats whose children ought to have been sacrificed to the god had been in the habit of purchasing poor children as substitutes; the practice was now sternly repressed, since Moloch was known to be more gratified by the sacrifice of aristocratic children. After this reform the fortunes of the Carthaginians began to mend.

Agathocles, feeling the need of reinforcements, sent envoys to Cyrene, which was at that time held, under Ptolemy, by Ophelas, one of Alexander's captains. The envoys were instructed to say that, with the help of Ophelas, Carthage could be destroyed; that Agathocles wished only to be secure in Sicily, and had no African ambitions; and that all their joint conquests in Africa should be the share of Ophelas. Tempted by these offers, Ophelas marched across the desert with his army, and after great hardship effected a junction with Agathocles. Agathocles thereupon murdered him, and pointed out to his army that their only hope of safety was to take service under the murderer of their late commander.

He then besieged Utica, where, arriving unexpectedly, he captured three hundred prisoners in the fields; these he bound to the front of his siege engines, so that the Uticans, to defend themselves, had to kill their own people. Although successful in this enterprise, his position was difficult, the more so as he had reason to fear that his son Archagathus was stirring up disaffection in the army. So he fled secretly back to Sicily, and the army, in fury at his desertion, murdered both Archagathus and his other son. This so enraged him that he killed every man, woman, and child in Syracuse that was related to any soldier in the mutinous army.

His power in Sicily, for some time, survived all these vicissitudes. He took Aegesta, killed all the poorer males in that city, and tortured the rich till they revealed where their wealth was concealed. The young women and children he sold as slaves to the Bruttii on the mainland.

His home life, I regret to say, was not altogether happy. His wife had an affair with his son, one of his two grandsons murdered the other, and then induced a servant of the old tyrant to poison grandpapa's toothpick. The last act of Agathocles, when he saw he must die, was to summon the senate and demand vengeance on his grandson. But his gums, owing to the poison, became so sore that he could not speak. The citizens rose, he was hurried on to his funeral pyre before he was dead, his goods were confiscated, and we are told that democracy was restored.

Renaissance Italy presents a very close parallel to ancient Greece, but the confusion is even greater. There were oligarchical commercial republics, tyrannies, after the Greek model, principalities of feudal origin, and, in addition, the States of the Church. The Pope, except in Italy, commanded reverence, but his sons did not, and Cesare Borgia had to rely upon naked power.

Cesare Borgia and his father Alexander VI are important, not only on their own account, but as having inspired Machiavelli. One incident in their career, with Creighton's comments, will serve to illustrate their age. The Colonna and Orsini had been the bane of the Popes for centuries; the Colonna had already fallen, but the Orsini remained. Alexander VI made a treaty with them, and invited their chief, Cardinal Orsini, to the Vatican, on hearing that Cesare had captured two important Orsini by treachery. Cardinal Orsini was arrested as soon as he came into the Pope's presence; his mother paid the Pope two thousand ducats for the privilege of sending him food, and his mistress presented His Holiness with a costly pearl which he had coveted. Nevertheless Cardinal Orsini died in prison – of poisoned wine given by the orders of Alexander VI, it was said. Creighton's comments on this occurrence[1] illustrate the character of a régime of naked power:

'It is amazing that this treacherous deed should have awakened no remonstrances, and should have been so completely successful; but in the artificial politics of Italy everything depended on the skill of the players of the game. The condottieri represented only themselves, and when they were removed by any means, however treacherous, nothing remained. There was no party, no interest, which was outraged by the fall of the Orsini and Vitellozzo. The armies of the condottieri were formidable so long as they followed their generals; when the generals were removed, the soldiers dispersed and entered into other engagements ... Most men admired Cesare's consummate coolness in the matter ... No outrage was done to current morality ... Most men in Italy accepted as sufficient Cesare's remark to Machiavelli: "It is well to beguile those who have shown themselves masters of treachery." Cesare's conduct was judged by its success.'

In Renaissance Italy, as in ancient Greece, a very high level of civilisation was combined with a very low level of morals: both ages exhibit the greatest heights of genius and the greatest depths of scoundrelism, and in both the scoundrels and the men of genius are by no means antagonistic to each other. Leonardo erected fortifications for Cesare Borgia; some of the pupils of Socrates were among the worst of the thirty tyrants; Plato's disciples were mixed up in shameful doings in Sycracuse, and Aristotle married a tyrant's niece. In both ages, after art, literature, and murder had flourished side by side for about a hundred and fifty years, all were extinguished together by less civilised but more cohesive nations from the West and North. In both cases the loss of political independence involved not only cultural decay, but loss of commercial supremacy and catastrophic impoverishment.

Periods of naked power are usually brief. They end, as a rule, in one or other of three ways. The first is foreign conquest, as in the cases of Greece and Italy which we have already considered. The second is the establishment of a stable dictatorship, which soon becomes traditional; of this the most notable instance is the empire of Augustus, after the period of civil wars from Marius to the defeat of Antony. The third is the rise of a new religion, using the word in its widest sense. Of this, an obvious instance is

[1] M. Creighton, *History of the Papacy*, Vol. V, p. 42.

the way in which Mohammed united the previously warring tribes of Arabia. The reign of naked force in international relations after the Great War might have been ended by the adoption of communism throughout Europe, if Russia had had an exportable surplus of food.

Where power is naked, not only internationally, but in the internal government of single States, the methods of acquiring power are far more ruthless than they are elsewhere. This subject has been treated, once for all, by Machiavelli. Take, for example, his laudatory account of Cesare Borgia's measures to protect himself in case of the death of Alexander VI:

'He decided to act in four ways. Firstly, by exterminating the families of those lords whom he had despoiled, so as to take away that pretext from the Pope. Secondly, by winning to himself all the gentlemen of Rome, so as to be able to curb the Pope with their aid. Thirdly, by converting the college more to himself. Fourthly, by acquiring so much power before the Pope should die that he could by his own measures resist the first shock. Of these four things, at the death of Alexander, he had accomplished three. For he had killed as many of the dispossessed lords as he could lay hands on, and few had escaped,' etc.

The second, third, and fourth of these methods might be employed at any time, but the first would shock public opinion in a period of orderly government. A British Prime Minister could not hope to consolidate his position by murdering the Leader of the Opposition. But where power is naked such moral restraints become inoperative.

Power is naked when its subjects respect it solely because it is power, and not for any other reason. Thus a form of power which has been traditional becomes naked as soon as the tradition ceases to be accepted. It follows that periods of free thought and vigorous criticism tend to develop into periods of naked power. So it was in Greece, and so it was in Renaissance Italy. The theory appropriate to naked power has been stated by Plato in the first book of the *Republic*, through the mouth of Thrasymachus, who gets annoyed with Socrates for his amiable attempts to find an ethical definition of justice. 'My doctrine is,' says Thrasymachus, 'that justice is simply the interest of the stronger'. He proceeds:

'Each government has its laws framed to suit its own interests; a democracy making democratical laws; an autocrat despotic laws, and so on. Now by this procedure these governments have pronounced that what is for the interest of themselves is just for their subjects; and whoever deviates from this, is chastised by them as guilty of illegality and injustice. Therefore, my good sir, my meaning is, that in all cities the same thing, namely, the interest of the established government, is just. And superior strength I presume is to be found on the side of the government. So that the conclusion of right reasoning is that the same thing, namely, the interest of the stronger, is everywhere just.'

Whenever this view is generally accepted, rulers cease to be subject to moral restraints, since what they do in order to retain power is not felt to be shocking except to those who suffer directly. Rebels, equally, are only restrained by the fear of failure; if they can succeed by ruthless means, they need not be afraid that this ruthlessness will make them unpopular.

The doctrine of Thrasymachus, where it is generally accepted, makes the existence of an orderly community entirely dependent upon the direct physical force at the disposal of the government. It thus makes a military tyranny inevitable. Other forms of government can only be stable where there is some widespread belief which inspires respect for the existing distribution of power. Beliefs which have been successful in this respect have usually been such as cannot stand against intellectual criticism. Power has at various times been limited, with general consent, to royal families, to aristocrats, to rich men, to men as opposed to women, and to white men as opposed to those with other pigmentations. But the spread of intelligence among subjects has caused them to reject such limitations, and the holders of power have been obliged either to yield or to rely upon naked force. If orderly government is to command general consent, some way must be found of persuading a majority of mankind to agree upon some doctrine other than that of Thrasymachus.

I postpone to a later chapter the consideration of methods of winning general consent to a form of government otherwise than by superstition, but a few preliminary remarks will be appropriate at this stage. In the first place, the problem is not essentially insoluble, since it has been solved in the United States. (It can hardly be said to have been solved in Great Britain, since respect for the Crown has been an essential element in British stability.) In the second place, the advantages of orderly government must be generally realised; this will usually involve the existence of opportunities for energetic men to become rich or powerful by constitutional means. Where some class containing individuals of energy and ability is debarred from desirable careers, there is an element of instability which is likely to lead to rebellion sooner or later. In the third place, there will be need of some social convention deliberately adopted in the interests of order, and not so flagrantly unjust as to arouse widespread opposition. Such a convention, if successful for a time, will soon become traditional, and will have all the strength that belongs to traditional power.

Rousseau's 'Social Contract', to a modern reader, does not seem very revolutionary, and it is difficult to see why it was so shocking to governments. The chief reason is, I think, that it sought to base governmental power upon a convention adopted on rational grounds, and not upon superstitious reverence for monarchs. The effect of Rousseau's doctrines upon the world shows the difficulty of causing men to agree upon some non-superstitious basis for government. Perhaps this is not possible when superstition is swept away very suddenly: some practice in voluntary co-operation is necessary as a preliminary training. The great difficulty is that respect for law is essential to social order, but is impossible under a traditional régime which no longer commands assent, and is necessarily disregarded in a revolution. But although the problem is difficult it must be solved if the existence of orderly communities is to be compatible with the free exercise of intelligence.

The nature of this problem is sometimes misapprehended. It is not sufficient to find, in thought, a form of government which, to the theorist, appears to afford no adequate motive for revolt; it is necessary to find a form of government which can be actually brought into existence, and further, if it exists, will command sufficient loyalty to be able to suppress or prevent revolution. This is a problem of practical statesmanship, in which account must be taken of all the beliefs and prejudices of the population concerned. There are those who believe that almost any group of men, when once it has seized the machinery of the State, can, by means of propaganda, secure general acquiescence. There are, however, obvious limitations to this doctrine. State propaganda has, in recent times, proved powerless when opposed to national feeling, as in India and (before 1921) in Ireland. It has difficulty in prevailing against strong religious feeling. How far, and for how long, it can prevail against the self-interest of the majority, is still a doubtful question. It must be admitted, however, that State propaganda becomes steadily more effective; the problem of securing acquiescence is therefore becoming easier for governments. The questions we have been raising will be considered more fully at later stages; for the present, they are merely to be borne in mind.

I have spoken hitherto of political power, but in the economic sphere naked power is at least equally important. Marx regarded all economic relations, except in the socialist community of the future, as entirely governed by naked power. *Per contra*, the late Élie Halévy, the historian of Benthamism, once maintained that, broadly speaking, what a man is paid for his work is what he himself believes it to be worth. I am sure this is not true of authors: I have always found, in my own case, that the more I thought a book was worth, the less I was paid for it. And if successful business men really believe that their work is worth what it brings in, they must be even stupider than they seem. None the less, there is an element of truth in Halévy's theory. In a stable community, there must be no considerable class with a burning sense of injustice; it is therefore to be supposed that, where there is no great economic discontent, most men do not feel themselves grossly underpaid. In undeveloped communities, in which a man's livelihood depends upon status rather than upon contract, he will, as a rule, consider that whatever is customary is just. But even then Halévy's formula inverts cause and effect: the custom is the cause of man's feeling as to what is just, and not vice versa. In this case, economic power is traditional; it only becomes naked when old customs are upset, or, for some reason, become objects of criticism.

In the infancy of industrialism, there were no customs to regulate the wages that should be paid, and the employees were not yet organised. Consequently the relation of employer and employed was one of naked power, within the limits allowed by the State; and at first these limits were very wide. The orthodox economists had taught that the wages of unskilled labour must always tend to fall to subsistence level, but they had not realised that this depended upon the exclusion of wage-earners from political power and from the benefits of combination. Marx saw that the question was one of power, but I think he underestimated political as compared with economic power. Trade unions, which immeasurably increase the bargaining power of wage-earners, can be suppressed if wage-earners have no share in political power; a series of legal decisions would have crippled them in England but for the fact that, from 1868 onward, urban working men had votes. Given trade union organisation, wages are no longer determined by naked power, but by bargaining, as in the purchase and sale of commodities.

The part played by naked power in economics is much greater than it was thought to be before the influence of Marx had become operative. In certain cases, this is obvious. The booty extracted by a highwayman from his victim, or by a conqueror from a vanquished nation, is obviously a matter of naked power. So is slavery, when the slave does not acquiesce from long habit. A payment is extorted by naked power, if it has to be made in spite of the indignation of the person making it. Such indignation exists in two classes of cases: where the payment is not customary, and where, owing to a change of outlook, what is customary has come to be thought unjust. Formerly, a man had complete control of the property of his wife, but the feminist movement caused a revolt against this custom, which led to a change in the law. Formerly, employers had no liability for accidents to their employees; here, also, sentiment changed, and brought about an alteration in the law. Examples of this kind are innumerable.

A wage-earner who is a Socialist may feel it unjust that his income is less than that of his employer; in that case, it is naked power that compels him to acquiesce. The old system of economic inequality is traditional, and does not, in itself, rouse indignation, except in those who are in revolt against the tradition. Thus every increase of socialistic opinion makes the power of the capitalist more naked; the case is analogous to that of heresy and the power of the Catholic Church. There are, as we have seen, certain evils that are inherent in naked power, as opposed to power which wins acquiescence; consequently every increase in socialist opinion tends to make the power of capitalists more harmful, except in so far as the ruthlessness of its exercise may be mitigated by fear. Given a community completely on the Marxist pattern, in which all wage-earners were convinced socialists and all others were equally convinced upholders of the capitalist system, the victorious party, whichever it might be, would have no escape from the exercise of naked force towards its opponents. This situation, which Marx prophesied, would be a very grave one. The propaganda of his disciples, in so far as it is successful, is tending to bring it about.

Most of the great abominations in human history are connected with naked power – not only those associated with war, but others equally terrible if less spectacular. Slavery and the slave trade, the exploitation of the Congo, the horrors of early indus-trialism, cruelty to children, judicial torture, the criminal law, prisons, workhouses, religious persecution, the atrocious treat-ment of the Jews, the merciless frivolities of despots, the unbe-lievable iniquity of the treatment of political opponents in Germany and Russia at the present day – all these are examples of the use of naked power against defenceless victims.

Many forms of unjust power which are deeply rooted in tradition must at one time have been naked. Christian wives, for many centuries, obeyed their husbands because St Paul said they should; but the story of Jason and Medea illustrates the difficulties that men must have had before St Paul's doctrine was generally accepted by women.

There must be power, either that of governments, or that of anarchic adventurers. There must even be naked power, so long as there are rebels against governments, or even ordinary crimi-nals. But if human life is to be, for the mass of mankind, anything better than a dull misery punctuated with moments of sharp horror, there must be as little naked power as possible. The ex-ercise of power, if it is to be something better than the infliction of wanton torture, must be hedged round by safeguards of law and custom, permitted only after due deliberation, and entrusted to men who are closely supervised in the interests of those who are subjected to them.

I do not pretend that this is easy. It involves, for one thing, the elimination of war, for all war is an exercise of naked power. It involves a world free from those intolerable oppressions that give rise to rebellions. It involves the raising of the standard of life throughout the world, and particularly in India, China, and Japan, to at least the level which had been reached in the United States before the depression. It involves some institution anal-ogous to the Roman tribunes, not for the people as a whole, but for every section that is liable to oppression, such as minorities and criminals. It involves, above all, a watchful public opinion, with opportunities of ascertaining the facts.

It is useless to trust in the virtue of some individual or set of individuals. The philosopher king was dismissed long ago as an idle dream, but the philosopher party, though equally fallacious, is hailed as a great discovery. No real solution of the problem of power is to be found in irresponsible government by a minority, or in any other short cut. But the further discussion of this matter must be left for a later chapter.

Chapter 7

Revolutionary Power

A traditional system, we observed, may break up in two different ways. It may happen that the creeds and mental habits upon which the old régime was based give way to mere scepticism; in that case, social cohesion can only be preserved by the exercise of naked power. Or it may happen that a new creed, involving new mental habits, acquires an increasing hold over men, and at last becomes strong enough to substitute a government in harmony with the new convictions in place of the one which is felt to have become obsolete. In this case the new revolutionary power has characteristics which are different both from traditional and from naked power. It is true that, if the revolution is successful, the system which it establishes soon becomes traditional; it is true, also, that the revolutionary struggle, if it is severe and prolonged, often degenerates into a struggle for naked power. Nevertheless, the adherents of a new creed are psychologically very different from ambitious adventurers, and their effects are apt to be both more important and more permanent.

I shall illustrate revolutionary power by considering four examples: (I) Early Christianity; (II) The Reformation; (III) The French Revolution and Nationalism; (IV) Socialism and the Russian Revolution.

I. *Early Christianity.* I am concerned with Christianity only as it affected power and social organisation, not, except incidentally, on the side of personal religion.

Christianity was, in its earliest days, entirely unpolitical. The best representatives of the primitive tradition in our time are the Christadelphians, who believe the end of the world to be imminent, and refuse to have any part or lot in secular affairs. This attitude, however, is only possible to a small sect. As the number of Christians increased and the Church grew more powerful, it was inevitable that a desire to influence the State should grow up. Diocletian's persecution must have very much strengthened this desire. The motives of Constantine's conversion remain more or less obscure, but it is evident that they were mainly political, which implies that the Church had become politically influential. The difference between the teachings of the Church and the traditional doctrines of the Roman State was so vast that the revolution which took place at the time of Constantine must be reckoned the most important in known history.

In relation to power, the most important of Christian doctrines was: 'We ought to obey God rather than man.' This was a precept to which nothing analogous had previously existed, except among the Jews. There were, it is true, religious duties, but they did not conflict with duty to the State except among Jews and Christians. Pagans were willing to acquiesce in the cult of the Emperor, even when they regarded his claim to divinity as wholly devoid of metaphysical truth. To the Christians, on the contrary, metaphysical truth was of the utmost moment: they believed that if they performed an act of worship to any but the one true God they incurred the risk of damnation, to which martyrdom was preferable as the lesser evil.

The principle that we ought to obey God rather than man has been interpreted by Christians in two different ways. God's commands may be conveyed to the individual conscience either directly, or indirectly through the medium of the Church. No one except Henry VIII and Hegel has ever held, until our own day, that they could be conveyed through the medium of the State. Christian teaching has thus involved a weakening of the State, either in favour of the right of private judgement, or in favour of the Church. The former, theoretically, involves anarchy; the latter involves two authorities, Church and State, with no clear principle according to which their spheres are to be delimited. Which are the things that are Caesar's and which are the things that are God's? To a Christian it is surely natural to say that all things are God's. The claims of the Church, therefore, are likely to be such as the State will find intolerable. The conflict between the Church and the State has never been theoretically resolved, and continues down to the present day in such matters as education.

It might have beeen supposed that the conversion of Constantine would lead to harmony between Church and State. This, however, was not the case. The first Christian Emperors were Arians, and the period of orthodox Emperors in the West was very brief, owing to the incursions of the Arian Goths and

Vandals. Later, when the adherence of the Eastern Emperors to the Catholic Faith had become unquestionable, Egypt was monophysite and much of Western Asia was Nestorian. The heretics in these countries welcomed the followers of the Prophet, as being less persecuting than the Byzantine government. As against the Christian State, the Church was everywhere victorious in these many contests; only the new religion of Islam gave the State power to dominate the Church.

The nature of the conflict between the Church and the Arian Empire of the late fourth century is illustrated by the struggle between the Empress Justina and Saint Ambrose, Archbishop of Milan, in the year 385. Her son Valentinian was a minor, and she was acting as regent; both were Arians. Being in Milan during Holy Week, the Empress 'was persuaded, that a Roman emperor might claim, in his own dominions, the public exercise of his religion; and she proposed to the Archbishop, as a moderate and reasonable concession, that he should resign the use of a single church, either in the city or suburbs of Milan. But the conduct of Ambrose was governed by very different principles. The palaces of the earth might indeed belong to Caesar; but the churches were the houses of God; and, within the limits of his diocese, he himself, as the lawful successor of the apostles, was the only minister of God. The privileges of Christianity, temporal as well as spiritual, were confined to the true believers; and the mind of Ambrose was satisfied that his own theological opinions were the standard of truth and orthodoxy. The archbishop, who refused to hold any conference, or negotiation, with the instruments of Satan, declared, with modest firmness, his resolution to die a martyr, rather than yield to the impious sacrilege.'[1]

It soon appeared, however, that he had no need to fear martyrdom. When he was summoned before the Council, he was followed by a vast and angry mob of supporters, who threatened to invade the palace and perhaps kill the Empress and her son. The Gothic mercenaries, through Arian, hesitated to act against so holy a man, and to avoid revolution the Empress was obliged to give way. 'The mother of Valentinian could never forgive the triumph of Ambrose; and the royal youth uttered a passionate exclamation, that his own servants were ready to betray him into the hands of an insolent priest' (ibid.).

In the following year (386) the Empress again attempted to

[1] E. Gibbon, Ch. XXVII.

overcome the Saint. An edict of banishment was pronounced against him. But he took refuge in the cathedral, where he was supported, day and night, by the faithful and the recipients of ecclesiastical charity. To keep them awake, he 'introduced into the church of Milan the useful institution of a loud and regular psalmody'. The zeal of his followers was further reinforced by miracles, and in the end 'the feeble sovereign of Italy found himself unable to contend with the favourite of heaven'.

Such contests, of which there were many, established the independent power of the Church. Its victory was due partly to almsgiving, partly to organisation, but mainly to the fact that no vigorous creed or sentiment was opposed to it. While Rome was conquering, a Roman could feel strongly about the glory of the State, because it gratified his imperial pride; but in the fourth century this sentiment had been long extinct. Enthusiasm for the State, as a force comparable with religion, revived only with the rise of nationalism in modern times.

Every successful revolution shakes authority and makes social cohesion more difficult. So it was with the revolution that gave power to the Church. Not only did it greatly weaken the State, but it set the pattern for subsequent revolutions. Moreover, the individualism, which had been an important element of Christian teaching in its early days, remained as a dangerous source of both theological and secular rebellion. The individual conscience, when it could not accept the verdict of the Church, was able to find support in the Gospels for a refusal to submit. Heresy might be annoying to the Church, but was not, as such, contrary to the spirit of primitive Christianity.

This difficulty is inherent in every authority that owes its origin to revolution. It must maintain that the original revolution was justified, and it cannot, logically, contend that all subsequent revolutions must be wicked.[1] The anarchic fire in Christianity

---

[1] The attempt to do so sometimes has strange results. The young in Russia at the present day are carefully sheltered from laudatory accounts of the revolutionary movement in Tsarist days. *The Letter of an Old Bolshevik* (George Allen & Unwin), after telling of a supposed plot by some students to murder Stalin, continues: 'From the accused students, threads were drawn to *professors of political science and party history*. It is easy to find pages in any lectures on the history of the Russian revolutionary movement highly conducive nowadays to the cultivation of critical attitudes in respect to the Government, and young hotheads always like to buttress their conclusions concerning the present by citing facts which they have been

remained alive, though deeply buried, throughout the Middle Ages; at the Reformation, it suddenly shot up into a great conflagration.

II. *The Reformation*. From the point of view of power, the Reformation has two aspects that concern us: on the one hand, its theological anarchism weakened the Church; on the other hand, by weakening the Church it strengthened the State. The Reformation was chiefly important as the partial destruction of a great international organisation, which had repeatedly proved itself stronger than any secular government. Luther, in order to succeed against the Church and the extremists, was obliged to rely upon the support of secular princes[1]; the Lutheran Church never, until the time of Hitler, showed any disloyalty to governments that were not Catholic. The peasants' revolt gave Luther another reason for preaching submission to princes. The Church, as an independent power, practically ceased to exist in Lutheran countries, and became part of the machinery for preaching submission to the secular government.

In England, Henry VIII took the matter in hand with characteristic vigour and ruthlessness. By declaring himself Head of the

---

taught in school to regard as officially established. All Agranov had to do was to pick the professors who, in his opinion, were to be regarded as fellow conspirators. This was how the first batch of defendants *in the trial of the sixteen* was recruited.'

[1] 'The Peasants' War,' says Tawney in *Religion and the Rise of Capitalism*, 'with its touching appeal to the Gospel and its frightful catastrophe, not only terrified Luther into his outburst: "Whoso can, strike, smite, strangle, or stab, secretly or publicly . . . such wonderful times are these that a prince can better merit Heaven with bloodshed than another with prayer"; it also helped to stamp on Lutheranism an almost servile reliance on the secular authorities.' A few pages later he quotes another saying of Luther's: 'No one need think that the world can be ruled without blood. The civil sword shall and must be red and bloody.' Tawney's comment is as follows: 'Thus the axe takes the place of the stake, and authority, expelled from the altar, finds a new and securer home upon the throne. The maintenance of Christian morality is to be transferred from the discredited ecclesiastical authorities to the hands of the State. Sceptical as to the existence of unicorns and salamanders, the age of Machiavelli and Henry VIII found food for its credulity in the worship of that rare monster, the God-fearing Prince.' Some such credulity is characteristic of revolutionary epochs.

Church of England, he set to work to make religion secular and national. He had no wish that the religion of England should be part of the universal religion of Christendom; he wished English religion to minister to his glory rather than to the glory of God. By means of subservient Parliaments, he could alter dogmas as he chose; and he had no difficulty in executing those who disliked his alterations. The dissolution of the monasteries brought him revenue, which enabled him easily to destroy such Catholic insurrections as the Pilgrimage of Grace. Gunpowder and the Wars of the Roses had weakened the old feudal aristocracy, whose heads he cut off whenever he felt so disposed. Wolsey, who relied upon the ancient power of the Church, fell; Cromwell and Cranmer were Henry's subservient tools. Henry was a pioneer, who first showed the world what, in the eclipse of the Church, the power of the State could be.

The work of Henry VIII might not have been permanent, but for the fact that, under Elizabeth, a form of nationalism associated with Protestantism became at once necessary and lucrative. Self-preservation demanded the defeat of Catholic Spain, and took the pleasant form of capturing Spanish treasure-ships. After that time, the only danger to the Anglican Church was from the Left, not from the Right. But the attack from the Left was defeated, and was succeeded by

> Good King Charles's golden days,
> When loyalty no harm meant.

The *Vicar of Bray* illustrates the defeat of the Church by the State in Protestant countries. So long as religious toleration was not thought possible, Erastianism was the only available substitute for the authority of the Pope and General Councils.

Erastianism, however, could never be satisfactory to men in whom personal religion was strong. There was something grotesque in asking men to submit to the authority of Parliament on such questions as the existence of Purgatory. The Independents rejected the State and the Church equally as theological authorities, and claimed the right of private judgement, with the corollary of religious toleration. This point of view readily associated itself with revolt against secular despotism. If each individual had a right to his own theological opinions, had he not, perhaps, other rights as well? Were there not assignable limits to what governments might legitimately do to private citizens? Hence the doctrine of the Rights of Man, carried across the Atlantic by the defeated followers of Cromwell, embodied by Jefferson in the American Constitution, and brought back to Europe by the French Revolution.

III. *The French Revolution and Nationalism.* The Western world, from the Reformation until 1848, was undergoing a continuous upheaval which may be called the Rights-of-Man Revolution. In 1848, this movement began to transform itself into nationalism east of the Rhine. In France, the association had existed since 1792, and in England from the beginning; in America, it had existed since 1776. The nationalist aspect of the movement has gradually overpowered the Rights-of-Man aspect, but this latter was at first the more important.

It is customary in our day to pour scorn on the Rights of Man, as a piece of shallow eighteenth-century rhetoric. It is true that, philosophically considered, the doctrine is indefensible; but historically and pragmatically it was useful, and we enjoy many freedoms which it helped to win. A Benthamite, to whom the abstract conception of 'rights' is inadmissible, can state what is, for practical purposes, the same doctrine in the following terms: 'The general happiness is increased if a certain sphere is defined within which each individual is to be free to act as he chooses, without the interference of any external authority.' The administration of justice was also a matter that interested the advocates of the Rights of Man; they held that no man should be deprived of life or liberty without due process of law. This is an opinion which, whether true or false, involves no philosophical absurdity.

It is obvious that the doctrine is, in origin and sentiment, antigovernmental. The subject of a despotic government holds that he should be free to choose his religion as he pleases, to exercise his business in all lawful ways without bureaucratic interference, to marry where he loves, and to rebel against an alien domination. Where governmental decisions are necessary, they should – so the advocate of the Rights of Man contends – be the decisions of a majority or of their representatives, not of an arbitrary and merely traditional authority such as that of kings and priests. These views gradually prevailed throughout the civilised world, and produced the peculiar mentality of Liberalism, which retains even when in power a certain suspicion of governmental action.

Individualism has obvious logical and historical relations to Protestantism, which asserted its doctrines in the theological sphere, although it often abandoned them when it acquired power. Through Protestantism, there is a connection with early Christianity, and with its hostility to the pagan State. There is also a deeper connection with Christianity, owing to its concern with the individual soul. According to Christian ethics, no State necessity can justify the authorities in compelling a man to perform a sinful action. The Church holds that a marriage is null if either party is subject to compulsion. Even in persecution the theory is still individualistic: the purpose is to lead the individual heretic to recantation and repentance, rather than to effect a benefit to the community. Kant's principle, that each man is an end in himself, is derived from Christian teaching. In the Catholic Church, a long career of power had somewhat obscured the individualism of early Christianity; but Protestantism, especially in its more extreme forms, revived it, and applied it to the theory of government.

When a revolutionary and a traditional creed fight for mastery, as happened in the French Revolution, the power of the victors over the vanquished is naked power. The revolutionary and Napoleonic armies exhibited a combination of the propagandist force of a new creed with naked power on a larger scale than had been seen before in Europe, and the effect upon the imagination of the Continent has lasted to the present day. Traditional power everywhere was challenged by the Jacobins, but it was Napoleon's armies that made the challenge effective. Napoleon's enemies fought in defence of ancient abuses, and established a reactionary system when they were at last victorious. Under their dull repression his violence and extortion were forgotten; the deadness of the Great Peace made war seem splendid and bayonets the harbingers of freedom. A Byronic cult of violence grew up during the years of the Holy Alliance, and gradually moulded men's daily thoughts. All this is traceable to the naked power of Napoleon, and its connection with the emancipating war-cries of the Revolution. Hitler and Mussolini, no less than Stalin, owe their success to Robespierre and Napoleon.

Revolutionary power, as the case of Napoleon shows, is very apt to degenerate into naked power. The clash of rival fanaticism, whether in foreign conquest, in religious persecution, or in the class war, is distinguished, it is true, from naked power by the fact that it is a group, not an individual, that seeks power, and that it seeks it, not for its own sake, but for the sake of its creed. But since power is its means, and in a long conflict the end is apt to be forgotten, there is a tendency, especially if the struggle is long and severe, for fanaticism to become gradually transformed into the mere pursuit of victory. The difference between revolutionary and naked power is therefore often less than it seems to be at first sight. In Latin America, the revolt against Spain was led, at first, by Liberals and democrats, but ended, in most cases, in the establishment of a series of unstable military dictatorships separated by mutinies. Only where the revolutionary faith is strong and widespread, and victory is not too long delayed, can the habit of co-operation survive the shock involved in revolution, and enable the new government to rest upon consent rather than upon mere military force. A government without psychological authority must be a tyranny.

IV. *The Russian Revolution.* Of the importance of the Russian Revolution in the history of the world, it is as yet too soon to judge; we can only speak, as yet, of some of its aspects. Like early Christianity, it preaches doctrines which are international and even anti-national; like Islam, but unlike Christianity, it is essentially political. The only part of its creed, however, which, so far, has proved effective, is the challenge to Liberalism. Until November 1917, Liberalism had only been combated by reactionaries; Marxists, like other progressives, advocated democracy, free speech, free press, and the rest of the Liberal political apparatus. The Soviet Government, when it seized power, reverted to the teaching of the Catholic Church in its great days: that it is the business of Authority to propagate Truth, both by positive teaching and by the suppression of all rival doctrines. This involved, of course, the establishment of an undemocratic dictatorship, depending for its stability upon the Red Army. What was new was the amalgamation of political and economic power, which made possible an enormous increase of governmental control.

The international part of Communist doctrine has proved ineffective, but the rejection of Liberalism has had an extraordinary success. From the Rhine to the Pacific Ocean, all its chief doctrines are rejected almost everywhere; Italy first, and then Germany, adopted the political technique of the Bolsheviks; even in the countries that remain democratic, the Liberal faith has lost its fervour. Liberals hold, for example, that when public buildings are destroyed by incendiaries, an attempt should be made by the police and the law-courts to discover the actual culprits; but the modern-minded man holds, like Nero, that the guilt should be attributed, by means of manufactured evidence, to whatever party he personally dislikes. As regards such matters as free speech, he holds, like St Ambrose, that there should be freedom for his own party, but not for any other.

The result of such doctrines is to transform all power, first, into revolutionary power, and then, by inevitable gradations, into naked power. This danger is imminent; but as to the means of averting it I shall say no more until a later stage.

The decay of Liberalism has many causes, both technical and psychological. They are to be found in the technique of war, in the technique of production, in the increased facilities for propaganda, and in nationalism, which is itself an outcome of Liberal doctrines. All these causes, especially where the State has economic as well as political power, have immensely increased the power of governments. The problems of our time, as regards the relation of the individual to the State, are new problems, which Locke and Montesquieu will not enable us to solve. A modern community, just as much as those of the eighteenth century, requires, if it is to remain happy and prosperous, a sphere for individual initiative, but this sphere must be defined afresh, and safeguarded by new methods.

Chapter 8

Economic Power

Economic power, unlike military power, is not primary, but derivative. Within one State, it depends on law; in international dealings it is only on minor issues that it depends on law, but when large issues are involved it depends upon war or the threat of war. It has been customary to accept economic power without analysis, and this has led, in modern times, to an undue emphasis upon economics, as opposed to war and propaganda, in the causal interpretation of history.

Apart from the economic power of labour, all other economic power, in its ultimate analysis, consists in being able to decide, by the use of armed force if necessary, who shall be allowed to stand upon a given piece of land and to put things into it and take things from it. In some cases this is obvious. The oil of Southern Persia belongs to the Anglo-Persian Oil Company, because the British Government has decreed that no one else shall have access to it, and has hitherto been strong enough to enforce its will; but if Great Britain were defeated in a serious war, the ownership would probably change. Rhodesian goldfields belong to certain rich men because the British democracy thought it worth while to make these men rich by going to war with Lobengula. The oil of the United States belongs to certain companies because they have a legal title to it, and the armed forces of the United States are prepared to enforce the law; the Indians, to whom the oil regions originally belonged, have no legal title, because they were defeated in war. The iron ore of Lorraine belongs to the citizens of France or Germany according to which has been victor in the most recent war between those two countries. And so on.

But the same analysis applies in less obvious cases. Why must a tenant farmer pay rent for his farm, and why can he sell his crop? He must pay rent because the land 'belongs' to the landowner. The landowner owns the land because he has acquired it by purchase or inheritance from someone else. Pursuing the history of his title backwards, we come ultimately to some man who acquired the land by force – either the arbitrary power of a king exercised in favour of some courtier, or a large-scale conquest such as those of the Saxons and Normans. In the intervals between such acts of violence, the power of the State is used to ensure that ownership shall pass according to law. And ownership of land is power to decide who shall be permitted to be on the land. For this permission the farmer pays rent, and in virtue of it he can sell his crop.

The power of the industrialist is of the same sort; it rests, in the last analysis, upon the lock-out, that is to say, upon the fact that the owner of a factory can call upon the forces of the State to prevent unauthorised persons from entering it. In certain states of public opinion, the State may be reluctant to do the bidding of the owner in this respect; the consequence is that stay-in strikes become possible. As soon as they are tolerated by the State, ownership ceases to be vested wholly in the employer, and begins to be shared, in some degree, with the employees.

Credit is more abstract than other kinds of economic power, but is not essentially different; it depends upon the legal right to transfer a surplus of consumable commodities from those who have produced them to others who are engaged in work which is not immediately productive. In the case of a private person or corporation which borrows money, the obligations can be enforced by law, but in the case of a government the ultimate sanction is the military power of other governments. This sanction may fail, as in Russia after the Revolution; when it fails, the borrower simply acquires the property of the lender. For example, it is the Soviet Government, not the pre-war shareholders, that has power to decide who shall have access to the Lena goldfields.

Thus the economic power of private persons depends upon the decision of their government to employ its armed forces, if necessary, in accordance with a set of rules as to who shall be allowed access to land; while the economic power of governments depends in part upon their armed forces, and in part upon the respect of other governments for treaties and international law.

The connection of economic power with government is to some extent reciprocal; that is to say, a group of men may, by combination, acquire military power, and, having acquired it, may possess economic power. The ultimate acquisition of economic power may, in fact, be their original motive in combining.

Consider, for example, the semi-anarchic conditions prevailing in a gold-rush such as that in California in 1849, or in Victoria a few years later. A man who possessed gold which he had acquired legally on his own holding could not be said to possess economic power until he had lodged his gold in a bank. Until then, he was liable to be robbed and murdered. In a state of *complete* anarchy, involving a war of all against all, gold would be useless except to a man so quick and sure with his revolver as to be able to defend himself against every assailant; and even to him, it could only be a pleasant object to contemplate, since he could satisfy his needs by the threat of murder, without having to make any payment. Such a state of affairs would necessarily be unstable, except possibly in a very sparse food-gathering population. Agriculture is impossible unless there are means of preventing trespass and the theft of crops. It is obvious that an anarchic community composed of more or less civilised individuals, like the men in a gold rush, will soon evolve a government of some kind, such as a committee of Vigilantes. Energetic men will combine to prevent others from plundering them; if there is no outside authority to interfere, they may also plunder others, but they will do so with moderation, for fear of killing the goose that lays the golden eggs. They may, for example, sell protection in return for a percentage of a man's earnings. This is called income tax. As soon as there are rules determining the giving of protection, the reign of military force is disguised as the reign of law, and anarchy has ceased to exist. But the ultimate basis of law and of economic relations is still the military power of the Vigilantes.

The historical development has, of course, been different from this, because it has been gradual, and not dependent, as a rule, upon men accustomed to more civilised institutions than those under which they were living at the moment. None the less, something very much of the above sort occurs whenever there is foreign conquest, particularly if the conquerors are a small minority; and ownership of land can usually be traced back to some such conquest. In international economic relations, we have not yet reached the stage represented by the first formation of the committee of Vigilantes: the stronger nations, individually, each still extract money from the weaker by the threat of death. This is illustrated by recent British dealings with Mexico in the matter of oil, or rather would be but for the Monroe Doctrine. A more forcible illustration was the Reparation Clauses of the Versailles

Treaty. But in the internal economic systems of civilised countries the legal foundations are complex. The wealth of the Church depends upon tradition; wage-earners have profited to some extent by trade unionism and by political action; wives and children have rights which are based upon the moral sentiments of the community. But whatever the economic rules made by the State may be, military power in the background is essential to their enforcement.

In the case of private persons, the rules made by the State constitute the relevant part of the Law. This part of the Law, like every other, is only effective when it is supported by public opinion. Public opinion, in accordance with the eighth commandment, reprobates theft, and defines 'theft' as taking property in a manner condemned by the law. Thus the economic power of private persons rests ultimately on opinion, namely on the moral condemnation of theft, together with the sentiment which allows theft to be defined by the law. Where this sentiment is weak or non-existent, property is endangered; Stalin, for instance, began his career as a virtuous bandit practising his vocation in the interests of Communism. We have seen how the power of the Pope to release men from the moral obligation of the eighth commandment enabled him to control the Italian bankers in the thirteenth century.

Economic power within a State, although ultimately derived from law and public opinion, easily acquires a certain independence. It can influence law by corruption and public opinion by propaganda. It can put politicians under obligations which interfere with their freedom. It can threaten to cause a financial crisis. But there are very definite limits to what it can achieve. Caesar was helped to power by his creditors, who saw no hope of repayment except through his success; but when he had succeeded he was powerful enough to defy them. Charles V borrowed from the Fuggers the money required to buy the position of Emperor, but when he had become Emperor he snapped his fingers at them and they lost what they had lent.[1] The City of

[1] The Fuggers never could resist a Hapsburg borrower. They lent money, not only to Charles V, but to the Emperor Maximilian before him, and to his Spanish descendants after him. The Introduction to the *Fugger News Letters* says: 'At least four million ducats had been borrowed from the Fuggers by the Spanish kings and never repaid, and it is not exaggeration if the losses accruing from their business transactions with the Hapsburgs in the west and east are estimated at

London, in our own day, has had a similar experience in helping German recovery; and so has Thyssen in helping to put Hitler into power.

Let us consider, for a moment, the power of the plutocracy in a democratic country. It has been unable to introduce Asiatic labour in California or Australia, except in early days in small numbers. It has been unable to destroy trade unionism. It has been unable, especially in Great Britain, to avoid heavy taxation of the rich. And it has been unable to prevent socialist propaganda. *Per contra*, it can prevent governments composed of Socialists from introducing Socialism, and if they are obstinate it can bring about their downfall by engineering a crisis and by propaganda. If these means were to fail, it could stir up a civil war to prevent the establishment of Socialism. That is to say, where the issue is simple and public opinion is definite, the plutocracy is powerless; but where public opinion is undecided, or baffled by the complexity of the issue, the plutocracy can secure a desired political result.

The power of trade unions is the converse of the power of the rich. Trade unions can keep out coloured labour, prevent their own extinction, secure heavy death duties and income tax, and preserve freedom for their own propaganda. But they have failed hitherto to bring about Socialism, or to keep in power governments which they liked but which a majority of the nation distrusted.

Thus the power of economic organisations to influence political decisions in a democracy is limited by public opinion, which, on many important issues, refuses to be swayed even by very intensive propaganda. Democracy, where it exists, has more reality than many opponents of capitalism are willing to admit.

Although economic power, in so far as it is regulated by law, ultimately depends upon ownership of land, it is not the nominal landowners who have the greatest share of it in a modern community. In feudal times, the men who owned the land had the power; they could deal with wages by such measures as the Statute of Labourers, and with the nascent power of credit by

eight million florins. . . . But for them (the Fuggers) the Reformation in Germany would probably have triumphed without opposition. The most capable members of this House strove for a century, but nothing remained to their innumerable heirs but an inordinately costly pile of parchments and heavily mortgaged landed property.'

pogroms. But where industrialism has developed, credit has become stronger than nominal ownership of land. Landowners borrow, wisely or unwisely, and in doing so become dependent upon the banks. This is a commonplace, and usually regarded as entirely a consequence of changes in the technique of production. In fact, however, as may be seen from its having happened in India, where agricultural technique is not modern, it is quite as much a result of the power and determination of the State to enforce the law. Where Law is not all-powerful, money-lenders are, at intervals, murdered by their debtors, who at the same time burn all documents giving evidence of indebtedness. Everybody connected with the land, from prince to peasant, has been addicted to borrowing ever since there first were willing lenders; but it is only where Law is respected and enforced that the borrower has to go on paying interest until he is ruined. Where that happens, the economic power derived from landed property passes from the borrower to the lender. And in a modern community the lender is usually a bank.

In a modern large corporation, ownership and power are by no means necessarily combined. This matter, as it affects the United States, is authoritatively dealt with in a very important book, *The Modern Corporation and Private Property*, by Berle and Means (1932). They contend that, although ownership is centrifugal, economic power is centripetal; by a very careful and exhaustive investigation they arrive at the conclusion that two thousand individuals control half the industry of the United States (p. 33). They regard the modern executive as analogous to the kings and Popes of former times; in their opinion, more is to be learnt as to his motives by studying such men as Alexander the Great than by considering him as the successor of the tradesmen who appear in the pages of Adam Smith. The concentration of power in these vast economic organisations is analogous – so they argue – to that in the mediaeval Church or in the National State, and is such as to enable corporations to compete with States on equal terms.

It is easy to see how this concentration has come about. The ordinary shareholder in a railway company, for example, has no voice in the management of the railway; he may, in theory, have about as much as the average voter at a Parliamentary election has in the management of the country, but in practice he has even less than this. The economic power of the railway is in the hands of a very few men; in America, it has usually been in the hands of one man. In every developed country, the bulk of economic power belongs to a small body of individuals. Some-times these men are private capitalists, as in America, France, and Great Britain; sometimes they are politicians, as in Germany, Italy and Russia. The latter system arises where economic and political power have coalesced. The tendency for economic power to become concentrated in few hands is a commonplace, but this tendency applies to power in general, not only to economic power. A system in which economic and political power have coalesced is at a later stage of development than one in which they are separate, just as a Steel Trust belongs to a later stage than a number of competing small steel manufacturers. But I do not wish, as yet, to discuss the totalitarian State.

The possession of economic power may lead to the possession of military or propaganda power, but the opposite process is just as apt to occur. Under primitive conditions, military power is usually the source of other kinds, in so far as the relations between different countries are concerned. Alexander was not as rich as the Persians, and the Romans were not as rich as the Carthaginians; but by victory in war the conquerors, in each case, made themselves richer than their enemies. The Mohammedans, at the beginning of their career of conquest, were very much poorer than the Byzantines, and the Teutonic invaders were poorer than the Western Empire. In all these cases, military power was the source of economic power. But within the Arab nation, the military and economic power of the Prophet and his family was derived from propaganda; so was the power and wealth of the Church in the West.

There are a number of instances of States which have acquired military power because of their economic strength. In antiquity, the Greek maritime cities and Carthage are the most notable examples; in the Middle Ages, the Italian republics; and in modern times, first Holland and then England. In all these instances, with the partial exception of England after the industrial revolution, economic power was based upon commerce, not upon the ownership of raw materials. Certain cities or States acquired a partial monopoly of commerce through a combination of skill with geographical advantages. (The latter alone were not sufficient, as may be seen in the decline of Spain during the seventeenth century.) The wealth obtained by commerce was spent, in part, on the hire of mercenaries, and was thus made into a means of obtaining military power. This method had, however, the drawback that it involved a constant danger of mutiny or large-scale treachery; for this reason, Machiavelli disapproves of it, and advises armies composed of citizens. The advice would be sound in the case of a large country enriched by commerce, but in the case of a Greek City State or a small Italian Republic it was useless. Economic power based on commerce can only be stable when it belongs to a large community, or to one which is much more civilised than its neighbours.

Commerce, however, has lost its importance. Owing to improvement in the means of communication, geographical situation is less important than it used to be; and owing to imperialism, the important States have less need of external trade than they formerly had. The important form of economic power, in international relations, is now the possession of raw materials and food; and the most important raw materials are those required in war. Thus military and economic power have become scarcely distinguishable. Take oil, for example: a country cannot fight without oil, and cannot own oil fields unless it is able to fight. Either condition may fail: the oil of Persia was useless to the Persians because they had no adequate armies, and the armed forces of Germany will be useless to the Germans unless they can obtain oil. A similar state of affairs exists in regard to food: a powerful war-machine requires an immense diversion of national energies from food production, and therefore depends upon military control of large fertile areas.

Economic and military power have never, in the past, been so closely interconnected as they are at present. No nation can be powerful without developed industrialism and access to raw materials and food. *Per contra*, it is by means of military power that nations acquire access to such raw materials as are not obtainable on their own territory. The Germans, during the War, acquired by conquest the oil of Rumania and the harvest of the Ukraine; and States which derive raw materials from the tropics hold their colonies by their military strength or by that of their allies.

The part played by propaganda in national power has increased with the spread of education. A nation cannot succeed in modern war unless most people are willing to suffer hardship and many people are willing to die. In order to produce this willingness, the rulers have to persuade their subjects that the war is about something important – so important, in fact, as to be worthy of martyrdom. Propaganda was a large part of the cause of the Allied victory in the War, and almost the sole cause of the Soviet victory in the years 1918 to 1920. It is obvious that the same causes which are leading to a coalescence of military and economic power are also tending towards a unification of both with propaganda power. There is, in fact, a general tendency towards the combination of all forms of power in a single organisation, which must necessarily be the State. Unless counteracting forces come into play, the distinction between different kinds of power will soon be of only historical interest.

At this point, we must consider a view which Marxism has made familiar, namely that capitalism tends to generate a war of classes which will ultimately dominate all other forms of conflict. It is not by any means easy to interpret Marx, but he seems to have thought that, in times of peace, all economic power belongs to landowners and capitalists, who will exploit their control to the uttermost, thereby stirring the proletariat to revolt. The proletariat, being the vast majority, will win in war as soon as they are united, and will institute a system in which the economic power derived from land and capital will be transferred to the community as a whole. Whether or not this theory is exactly that of Marx, it is, broadly, that of present-day communists, and therefore deserves to be examined.

The view that all economic power belongs to landowners and capitalists is one which, though roughly true, and though I have hitherto assumed it, has important limitations. Landowners and capitalists are helpless without labour, and strikes, when they are sufficiently determined and widespread, can secure for labour a share of economic power. But the possibilities of the strike are such a familiar theme that I shall say no more about them.

The second question that arises is: Will capitalists, in fact, exploit their control to the uttermost? Where they are prudent, they do not do so, for fear of just such consequences as Marx foresaw. If they allow the workers some share in prosperity they may prevent them from becoming revolutionary; of this the most notable example is in the United States, where the skilled workers are on the whole Conservative.

The assumption that the proletariat are the majority is very questionable. It is definitely untrue in agricultural countries where peasant proprietorship prevails. And in countries where there is much settled wealth, many men who, from an economic point of view, are proletarians, are politically on the side of the rich, because their employment depends upon the demand for luxuries. A class-war, if it occurs, is therefore by no means certain to be won by the proletariat.

Finally, most people, at a crisis, feel more loyalty to their nation than to their class. This may not always be the case, but there is as yet no sign of any change since 1914, when almost all nominal internationalists became patriotic and bellicose. The class-war, therefore, though it remains a possibility of the distant future, is hardly to be expected while the danger of nationalist wars remains as great as it is at present.

It may be said that the present civil war in Spain, and its repercussion in other countries, proves that the class-war is now dominant over nationalist considerations. I do not think, however, that the course of events bears out this view. Germany and Italy have nationalistic grounds for siding with Franco; England and France have nationalistic grounds for opposing him. It is true that British opposition to Franco has been much less, hitherto, than it would have been if British interest alone had determined the action of Government, because Conservatives naturally sympathise with him. Nevertheless, as soon as such matters as Moroccan ore or naval control of the Mediterranean are in question, British interests override political sympathies. The grouping of the Great Powers is again what it was before 1914, in spite of the Russian Revolution. Liberals disliked the Tsar, and Conservatives dislike Stalin; but neither Sir E. Grey nor the present Government could permit such matter of taste to interfere with the pursuit of British interests.

To sum up what has been said in this chapter: the economic power of a military unit (which may be composed of several independent States) depends upon (*a*) its capacity to defend its own territory, (*b*) its ability to threaten the territory of others, (*c*) its possession of raw materials, food, and industrial skill, (*d*) its power of supplying goods and services needed by other military units. In all this, military and economic factors are inextricably mingled; for example, Japan, by purely military means, has acquired in China raw materials which are essential to *great* military strength, and in like manner England and France have acquired oil in the Near East, but both would have been impossible without a considerable degree of previous industrial development. The importance of economic factors in war steadily increases as war becomes more mechanised and scientific, but it is not safe to assume that the side with superior economic resources must necessarily be victorious. The importance of propaganda in generating national feeling has increased as much as that of economic factors.

In the internal economic relations of a single State, the law sets limits to what can be done in the way of extracting wealth from others. An individual or a group must possess a complete or partial monopoly of something desired by others. Monopolies can be created by law; for example, patents, copyrights, and ownership of land. They can also be created by combination, as in the cases of trusts and trade unions. Apart from what private individuals or groups can extract by bargaining, the State retains the right to take by force whatever it considers necessary. And influential private groups can induce the State to use this right, as well as the power of making war, in a manner which is advantageous to themselves though not necessarily to the nation as whole; they can also cause the law to be such as is convenient to themselves, e.g. by allowing combinations of employers but not of wage-earners. Thus the actual degree of economic power possessed by an individual or group depends upon military strength and influence through propaganda quite as much as upon the factors usually considered in economics. Economics as a separate science is unrealistic, and misleading if taken as a guide in practice. It is one element – a very important element, it is true – in a wider study, the science of power.

Chapter 9

Power over Opinion

It is easy to make out a case for the view that opinion is omnipotent, and that all other forms of power are derived from it. Armies are useless unless the soldiers believe in the cause for which they are fighting, or, in the case of mercenaries, have confidence in the ability of their commander to lead them to victory. Law is impotent unless it is generally respected. Economic institutions depend upon respect for the law; consider, for example, what would happen to banking if the average citizen had no objection to forgery. Religious opinion has often proved itself more powerful than the State. If, in any country, a large majority were in favour of Socialism, Capitalism would become unworkable. On such grounds it might be said that opinion is the ultimate power in social affairs.

But this would be only a half-truth, since it ignores the forces which cause opinion. While it is true that opinion is an essential element in military force, it is equally true that military force may generate opinion. Almost every European country has, at this moment, the religion which was that of its government in the late sixteenth century, and this must be attributed mainly to the control of persecution and propaganda by means of the armed forces in the several countries. It is traditional to regard opinion as due to mental causes, but this is only true of the immediate causes: in the background, there is usually force in the service of some creed.

Per contra, a creed never has force at its command to begin with, and the first steps in the production of a wide-spread opinion must be taken by means of persuasion alone.

We have thus a kind of see-saw: first, pure persuasion leading to the conversion of a minority; then force exerted to secure that the rest of the community shall be exposed to the right propaganda; and finally a genuine belief on the part of the great majority, which makes the use of force again unnecessary. Some bodies of opinion never get beyond the first stage, some reach the second and then fail, others are successful in all three. The Society of Friends has never got beyond persuasion. The other nonconformists acquired the forces of the State in the time of Cromwell, but failed in their propaganda after they had seized power. The Catholic Church, after three centuries of persuasion, captured the State in the time of Constantine, and then, by force, established a system of propaganda which converted almost all the pagans and enabled Christianity to survive the barbarian invasion. The Marxist creed has reached the second stage, if not the third, in Russia, but elsewhere is still in the first stage.

There are, however, some important instances of influence on opinion without the aid of force at any stage. Of these the most notable is the rise of science. At the present day, science, in civilised countries, is encouraged by the State, but in its early days this was not the case. Galileo was made to recant, Newton was stopped by being made Master of the Mint, Lavoisier was guillotined on the grounds that 'la République n'pas besoin de savants'. Nevertheless these men, and a few others like them, were the creators of the modern world; their effect upon social life has been greater than that of any other men known to history, not excluding Christ and Aristotle. The only other man whose influence was of comparable importance was Pythagoras, and his existence is doubtful.

It is customary nowadays to decry Reason as a force in human affairs, yet the rise of science is an overwhelming argument on the other side. The men of science proved to intelligent laymen that a certain kind of intellectual outlook ministers to military prowess and to wealth; these ends were so ardently desired that the new intellectual outlook overcame that of the Middle Ages, in spite of the force of tradition and the revenues of the Church and the sentiments associated with Catholic theology. The world ceased to believe that Joshua caused the sun to stand still, because Copernican astronomy was useful in navigation; it abandoned Aristotle's physics, because Galileo's theory of falling bodies made it possible to calculate the trajectory of a cannon-ball; it rejected the story of the flood, because geology is useful in mining; and so on. It it is now generally recognised that science is indispensable both in war and in peace-time industry, and that, without science, a nation can be neither rich nor powerful.

All this effect on opinion has been achieved by science merely through appeal to fact: what science had to say in the way of general theories might be questionable, but its results in the way of technique were patent to all. Science gave the white man the mastery of the world, which he has begun to lose only since the Japanese acquired his technique.

From this example, something may be learnt as to the power of Reason in general. In the case of science, Reason prevailed over prejudice because it provided means of realising existing purposes, and because the proof that it did so was overwhelming. Those who maintain that Reason has no power in human affairs overlook these two conditions. If, in the name of Reason, you summon a man to alter his fundamental purposes – to pursue, say, the general happiness rather than his own power – you will fail, and you will deserve to fail, since Reason alone cannot determine the ends of life. And you will fail equally if you attack deep-seated prejudices while your argument is still open to question, or is so difficult that only men of science can see its force. But if you can prove, by evidence which is convincing to every sane man who takes the trouble to examine it, that you possess a means of facilitating the satisfaction of existing desires, you may hope, with a certain degree of confidence, that men will ultimately believe what you say. This, of course, involves the proviso that the existing desires which you can satisfy are those of men who have power or are capable of acquiring it.

So much for the power of Reason in human affairs. I come now to another form of un-forceful persuasion, namely that of the founders of religions. Here the process, reduced to its bare formula, is this: if a certain proposition is true, I shall be able to realise my desires; therefore I wish this proposition to be true; therefore, unless I have exceptional intellectual self-control, I believe it to be true. Orthodoxy and a virtuous life, I am told, will enable me to go to heaven when I die; there is pleasure in believing this, and therefore I shall probably believe it if it is forcibly presented to me. The cause of belief, here, is not, as in science, the evidence of fact, but the pleasant feelings derived from belief, together with sufficient vigour of assertion in the environment to make the belief seem not incredible.

The power of advertisement comes under the same head. It is pleasant to believe in so-and-so's pills, since it gives you hope of better health; it is possible to believe in them, if you find their excellence very frequently and emphatically asserted. Non-rational propaganda like the rational sort, must appeal to existing desires, but it substitutes iteration for the appeal to fact.

The opposition between a rational and an irrational appeal is, in practice, less clear-cut than in the above analysis. Usually there is *some* rational evidence, though not enough to be conclusive; the irrationality consists in attaching too much weight to it. Belief, when it is not simply traditional, is a product of several factors: desire, evidence, and iteration. When either the desire or the evidence is nil, there will be no belief; when there is no outside assertion, belief will only arise in exceptional characters, such as founders of religions, scientific discoverers, and lunatics. To produce a mass belief, of the sort that is socially important, all three elements must exist in some degree; but if one element is increased while another is diminished, the resulting amount of belief may be unchanged. More propaganda is necessary to cause acceptance of a belief for which there is little evidence than of one for which the evidence is strong, if both are equally satisfactory to desire; and so on.

It is through the potency of iteration that the holders of power acquire their capacity of influencing belief. Official propaganda has old and new forms. The Church has a technique which is in many ways admirable, but was developed before the days of printing, and is therefore less effective than it used to be. The State had employed certain methods for many centuries: the King's head on coins; coronations and jubilees; the spectacular aspects of the army and navy, and so on. But these are far less potent than the more modern methods: education, the press, the cinema, the radio, etc. These are employed to the utmost in totalitarian States, but it is too soon to judge of their success.

I said that propaganda must appeal to desire, and this may be confirmed by the failure of State propaganda when opposed to national feeling, as in large parts of Austria-Hungary before the War, in Ireland until 1922, and in India down to the present time. Propaganda is only successful when it is in harmony with something in the patient: his desire for an immortal soul, for health, for the greatness of his nation, or what not. Where there is no such fundamental reason for acquiescence, the assertions of authority are viewed with cynical scepticism. One of the advantages of democracy, from the governmental point of view, is that it makes the average citizen easier to deceive, since he regards the government as *his* government. Opposition to a war which is not swiftly successful arises much less readily in a democracy than under any other form of constitution. In a democracy, a majority can only turn against the government by first admitting to themselves that they were mistaken in formerly thinking well of their chosen leaders, which is difficult and unpleasant.

Systematic propaganda, on a large scale, is at present, in democratic countries, divided between the Churches, business advertisers, political parties, the plutocracy, and the State. In the main, all these forces work on the same side, with the exception of political parties in opposition, and even they, if they have any hope of office, are unlikely to oppose the fundamentals of State propaganda. In the totalitarian countries, the State is virtually the sole propagandist. But, in spite of all the power of modern propaganda, I do not believe that the official view would be widely accepted in the event of defeat in war. This situation suddenly gives to a government the kind of impotence that belongs to alien governments opposed by nationalist feeling; and the more the expectation of victory has been used to stimulate warlike ardour, the greater will be the reaction when it is found that victory is unobtainable. It is therefore to be expected that the next war, like the last, will end with a crop of revolutions, which will be more fierce than those of 1917 and 1918 because the war will have been more destructive. It is to be hoped that rulers realise the risk they will run of being put to death by the mob, which is at least as great as the risk that soldiers will run of death at the hands of the enemy.

It is easy to overestimate the power of official propaganda, especially when there is no competition. In so far as it devotes itself to causing belief in false propositions of which time will prove the falsity, it is in as bad a position as the Aristotelians in their opposition to Galileo. Given two opposing groups of States, each of which endeavours to instil the certainty of victory in war, one side, if not both, must experience a dramatic refutation of official statements. When all opposing propaganda is forbidden, rulers are likely to think that they can cause anything to be believed, and so to become over-weening and careless. Lies need competition if they are to retain their vigour.

Power over opinion, like all other forms of power, tends to coalescence and concentration, leading logically to a State monopoly. But even apart from war it would be rash to assume that a State monopoly of propaganda must make a government invulnerable. In the long run, those who possess the power are likely to become too flagrantly indifferent to the interests of the common man, as the Popes were in the time of Luther. Sooner or later, some new Luther will challenge the authority of the State, and, like his predecessor, be so quickly successful that it will be impossible to suppress him. This will happen because the rulers will believe that it cannot happen. But whether the change will be for the better it is impossible to foresee.

The effect of organisation and unification, in the matter of propaganda as in other matters, is to delay revolution, but to make it more violent when it comes. When only one doctrine is officially allowed, men get no practice in thinking or in weighing alternatives; only a great wave of passionate revolt can dethrone orthodoxy; and in order to make the opposition sufficiently whole-hearted and violent to achieve success, it will seem necessary to deny even what was true in governmental dogma. The only thing that will not be denied will be the importance of immediately establishing *some* orthodoxy, since this will be considered necessary for victory. From a rationalist standpoint, therefore, the likelihood of revolution in a totalitarian State is not necessarily a ground for rejoicing. What is more to be desired is a gradual increase in the sense of security, leading to a lessening of zeal, and giving an opening for laziness – the greatest of all virtues in the ruler of a totalitarian State, with the sole exception of non-existence.

Chapter 10

Creeds as Sources of Power

The power of a community depends not only upon its numbers and its economic resources and its technical capacity, but also upon its beliefs. A fanatical creed, held by all the members of a community, often greatly increases its power; sometimes, however, it diminishes it. As fanatical creeds are much more in the fashion than they were during the nineteenth century, the question of their effect on power is one of great practical importance. One of the arguments against democracy is that a nation of united fanatics has more chance of success in war than a nation containing a large proportion of sane men. Let us examine this argument in the light of history.

It should be observed, to begin with, that the cases in which fanaticism has led to success are naturally better known than those in which it has led to failure, since the cases of failure have remained comparatively obscure. Thus a too rapid survey is apt to be misleading; but if we are aware of this possible source of error, it is not difficult to avoid.

The classic example of power through fanaticism is the rise of Islam. Mohammed added nothing to the knowledge or to the material resources of the Arabs, and yet, within a few years of his death, they had acquired a large empire by defeating their most powerful neighbours. Undoubtedly, the religion founded by the Prophet was an essential element in the success of his nation. At the very end of his life, he declared war on the Byzantine Empire. 'The Moslems were discouraged: they alleged the want of money, or horses, or provisions: the season of harvest, and the intolerable heat of the summer: "Hell is much hotter," said the indignant prophet. He disdained to compel their service; but on his return he admonished the most guilty, by an excommunication of fifty days'.[1] Fanaticism, while Mohammed lived, and for a few

[1] E. Gibbon, Ch. L.

years after his death, united the Arab nation, gave it confidence in battle, and promoted courage by the promise of Paradise to those who fell fighting the infidel.

But although fanaticism inspired the first attempts of the Arabs, it was to other causes that they owed their prolonged career of victory. The Byzantine and Persian Empires were both weakened by long and indecisive wars; and Roman armies, at all times, were weak and against cavalry. The Arab horsemen were incredibly mobile, and were inured to hardships which their more luxurious neighbours found intolerable. These circumstances were essential to the first successes of the Muslim.

Very soon – sooner than in the beginning of any other great religion – fanaticism was dethroned from the government. Ali, the Prophet's son-in-law, kept alive the original enthusiasm among a section of the faithful, but he was defeated in civil war, and finally assassinated. He was succeeded in the Caliphate by the family of Ommiyah, who had been Mohammed's bitterest opponents, and had never yielded more than a political assent to his religion. 'The persecutors of Mahomet usurped the inheritance of his children; and the champions of idolatry became the supreme heads of his religion and empire. The opposition of Abu Sophian[1] had been fierce and obstinate; his conversion was tardy and reluctant; his new faith was fortified by necessity and interest; he served, he fought, perhaps he believed; and the sins of the time of ignorance were expiated by the recent merits of the family of Ommiyah'.[2] From that moment onwards, for a long time, the Caliphate was distinguished by free-thinking latitudinarianism, while the Christians remained fanatical. From the first, the Mohammedans showed themselves tolerant in their dealings with conquered Christians, and to this toleration – which was in strong contrast to the persecuting zeal of the Catholic Church – the ease of their conquest and the stability of their Empire were mainly due.

Another case of the apparent success of fanaticism is the victory of the Independents under Cromwell. But it may be questioned how much fanaticism had to do with Cromwell's achievements. In the contest with the King, Parliament won mainly because it held London and the Eastern Counties; both its manpower and its economic resources far exceeded those of the King. The Presbyterians – as always happens with the mod-

[1] Father of the new Caliph Moawiyah.
[2] E. Gibbon, op. cit.

erates in a revolution – were gradually thrust aside because they did not wholeheartedly desire victory. Cromwell himself, when he had achieved power, turned out to be a practical politician, anxious to make the best of a difficult situation; but he could not ignore the fanaticism of his followers, which was so unpopular as to lead, in the end, to the complete downfall of his party. It cannot be said that, in the long run, fanaticism did anything more to bring success to the English Independents than to their predecessors, the Anabaptists of Münster.

On a larger scale, the history of the French Revolution is analogous to that of the Commonwealth in England: fanaticism, victory, despotism, collapse, and reaction. Even in these two most favourable instances, the success of the fanatics was short-lived.

The cases in which fanaticism has brought nothing but disaster are much more numerous than those in which it has brought even temporary success. It ruined Jerusalem in the time of Titus, and Constantinople in 1453, when the West was rebuffed on account of the minute doctrinal differences between the Eastern and Western Churches. It brought about the decay of Spain, first through the expulsion of the Jews and Moors, and then by causing rebellion in the Netherlands and the long exhaustion of the Wars of Religion. On the other hand, the most successful nations, throughout modern times, have been those least addicted to the persecution of heretics.

Nevertheless, there is now a widespread belief that doctrinal uniformity is essential to national strength. This view is held and acted upon, with the utmost rigour, in Germany and Russia, and with slightly less severity in Italy and Japan. Many opponents of Fascism, in France and Great Britain are inclined to concede that freedom of thought is a source of military weakness. Let us therefore examine this question once more, in a more abstract and analytic fashion.

The question I am asking is not the broad one: should freedom of thought be encouraged, or at least tolerated? I am asking a narrower question: To what extent is a uniform creed, whether spontaneous or imposed by authority, a source of power? And to what extent, on the other hand, is freedom of thought a source of power?

When a British military expedition invaded Tibet in 1905, the Tibetans at first advanced boldly, because the Lamas had given them magic charms against bullets. When they nevertheless had casualties, the Lamas observed that the bullets were nickel-pointed, and explained that their charms were only effective against lead. After this, the Tibetan armies showed less valour. When Bela Kun and Kurt Eisner made Communist revolutions, they were confident that Dialectical Materialism was fighting for them. I forget what explanation of their failure was offered by the Lamas of the Comintern. In these two instances, uniformity of creed did not lead to victory.

To arrive at the truth in this matter, it is necessary to find a compromise between two opposite truisms. The first of these is: men who agree in their beliefs can cooperate more whole-heartedly than men who disagree. The second is: men whose beliefs are in accordance with fact are more likely to succeed than men whose beliefs are mistaken. Let us examine each of these truisms.

That agreement is a help in cooperation is obvious. In the civil war in Spain, cooperation has been difficult between anarchists, communists, and Basque nationalists, though all equally desired the defeat of Franco. In the same manner, though in a lesser degree, on the other side, cooperation has been difficult between Carlists and modern-style Fascists. There is need of agreement as to immediate ends, and also of a certain temperamental con-geniality; but where these exist, great differences of opinion may become harmless. Sir William Napier, the historian of the Penin-sular War, admired Napoleon and disliked Wellington; his book shows that he considered the defeat of Napoleon regrettable. But his sentiment of caste and his feeling of military duty overrode such purely intellectual convictions, and he fought the French as competently as if he had been a high Tory. In like manner, should the occasion arise, British Tories of the present day will fight Hitler just as vigorously as they would if they did not admire him.

The uniformity which is needed to give power to a nation, a religion, or a party, is a uniformity in practice, depending upon sentiment and habit. Where this exists, intellectual convictions can be ignored. It exists in Great Britain at the present day, but it did not exist until after 1745. It did not exist in France in 1792, or in Russia during the Great War and the subsequent civil war. It does not exist in Spain at this moment. It is not difficult for a government to concede freedom of thought when it can rely upon loyalty in action; but when it cannot, the matter is more difficult. It is obvious that freedom of propaganda is impossible during a civil war; and when there is an imminent danger of civil war, the argument for restricting propaganda is only slightly less over-whelming. In dangerous situations, therefore, there is a strong case for an imposed uniformity.

Let us now take up our second truism: that it is advantageous to have beliefs which are in accordance with fact. So far as *direct* advantages are concerned, this is only true of a limited class of beliefs: first, technical matters, such as the properties of high explosives and poison gases; secondly, matters concerning the relative strengths of the opposing forces. Even as regards these matters, it may be said, only those who decide policy and military operations need have correct views: it is desirable that the popu-lace should feel sure of victory, and should underrate the dangers of attack from the air. Only the government, the military chiefs, and their technical staffs need know the facts; among all others, blind confidence and blind obedience are what is most to be desired.

If human affairs were as calculable as chess, and politicians and generals as clever as good chess players, there might be some truth in this view. The advantages of successful war are doubt-ful, but the disadvantages of unsuccessful war are certain. If, therefore, the supermen at the head of affairs could foresee who was going to win, there would be no wars. But in fact there are wars, and in every war the government on one side, if not on both, must have miscalculated its chances. For this there are many reasons: of pride and vanity, of ignorance, and of con-tagious excitement. When the populace is kept ignorantly confident, its confidence and its bellicose sentiment may easily be communicated to the rulers, who can hardly attach the same weight to unpleasant facts which they know but conceal as to the pleasant facts that are being proclaimed in every newspaper and in every conversation. Hysteria and megalomania are catching, and governments have no immunity.

When war comes, the policy of concealment may produce effects exactly opposite to those intended. Some, at least, of the unpleasant facts which had been kept dark are likely to become patent to all, and the more men have been made to live in a fool's paradise, the more they will be horrified and discouraged by the reality. Revolution or sudden collapse is much more probable in such circumstances than when free discussion has prepared the public mind for painful events.

An attitude of obedience, when it is exacted from subordinates, is inimical to intelligence. In a community in which men have to accept, at least outwardly, some obviously absurd doctrine, the best men must become either stupid or disaffected. There will be, in consequence, a lowering of the intellectual level, which must, before long, interfere with technical progress. This is especially true when the official creed is one which few intelligent men can honestly accept. The Nazis have exiled most of the ablest Germans, and this must, sooner or later, have disastrous effects upon their military technique. It is impossible for technique to remain long progressive without science, or for science to flourish where there is no freedom of thought. Consequently insistence on doctrinal uniformity, even in matters quite remote from war, is ultimately fatal to military efficiency in a scientific age.

We may now arrive at the practical synthesis of our two truisms. Social cohesion demands a creed, or a code of behaviour, or a prevailing sentiment, or, best, some combination of all three; without something of the kind, a community disintegrates, and becomes subject to a tyrant or a foreign conqueror. But if this means of cohesion is to be effective, it must be very deeply felt; it may be imposed by force upon a small minority, provided they are not specially important through exceptional intelligence or character, but it must be genuine and spontaneous in the great majority. Loyalty to a leader, national pride, and religious fervour have proved, historically, the best means of securing cohesion; but loyalty to a leader is less permanently effective than it used to be, owing to the decay of hereditary sovereignty, and religious fervour is threatened by the spread of free thought. Thus national pride is left, and has become relatively more important than in former times. It has been interesting to observe the revival of this sentiment in Soviet Russia, in spite of an official creed which should be inimical to it – though not more so, after all, than Christianity.

How much interference with freedom is necessary for the maintenance of national pride? The interferences which actually occur have mainly this end in view. In Russia, it is thought that those who disagree with the official orthodoxy are likely to behave in an unpatriotic manner; in Germany and Italy, the strength of the government depends upon its appeal to nationalism, and any opposition is considered to be in the interests of Moscow; in France, if liberty is lost, it will probably be to prevent pro-German treachery. In all these countries, the difficulty is that the class-conflict cuts across the conflicts of nations, causing the capitalists in democratic countries, and the Socialists and Communists in Fascist countries, to be guided, to some extent, by other considerations than those of the national interest. If this diversion from nationalist aims can be prevented, a country's strength is likely to be increased, but not if it is necessary, for the purpose, to lower the whole level of intelligence. For governments the problem is a difficult one, since nationalism is a stupid ideal, and intelligent people perceive that it is bringing Europe to ruin. The best solution is to disguise it under some international slogan, such as democracy or communism or collective security. Where this cannot be done, as in Italy and Germany, outward uniformity demands tyranny, and does not easily produce a genuine inward sentiment.

To sum up: a creed or sentiment of some kind is essential to social cohesion, but if it is to be a source of strength it must be genuinely and deeply felt by the great majority of the population, including a considerable percentage of those upon whom technical efficiency depends. Where these conditions are absent, governments may seek to produce them by censorship and persecution; but censorship and persecution, if they are severe, cause men to become out of touch with reality, and ignorant or oblivious of facts which it is important to know. Since the holders of power are biased by their power-impulses, the amount of interference with freedom that conduces most to national power will always be less than governments are inclined to believe; therefore a diffused sentiment against interference, provided it does not go so far as to lead to anarchy, is likely to add to the national strength. But it is impossible to go beyond these generalities except in relation to particular cases.

Throughout the above discussion, we have considered only the more immediate effects of a fanatical creed. The long-term effects are quite different. A creed which is used as source of power inspires, for a time, great efforts, but these efforts, especially if they are not very successful, produce weariness, and weariness produces scepticism – not, at first, definite disbelief, which is an energetic frame of mind, but mere absence of strong belief.[1] The

[1] On this subject, see the very interesting chapter 'Fog of Skepticism over Russia,' in E. Lyons's *Assignment in Utopia*. After telling of the enthusiasm with which the launching of the Five-Year Plan had been greeted, and of the gradual disillusionment as the promised comforts failed to be realised, he says: 'I watched skepticism spread

more the methods of propaganda have been used to produce excitement, the greater will be the reaction, until in the end a quiet life comes to seem the only thing worth having. When, after a period of repose, the population again becomes capable of excitement, it will need a new stimulus, since all the old stimuli have become boring. Hence creeds which are used too intensively are transitory in their effects. In the thirteenth century, men's imaginations were dominated by three great men: the Pope, the Emperor, and the Sultan. The Emperor and the Sultan have disappeared, and the Pope's power is a pale shadow of what it was. In the sixteenth and early seventeeth centuries, the wars between Catholics and Protestants filled Europe, and all large-scale propaganda was in favour of one or other of the two creeds. Yet ultimate victory went to neither party, but to those who thought the issues between them unimportant. Swift satirised the conflict in his wars of Big-Endians and Little-Endians; Voltaire's Huron, finding himself in prison with a Jansenist, thinks it equally silly of the government to demand his recantation and of him to refuse it. If the world, in the near future, becomes divided between Communists and Fascists, the final victory will go to neither, but to those who shrug their shoulders and say, like Candide, 'cela est bien dit, mais il faut cultiver notre jardin'. The ultimate limit to the power of creeds is set by boredom, weariness, and love of ease.

---

like a thick wet fog over Russia, soaking into the flesh and spirits of men and women. It chilled the hearts of the leaders no less than of the masses. Men who publicly spent all their time pumping up optimism, talked bitterly in private of the planlessness of the Plan, the terrible wastage of substance and energy, the dislocation of a national economy swollen in some of its limbs and shrunken in the rest. Doubts of the efficacy of enthusiasm were expressed in a constantly greater stress on cash rewards at one pole and harsh punishment at the other. . . . Draconic decrees were invented almost weekly to discipline and repress the common workers. One of them made a single day's absence from work punishable by loss of job, bread book, and living space: tantamount to a sentence of slow death.' In another chapter he writes: 'People under dictatorships, it has been well said, are condemned to a lifetime of enthusiasm. It is a wearing sentence. Gladly would they burrow into the heart of their misery and lick their wounds in private. But they dare not; sulking is next door to treason. Like soldiers weary unto death after a long march, they must line up smartly for parade.'

Chapter 11

The Biology of Organisations

We have been considering hitherto the sentiments which are the most important psychological sources of power: tradition, especially in the form of respect for priests and kings; fear and personal ambition, which are the sources of naked power; the substitution of a new creed for an old one, which is the source of revolutionary power; and the interactions between creeds and other sources of power. We come now to a new department of our subject: the study of the organisations through which power is exercised, considered first as organisms with a life of their own, then in relation to their forms of government, and finally as affecting the lives of the individuals who compose them. In this section of our subject, organisms are to be considered as far as possible without regard to their purposes, in the way in which men are considered in anatomy and biochemistry.

The subject to be discussed in this chapter, namely the biology of organisations, depends upon the fact that an organisation is also an organism, with a life of its own, and a tendency to growth and decay. Competition between organizations is analogous to competition between individual animals and plants, and can be viewed in a more or less Darwinian manner. But this analogy, like others, must not be pressed too far; it may serve to suggest and to illuminate, but not to demonstrate. For example, we must not assume that decay is inevitable where social organisations are concerned.

Power is dependent upon organisation in the main, but not wholly. Purely psychological power, such as that of Plato or Galileo, may exist without any corresponding social institution. But as a rule even such power is not important unless it is propagated by a Church, a political party, or some analogous social organism. For the present, I shall ignore power which is not connected with an organisation.

An organisation is a set of people who are combined in virtue of activities directed to common ends. It may be purely voluntary, like a club; it may be a natural biological group, like a family or a clan; it may be compulsory, like a State; or it may be a complicated mixture, like a railway company. The purpose of the organisation may be explicit or unexpressed, conscious or unconscious; it may be military or political, economic or religious, educational or athletic, and so on. Every organisation, whatever its character and whatever its purpose, involves some redistribution of power. There must be a government, which takes decisions in the name of the whole body, and has more power than the single members have, at any rate as regards the purposes for which the organisation exists. As men grow more civilised and technique grows more complicated, the advantages of combination become increasingly evident. But combination always involves some surrender of independence: we may acquire increased power over others, but they also acquire power over us. More and more, the important decisions are those of bodies of men, not of single individuals. And the decisions of bodies of men, unless the members are very few, have to be effected through governments. Thus government necessarily plays a much larger part in the life of a modern civilised community than in that of pre-industrial societies.

Even a completely democratic government – if such a thing were possible – involves a redistribution of power. If every man has an equal voice in joint decisions, and if there are (say) a million members, every man has a millionth part of the power over the whole million, instead of complete power over himself and none over others, as he would have if he were a solitary wild animal. This produces a very different psychology from that of an anarchic collection of individuals. And where – as must always be the case to some extent – the government is not completely democratic, the psychological effect is increased. The members of the government have more power than the others, even if they are democratically elected; and so do officials appointed by a democratically elected government. The larger the organisation, the greater the power of the executive. Thus every increase in the size of organisations increases inequalities of power by simultaneously diminishing the independence of ordinary members and enlarging the scope of the initiative of the government. The average man submits because much more can be achieved cooperatively than singly; the exceptionally power-loving man rejoices, since it provides his opportunity – unless indeed, the government is hereditary, or the power-loving individual belongs to a group (such as Jews in some countries) which is not allowed to occupy positions of importance.

Competition for power is of two sorts: between organisations, and between individuals for leadership within an organisation. Competition between organisations only arises when they have objects which are more or less similar, but incompatible; it may be economic, or military, or by means of propaganda, or may involve any two or all three of these methods. When Napoleon III was engaged in making himself Emperor, he had to create an organisation devoted to his interests, and then to secure its supremacy. For this purpose, he gave cigars to some people – this was economic; to others he pointed out that he was the nephew of his uncle – this was propaganda; finally he shot a number of opponents – this was military.[1] His opponents, meanwhile, had confined themselves to praising the Republican form of government, and had neglected the cigars and bullets. The technique of acquiring dictatorship over what has been a democracy has been familiar since Greek times, and always involves the same mixture of bribery, propaganda and violence. This, however, is not our present theme, which is the biology of organisations.

There are two important respects in which organisations may differ: one is size, the other is what one might call density of power, by which I mean the degree of control which they exert over their members. Owing to the love of power which is to be expected in those who acquire governmental posts, every organisation will, in the absence of any counteracting force, tend to grow both in size and in density of power. It is possible for either form of growth to be stopped by intrinsic causes; an international chess club, for example, may come to contain all chess-players of sufficient excellence, and is not likely to wish to control any of the activities of its members except those connected with chess. It might, under an energetic secretary, seek to make more people 'chess-conscious', but this would be unlikely to happen if the secretary were expected to be a good chess-player; and if it did happen, the club might be ruined by the defection of the best players. But such cases are exceptional; where the purpose of

[1] See F. A. Simpson, *The Rise of Louis Napoleon.*

the organisation is one making a general appeal – e.g. wealth, or political domination – growth in size is only stopped either by the pressure of other organisations, or by the organisation in question becoming world-wide; and growth in density is only stopped where love of personal independence becomes overwhelmingly strong.

The most obvious example of this is the State. Every State which is sufficiently powerful aims at foreign conquest; apparent instances to the contrary only arise where a State, from experience, knows itself to be less strong than it seems, or, from inexperience, believes itself to be less strong than it is. The broad rule is that a State conquers what it can, and stops only when it reaches a frontier at which some other State or States can exert a pressure as strong as its own. Great Britain has not acquired Afghanistan, because Russia is as powerful there as the British are; Napoleon sold Louisiana to the United States because it was impossible for him to defend it; and so on. So far as intrinsic forces are concerned, every State tends to become world-wide. But the power of a State is to a greater or smaller extent geographical: it usually radiates from a centre, and grows less as the distance from the centre increases. Consequently, at a greater or smaller distance from the centre, its power is in equilibrium with that of some other State, and there the frontiers will be, unless the force of tradition interferes.

What has just been said is too abstract to be true without modification. Small States exist, not by their own power, but through the jealousies of large ones; e.g. Belgium exists because its existence is convenient for England and France. Portugal has large colonies, because the Great Powers cannot agree about how to divide them. Since war is a serious business, a State may, for a considerable time, retain territory which it would lose if any strong State chose to take it. But such considerations do not destroy our general principle; they only introduce frictional forces which delay the operation of crude power.

It might be urged that the United States is an exception to the principle that a State conquers what it can. It is obvious that the conquest of Mexico, and indeed of all Latin America, would offer no serious difficulties if the United States cared to undertake the task. The usual motives for political conquest, however, are at present inhibited in this case by various counteracting forces. Before the Civil War, the Southern States had imperialistic tendencies, which found an outlet in the Mexican War, leading to the annexation of an immense territory. After the Civil

War, the settlement and economic development of the West was a sufficient task to absorb the energies of even the most energetic national. As soon as this business had been brought to some sort of conclusion, the Spanish-American War of 1898 gave vent to a fresh impulse of imperialism. But annexation of territory has difficulties under the American Constitution: it involves the admission of new voters, who may be thought undesirable, and – what is more important – it extends the area of internal free trade, and is therefore damaging to important economic interests. The Monroe Doctrine, which involves a virtual protectorate over Latin America, is therefore more satisfactory to the dominant interests than annexation would be. If political conquest were economically advantageous, no doubt it would soon take place.

Concentration of power, in the political sphere, has always been sought by rulers, and has not always been resisted by those over whom they ruled. Nominally, it was more complete in the great empires of antiquity than in even the most dictatorial of modern régimes, but in practice it was limited to what was technically possible. The most urgent problem for ancient monarchs was that of mobility. In Egypt and Babylonia, this was facilitated by the great rivers; but the Persian rule depended upon roads. Herodotus describes the great royal road from Sardis to Susa, a distance of about 1,500 miles, along which the King's messengers travelled in time of peace, and the King's armies in time of war. 'The true account of the road in question', he says, 'is the following: Royal stations exist along its whole length, and excellent caravanserais; and throughout, it traverses an inhabited tract, and is free from danger ... On leaving Phrygia the Halys has to be crossed; and here are gates through which you must needs pass ere you can traverse the stream. A strong force guards this post ... The boundary between Cilicia and Armenia is the river Euphrates, which it is necessary to cross in boats. In Armenia the resting-places are fifteen in number, and the distance is 56½ parasangs (about 180 miles). There is one place where a guard is posted. Four large streams intersect this district, all of which have to be crossed by means of boats ... The entire number of stations is raised to 111; so many are in fact the resting-places that one finds between Sardis and Susa.' He goes on to state that, 'travelling at the rate of 150 furlongs a day' (about the speed of an army), 'one will take exactly ninety days to perform the journey.'[1]

[1] Book V, Chapters 52, 53. Rawlinson's translation.

Such a road, though it made an extended empire possible, did not enable the King to exercise any detailed control over the satraps of distant provinces. A messenger on horseback might brings news from Sardis to Susa in a month, but an army would require three months to march from Susa to Sardis. When the Ionians revolted against Persia, they therefore had a number of months at their disposal before they had to meet any troops not already in Asia Minor. All ancient empires suffered from revolts, often led by provincial governors; and even when no overt revolt occurred, local autonomy was almost unavoidable except when conquest was recent, and was apt, in the course of time, to develop into independence. No large State of antiquity was governed from the centre to nearly the same extent as is now customary; and the chief reason for this was lack of rapid mobility.

The Roman Empire learnt from the Persians, through the Macedonians, how to fortify the central government by means of roads. Imperial messengers could travel at an average rate of ten miles an hour, day and night, throughout Western and Southern Europe, North Africa, and Western Asia. But in each province the imperial post was controlled by the military commander, who could therefore move his armies without the knowledge of anyone not in their line of march. The swiftness of the legions and the tardiness of news resulted often in advantage to rebels against the Emperor in Rome. Gibbon, in telling of Constantine's march from the north of Gaul to invade Italy, contrasts the ease of his movements with the difficulty of Hannibal's:

'When Hannibal marched from Gaul into Italy, he was obliged, first to discover, and then to open, a way over mountains and through savage nations that had never yielded a passage to a regular army. The Alps were then guarded by nature, they are now fortified by art. But in the course of the intermediate period, the generals, who have attempted the passage, have seldom experienced any difficulty or resistance. In the age of Constantine, the peasants of the mountains were civilised and obedient subjects; the country was plentifully stocked with provisions, and the stupendous highways, which the Romans had carried over the Alps, opened several communications between Gaul and Italy. Constantine preferred the road of the Cottian Alps, or as it is now called of Mount Cenis, and led his troops with such active diligence, that he descended into the plain of Piedmont before the court of Maxentius (in Rome) had received any certain intelligence of his departure from the banks of the Rhine.'

The result was that Maxentius was defeated and Christianity became the religion of the State. The history of the world might have been different if the Romans had had worse roads or a swifter means of transmitting news.

Steamships, railways, and finally aeroplanes have made it possible for governments to exercise power quickly at great distances. A revolt in the Sahara or in Mesopotamia can now be quelled within a few hours, whereas a hundred years ago it would have required months to send an army, and there would have been great difficulty in preventing it from dying of thirst, like Alexander's soldiers in Baluchistan.

Quite as important as the mobility of persons and goods is the rapidity in the transmission of news. In the war of 1812, the battle of New Orleans was fought after the conclusion of peace, though neither of the opposing armies was aware of this fact. At the end of the Seven Years War, British forces captured Cuba and the Philippines, but this was not known in Europe until peace had been signed. Until the invention of the telegraph, ambassadors in time of peace and generals in time of war had necessarily a very great latitude, since their instructions could not take account of the most recent occurrences. Agents of a distant government were very frequently called upon to act on their own judgement, and thus became much more than mere transmitters of a centrally directed policy.

It is not only the absolute rapidity in the transmission of messages that is important, but also, and still more, the fact that messages travel faster than human beings. Until little over a hundred years ago, neither messages nor anything else could travel faster than a horse. A highwayman could escape to a neighbouring town, and reach it before the news of his crime. Nowadays, since news arrives first, escape is more difficult. In time of war all rapid means of communication are controlled by governments, and this greatly increases their power.

Modern technique, not only through the rapidity in the transmission of messages, but also through railways, telegraph, motor traffic, and governmental propaganda, has made large empires much more capable of stability than they were in former times. Persian satraps and Roman proconsuls had enough independence to make rebellion easy. Alexander's empire fell apart at his death. The empires of Attila and Genghis Khan were transitory; and the nations of Europe lost most of their possessions in the New World. But with modern technique most empires are fairly safe except against external attack, and revolution is only to be expected after defeat in war.

Technical causes, it should be observed, have not operated *wholly* in the direction of making it easier to exercise the power of the State at a distance; in some respects they have had the opposite effect. Hannibal's army subsisted for many years without keeping open its line of communications, whereas a large modern army could not last more than two or three days in such conditions. Navies, so long as they depended upon sails, were world-wide in their operations; now, since they must frequently refuel, they are unable to operate long at a distance from some base. In Nelson's day, if the British commanded the seas in one region they commanded them everywhere; now, though they may have command of the home waters, they are weak in the Far East, and have no access to the Baltic.

Nevertheless, the broad rule is that it is easier now than in former days to exert power at a distance from the centre. The effect of this is to increase the intensity of competition between States, and to make victory more absolute, since the resulting increase of size need not impair efficiency. A World State is now a technical possibility, and might be established by a victor in some really serious world-war, or, more probably, by the most powerful of the neutrals.

As regards density of power, or intensity of organisation (as it may also be called), the questions involved are complex and very important. The State, in every civilised country, is far more active now than at any former time; in Russia, Germany, and Italy it interferes in almost all human concerns. Since men love power, and since, on the average, those who achieve power love it more than most, the men who control the State may be expected, in normal circumstances, to desire an increase of its internal activities just as much as an increase of its territory. Since there are solid reasons for augmenting the functions of the State, there will be a predisposition, on the part of ordinary citizens, in favour of acquiescing in the wishes of the government in this respect. There is, however, a certain desire for independence, which will, at some point, become strong enough to prevent, at least temporarily, any further increase in the intensity of the organisation. Consequently love of independence in the citizens and love of power in the officials will, when organisation reaches a certain intensity, be in at least temporary equilibrium, so that if organisation were increased love of independence would become the stronger force, and if it were diminished official love of power would be the stronger.

Love of independence is, in most cases, not an abstract dislike of external interference, but aversion from some one form of control which the government thinks desirable – prohibition, conscription, religious conformity, or what not. Sometimes such sentiments can be gradually overcome by propaganda and education, which can indefinitely weaken the desire for personal independence. Many forces conspire to make for uniformity in modern communities – schools, newspapers, cinema, radio, drill, etc. Density of population has the same effect. The position of momentary equilibrium between the sentiment of independence and the love of power tends, therefore, under modern conditions, to shift further and further in the direction of power, thus facilitating the creation and success of totalitarian States. By education, love of independence can be weakened to an extent to which, at present, no limits are known. How far the internal power of the State may be gradually increased without provoking revolt it is impossible to say; but there seems no reason to doubt that, given time, it can be increased far beyond the point at present reached even in the most autocratic States.

Organisations other than States are, in the main, subject to laws of the same kind as those that we have been considering, except that they cannot use force. I omit from consideration those that afford little outlet to power-impulses, such as clubs. The most important for our purposes are political parties, Churches, and business corporations. Most Churches aim at being world-wide, however little they may expect their aim to be realised; also most of them endeavour to regulate some of the most intimate concerns of their members, such as marriage and the education of children. When it has proved possible, Churches have usurped the functions of the State, as in Tibet and the patrimony of St Peter, and to some extent throughout Western Europe until the Reformation. The power impulses of Churches, with some exceptions, have been limited only by lack of opportunity, and by the fear of revolt in the shape of heresy or schism. Nationalism, however, has greatly diminished their power in many countries, and has transferred to the State many emotions which formerly found their outlet in religion.[1] The diminution in the strength of religion is partly the cause and partly the effect of nationalism and the increased strength of national States.

Political parties were, until recently, very loose organisations, which made only very slight attempts to control the activities of their members. Throughout the nineteenth century, Members of Parliament frequently voted against their Party leaders, with the consequence that the results of divisions were far more unpredictable than they are now. Walpole, North, and the younger Pitt controlled their supporters, to a certain extent, by means of corruption; but after the diminution of corruptions, and while politics was still aristocratic, governments and party leaders had no way of bringing effective pressure to bear. Now, especially in the Labour Party, men are pledged to orthodoxy, and failure to keep this pledge usually involves both political extinction and financial loss. Two kinds of loyalty are demanded: to the programme, in the opinions professed; and to the leaders, in the action taken from day to day. The programme is decided in a manner which is nominally democratic, but is very much influenced by a small number of wire-pullers. It is left to the leaders to decide, in their parliamentary or governmental activities, whether they shall attempt to carry out the programme; if they decide not to do so, it is the duty of their followers to support their breach of faith by their votes, while denying, in their speeches, that it has taken place. It is this system that has given to leaders the power to thwart their rank-and-file supporters, and to advocate reforms without having to enact them.

But although the density of organisation in all political parties has greatly increased, it is still immeasurably less, in democratic parties, than among Communists, Fascists, and Nazis. These latter are a development, historically and psychologically, not of the political party, but of the secret society. Under an autocratic government, men who aim at any radical change are driven to secrecy, and, when they combine, fear of treachery leads to a very strict discipline. It is natural to demand a certain way of life, as a safeguard against spies. The risk, the secrecy, the present suffering, and the hope of future triumph, produce a quasi-religious exaltation, and attract those to whom this mood comes

---

[1] The late W. A. S. Hewins, who was instrumental in the conversion of Joseph Chamberlain to tariff reform, told me that his ancestors had been ardent Roman Catholics, but that his emotions attached themselves to the British Empire as theirs had to the Church. This was a typical development.

easily. Hence within a revolutionary secret society, even if its aim is anarchism, there is likely to be a very severe despotism, and a supervision extending far beyond what would usually be considered political activity. Italy after the fall of Napoleon became filled with secret societies, to which some were attracted by revolutionary theory and others by criminal practice. The same thing happened in Russia with the rise of terrorism. Both Russian Communists and Italian Fascists were deeply impregnated with the mentality of the secret society, and the Nazis were modelled on them. When their several leaders acquired the government, they ruled the State in the same spirit in which they had formerly ruled their parties. And the correlative spirit of submission is demanded of their followers throughout the world.

The growth in the size of economic organisations suggested to Marx his views on the dynamics of power. Much of what he said on the subject has proved true, but is applicable to all organisations that give an outlet to power-impulses, not only to those that have economic functions. The tendency has been, in production, to give rise to trusts that are coextensive with some great State and its satellites, but seldom, outside the armament industry, to the formation of world-wide trusts. Tariffs and colonies have caused big business to be intimately associated with the State. Foreign conquest in the economic sphere has come to be dependent upon the military strength of the nation to which the trust in question belongs; it is no longer, except to a limited extent, conducted by the old methods of purely business competition. In Italy and Germany the relation between big business and the State is more intimate and obvious than in democratic countries, but it would be a mistake to suppose that big business, under Fascism, controls the State more than it does in England, France, or America. On the contrary, in Italy and Germany the State has used the fear of Communism to make itself supreme over big business as over everything else. For example, in Italy a very drastic capital levy is being introduced, whereas a much milder form of the same measure, when proposed by the British Labour Party, caused a capitalist outcry which was completely successful.

When two organisations with different but not incompatible objects coalesce, the result is something more powerful than either previous one, or even both together. Before the War, the Great Northern went from London to York, the North Eastern from York to Newcastle, and the North British from Newcastle to Edinburgh; now the LNER goes all the way, and is obviously stronger than the three older Companies put together. Similarly there is an advantage if the whole steel industry, from the extraction of the ore to ship-building, is controlled by one corporation. Hence there is a natural tendency to combination; and this is true not only in the economic sphere. The logical outcome of this process is for the most powerful organisation, usually the State, to absorb all others. The same tendency would lead in time to the creation of one World-State, if the purposes of different States were not incompatible. If the purpose of States were the wealth, health, intelligence, or happiness of their citizens there would be no incompatibility; but since these, singly and collectively, are thought less important than national power, the purposes of different States conflict, and cannot be furthered by amalgamation. Consequently a World-State is only to be expected, if at all, through the conquest of the world by some one national State, or through the universal adoption of some creed transcending nationalism, such as first socialism, and then communism, seemed to be in their early days.

The limitation to the growth of States owing to nationalism is the most important example of a limitation which may be seen also in party politics and in religion. I have been endeavouring in this chapter to treat organisations as having a life independent of their purpose. I think it important to note that, up to a point, this is possible; but of course it is *only* up to a point that it is possible. Beyond that point, it is necessary to consider the passion to which the organisation appeals.

The desires of an individual can be collected into groups, each group constituting what some psychologists call a 'sentiment'. There will be – to take politically important sentiments – love of home, of family, of country, love of power, love of enjoyment, and so on; there will also be sentiments of aversion, such as fear of pain, laziness, dislike of foreigners, hatred of alien creeds, and so on. A man's sentiments at any given moment are a complicated product of his nature, his past history, and his present circumstances. Each sentiment, in so far as it is one which many men can gratify cooperatively better than singly, will, given opportunity, generate one or more organisations designed for its gratification. Take, for example, family sentiment. This has given rise, or has helped to give rise, to organisations for housing, education, and life insurance, which are matters in which the interests of different families are in harmony. But it has also – in the past more than in the present – given rise to organisations representing the interests of one family at the expense of others, such as those of the retainers of the Montagues and Capulets respectively. The dynastic State was an organisation of this sort. Aristocracies are organisations of certain families to procure their own privileges at the expense of the rest of the community. Such organisations always involve, in a greater or less degree, sentiments of aversion: fear, hatred, contempt, and so on. Where such sentiments are strongly felt, they are an obstacle to the growth of organisations.

Theology affords illustrations of this limitation. The Jews, except during a few centuries round about the beginning of the Christian era, have had no wish to convert the Gentiles; they have been content with the feeling of superiority which they derived from being the Chosen People. Shinto, which teaches that Japan was created earlier than the rest of the world, is not intended or likely to appeal to those who are not Japanese. Everyone knows the story of the Auld Lichts arriving in heaven, and being prevented from discovering that there were other people there, for fear of spoiling their enjoyment of celestial bliss. The same kind of sentiment may take a more sinister form: persecution may be so pleasant to the persecutor that he would find a world without heretics intolerably dull. Similarly Hitler and Mussolini, since they teach that war is the noblest of human activities, could not be happy if they had conquered the world and had no enemies left to fight. In like manner, party politics become uninteresting as soon as one party has unquestionable supremacy.

Thus an organisation which derives its appeal to the individual from such motives as pride, envy, hate, contempt, or pleasure in contest,[1] cannot fulfil its purpose if it is world-wide. In a world where such passions are strong, an organisation which becomes world-wide is pretty sure to break up, since it will have lost its motive force.

It will be seen that, in what has just been said, we have been considering rather the sentiments of ordinary members of organisations than those of their governments. Whatever the purpose of an organisation, its government derives satisfaction from power, and has, in consequence, an interest not identical with that of the

---

[1] I am excluding merely sporting contests, which can be organised within a single governing authority such as the MCC.

members. The desire for universal conquest is therefore likely to be stronger in the government than in the members.

Nevertheless, there is an important difference between the dynamics of organisations embodying sentiments to be realised by cooperation and that of those whose purposes essentially involve conflict. This is a large subject, and for the present I am merely concerned to point out the limitations to the study of organisations without regard to their purposes.

I have spoken of the growth of an organisation, and of its competition with rivals. To complete the Darwinian analogy, something should be said about decay and old age. The fact that men are mortal is not, in itself, a reason for expecting organisations to die, and yet most of them do. Sometimes they suffer a violent death from without, but this is not what, at the moment, I wish to consider. What I wish to consider is the feebleness and slowness of movement, analogous to that of old men, which is often seen in old organisations. One of the best examples is the Chinese Empire before the revolution of 1911. It was by far the most ancient government in the world; it had shown military prowess at the time of the rise of Rome, and during the great days of the Caliphate; it had a continuous tradition of high civilisation, and a long-established practice of government by able men chosen through the medium of competitive examination. The strength of the tradition, the tyranny of centuries of habit, was the cause of collapse. It was impossible for the literati to understand that other knowledge than that of the Confucian classics was needed for coping with the nations of the West, or that the maxims which had been adequate against semi-barbarian frontier races were of no avail against Europeans. What makes an organisation grow old is habit based upon success; when new circumstances arise, the habit is too strong to be shaken off. In revolutionary times, those who have the habit of command never realise soon enough that they can no longer count upon the correlative habit of obedience. Moreover the respect exacted by exalted persons, originally with a view to confirming their authority, in time develops into a stiff etiquette that hampers them in action and prevents them from acquiring the knowledge needed for success. Kings can no longer lead in battle because they are too sacred; they cannot be told unpalatable truths, because they would execute the teller. In time they become mere symbols, and some day people wake up to the fact that they symbolise nothing of any value.

There is, however, no reason why *all* organisations should be mortal. The American Constitution, for example, does not invest any man or body of men with the kind of reverence that leads to ignorance and impotence, nor does it readily lend itself, except to some extent in relation to the Supreme Court, to the accumulation of habits and maxims which prevent adaptation to new circumstances. There is no obvious reason why an organisation of this sort should not persist indefinitely. I think, therefore, that, while most organisations perish sooner or later, either from rigidity or from external causes, there is no inherent reason which makes this unavoidable. At this point, the biological analogy, if pressed, becomes misleading.

Chapter 12

Powers and Forms of Governments

Apart from the purpose of an organisation, its most important characteristics are (1) size, (2) power over members, (3) power over non-members, (4) form of goverment. The question of size I shall consider in the next chapter; the others are to form our present topic.

Legally tolerated organisations other than the State have powers over their members which are strictly limited by law. If you are a barrister, a solicitor, a medical man, or an owner of racehorses, you may be disbarred, struck off the rolls, disqualified or warned off the turf. All these punishments involve disgrace, and the first three are likely to involve extreme economic hardship. But however unpopular you may be in your profession, your colleagues cannot legally do more than prevent you from practising it. If you are a politician, you must be of the machine; but you cannot be prevented from joining another party or from living a peaceful life remote from parliamentary contests. The powers of organisations other than the State over their members depend upon the right of expulsion, and are more or less severe according to the degree of obloquy and financial hardship attached to expulsion.

The powers of the State over its citizens are, on the contrary, unlimited, except in so far as constitutional provisions may forbid arbitrary arrest or spoliation. In the United States, no man can be deprived of life, liberty, or property except by due process of law, i.e. by the demonstration to the judicial authorities that he has been guilty of some act previously declared deserving of such punishment. In England, although the powers of the executive are similarly limited, the legislature is omnipotent: it can pass an Act to the effect that Mr John Smith is to be put to death, or deprived of his property, without the necessity of establishing that he has committed a crime. In the form of Acts of Attainder, this power was one of the means by which Parliament acquired control of the government. In India and in totalitarian States, this power belongs to the executive, and is freely exercised. This is in accordance with tradition, and where States have lost this omnipotence they have done so as a result of the doctrine of the Rights of Man.

The powers of organisations over non-members are less easy to define. The powers of a State in relation to foreigners depend upon war and the threat of war; this applies even to such matters as tariffs and immigration laws, both of which, in China, were regulated by treaties accepted as a result of military defeat. Nothing but lack of military force limits the power of one State over another; given sufficient preponderance, even extermination or removal of the whole population may be decreed, and often has been. Consider, for example, the Book of Joshua, the Babylonian captivity, and the confinement of North American Indians to reservations when not exterminated.

The external powers of private organisations are apt to be regarded by the State with jealousy, and are therefore largely extra-legal. They depend mainly upon the boycott and other more extreme forms of intimidation. Such terroristic influence is usually a prelude to revolution or anarchy. In Ireland, assassination brought about the downfall, first of the landlords, and then of the English domination. In Tsarist Russia, the revolutionaries depended very largely upon terroristic methods. The Nazis won their way by acts of illegal violence. At the present moment, in Czechoslovakia, those among the German population who will not join Henlein's party receive such notices as 'you are a marked man' or 'your turn will come'; and in view of what happened to opponents when the Germans occupied Austria, such threats are very effective. A State which cannot cope with this kind of illegality usually soon comes to grief. If the illegality is that of a single organisation with a definite political programme, the result is revolution, but if it is that of bands of brigands or mutinous soldiers, there may be a lapse into mere anarchy and chaos.

In democratic countries, the most important private organisations are economic. Unlike secret societies, they are able to exercise their terrorism without illegality, since they do not threaten to kill their enemies, but only to starve them. By means of such threats – which do not need to be explicitly uttered – they have frequently even defeated governments, for example recently in France. So long as private organisations can decide whether individuals not belonging to them shall, or shall not, have enough to eat, the power of the State is obviously subject to very serious limitations. In Germany and Italy, no less than in Russia, the State has become supreme over private capital in this respect.

I come now to the question of forms of government, and it is natural to begin with absolute monarchy, as the oldest, simplest, and most widespread of the constitutions known in historical times. I am not now distinguishing between the king and the tyrant; I am considering simply one-man rule, whether that of a hereditary king or that of a usurper. This form of government has prevailed in Asia at all times, from the beginning of Babylonian records through the Persian monarchy, the Macedonian and Roman domination, and the Caliphate, to the days of the Great Mogul. In China, it is true, the Emperor was not absolute, except during the reign of Shih Huang Ti (third century B.C.), who burnt the books; at other times, the literati could usually defeat him. But China has always been an exception to all rules. At the present day, though absolute monarchy is supposed to be in decline, something very like it prevails in Germany, Italy, Russia, Turkey, and Japan. It is evident that this form of government is one which men find natural.

Psychologically, its merits are clear. In general, the ruler leads some tribe or sect to conquest, and his followers feel themselves partakers in his glory. Cyrus led the Persians in revolt against the Medes; Alexander gave power and wealth to his Macedonians; Napoleon brought victory to the armies of the Revolution. The relations of Lenin and Hitler to their parties were of the same sort. The tribe or sect of which the conqueror is the head follows him willingly, and feels itself magnified by his successes; those whom he subdues feel fear mixed with admiration. No political training, no habit of compromise, is required; the only instinctive social cohesion that is necessary is that of the small inner band of followers, which is rendered easy by the fact that all depend upon the hero's achievements. When he dies, his work may fall to pieces, like that of Alexander; but with luck an able successor may carry it on until the new power has become traditional.

The difficulty of any other relation between men, as a bond uniting them in one community, except that of command and obedience, may be illustrated by the relations of States. There are innumerable instances of small States growing into great empires by conquest, but hardly any of voluntary federation. For Greece in the time of Philip, and Italy in the Renaissance, some degree of cooperation between different sovereign States was a matter of life or death, and yet it could not be brought about. The same thing is true of Europe in the present day. It is not easy to induce men who have the habit of command, or even only of independence, to submit voluntarily to an external authority. When this does happen, it is usually in such a case as a gang of pirates, where a small group hopes for great gains at the expense of the general public, and has such confidence in a leader as to be willing to leave the direction of the enterprise in his hands. It is only in this kind of situation that we can speak of government arising from a 'social contract', and in this case the contract is Hobbes's rather than Rousseau's – i.e. it is a contract which the citizens (or pirates) fake with each other, not a contract between them and their leader. The psychologically important point is that men are only willing to agree to such a contract when there are great possibilities of plunder or conquest. It is this psychological mechanism, though usually not in an overt form, which has enabled kings who were not absolute to become more nearly so by successful war.

The conclusion to be derived from these considerations is that, while something like voluntary consent to the arbitrary power of a monarch is necessary from a band of companions who are near the throne, the majority of his subjects usually submit, at first from fear, and afterwards as the result of custom and tradition. The 'social contract', in the only sense in which it is not *completely* mythical, is a contract among conquerors, which loses its *raison d'être* if they are deprived of the benefits of conquest. So far as the majority of subjects are concerned, fear, rather than consent, is the original cause of submission to a king whose power extends beyond a single tribe.

It is because the motives of loyalty in an inner group and fear in the general population are so simple and easy that almost all enlargement in the areas of sovereign States has been by conquest, not by voluntary federation; and it is also for this reason that monarchy has played such a great part in history.

Monarchy has, however, very great disadvantages. If it is hereditary, it is unlikely that the rulers will continue to be able; and if there is any uncertainty about the law of succession, there will be dynastic civil wars. In the East, a new ruler usually began by putting his brothers to death; but if one of them escaped he set up a claim to the throne as the only chance of avoiding execution. Read, for example, Mainucci's *Storia do Mogor*, which deals with the Great Moguls, and makes it evident that wars of succession did more than anything else to weaken their empire. In our own country the Wars of the Roses point the same moral.

If, on the other hand, the monarchy is not hereditary, there is even more likelihood of civil war. This danger is illustrated by the Roman Empire from the death of Commodus to the accession of Constantine. Only one really successful solution of this problem has ever been devised: it is the method by which the Pope is elected. But this is the ultimate term of a development which started from democracy; and even in this case the Great Schism shows that the method is not infallible.

A still more serious disadvantage of monarchy is the fact that it is usually indifferent to the interests of subjects, except when they are identical with those of the king. Identity of interest is likely to exist up to a point. The king has an interest in suppressing internal anarchy, and will therefore be supported by the law-abiding section of his subjects whenever the danger of anarchy is great. He has an interest in the wealth of his subjects, since it makes the taxes more productive. In foreign war, the interests of the king and his subjects will be thought to be identical so long as he is victorious. So long as he continues to extend his dominions, the inner group, to whom he is a leader rather than a master, will find his service profitable. But kings are led astray by two causes: pride, and reliance upon an inner group which has lost its power of command. As for pride: though the Egyptians endured the Pyramids, the French, in the end, grumbled about Versailles and the Louvre; and moralists have always inveighed against the luxury of courts. 'Wine is wicked, women are wicked, the king is wicked,' we are told in the Apocrypha.

The other cause for the decay of monarchy is more important. Kings acquire the habit of relying upon some section of the population: the aristocracy, the Church, the higher bourgeoisie, or perhaps a geographical group, such as the Cossacks. Gradually economic or cultural changes diminish the power of the favoured group, and the king shares their unpopularity. He may even, like Nicholas II, be so unwise as to lose the support of the groups that should be most completely on his side; but this is exceptional. Charles I and Louis XVI were supported by the aristocracy, but fell because the middle class was opposed to them.

A king or despot can maintain his power if he is astute in internal politics and successful externally. If he is quasi-divine, his dynasty may be prolonged indefinitely. But the growth of civilisation puts an end to belief in his divinity; defeat in war is not always avoidable; and political astuteness cannot be an invariable attribute of monarchs. Therefore sooner or later, if there is no external conquest, there is revolution, and the monarchy is either abolished or shorn of its power.

The natural successor to absolute monarchy is oligarchy. But oligarchy may be of many sorts; it may be the rule of a hereditary aristocracy, of the rich, or of a Church or political party. These produce very different results. A hereditary landed aristocracy is apt to be conservative, proud, stupid, and rather brutal; for these reasons among others, it is always worsted in a struggle with the higher bourgeoisie. A government of the rich prevailed in all the free cities of the Middle Ages, and survived in Venice until Napoleon extinguished it. Such governments have been, on the whole, more enlightened and astute than any others known to history. Venice, in particular, steered a prudent course through centuries of complicated intrigue, and had a diplomatic service far more efficient than that of any other State. Money made in commerce is made by cleverness which is not dictatorial, and this characteristic is displayed by governments composed of successful merchants. The modern industrial magnate is a totally different type, partly because he deals largely with the technical manipulation of materials, partly because his dealings with human beings are preponderantly with an army of employees rather than with equals who must be persuaded, not coerced.

Government by a Church or political party – which may be called a theocracy – is a form of oligarchy which has assumed a new importance in recent years. It had an older form, which survived in the Patrimony of St Peter and in the Jesuit régime in Paraguay, but its modern form begins with Calvin's rule in Geneva – apart from the very brief sway of the Anabaptists in Münster. Still more modern was the Rule of the Saints, which ended in England at the Restoration, but survived for a considerable period in New England. In the eighteenth and nineteenth centuries, this type of government might have been thought permanently extinct. But it was revived by Lenin, adopted in Italy and Germany, and seriously attempted in China.

In a country such as Russia or China, where the bulk of the population is illiterate and without political experience, the successful revolutionary found himself in a very difficult situation. Democracy on Western lines could not possibly succeed; it was attempted in China, but was a fiasco from the first. On the other hand, the revolutionary parties in Russia had nothing but contempt for the territorial aristocracy and the rich of the middle class; none of the objects they had in view could be achieved by an oligarchy chosen from these classes. They accordingly said: 'We, the party that has made the revolution, will retain political power until such time as the country is ripe for democracy; and meanwhile we will educate the country in our principles.'

The result, however, was not quite what the Old Bolsheviks had hoped. Under the stress of civil war, famine, and peasant discontent, the dictatorship became gradually more severe, while the struggle within the Communist Party after the death of Lenin transformed it from government by a Party to one-man rule. All this was not difficult to foresee. I wrote in 1920: 'The Bolshevik theory requires that every country, sooner or later, should go through what Russia is going through now. And in every country in such a condition we may expect to find the government falling into the hands of ruthless men, who have not by nature any love for freedom, and who will see little importance in hastening the transition from dictatorship to freedom ... Is it not almost inevitable that men placed as the Bolsheviks are placed in Russia ... will be loath to relinquish their monopoly of power, and will find reasons for remaining until some new revolution ousts them?' For such reasons, it is difficult to regard a theocracy as a step towards democracy, though in other respects it may have merits.

The merits of theocracies, when they represent some new creed, are sometimes very great, and sometimes almost non-existent. In the first place, the believers form a nucleus for social cohesion after revolution, and they can easily cooperate because they agree on fundamentals; it is therefore possible for them to establish a vigorous government that knows its own mind. In the second place, as already observed, the Party or Church is a minority not of birth or wealth, to which it is possible to entrust political power where democracy, for whatever reason, must fail.

In the third place, the believers are almost sure to be more energetic and politically conscious than the average of the population, to whom, in many instances, they have also been superior intellectually. Certain creeds, however – including some that have become powerful – attract only stupid people, apart from the leaven of adventurers in search of jobs. Intelligence, therefore, is a characteristic of only some among theocracies.

When power is confined to the members of one sect, there is inevitably a severe ideological censorship. Sincere believers will be anxious to spread the true faith; others will be content with outward conformity. The former attitude kills the free exercise of intelligence; the latter promotes hypocrisy. Education and literature must be stereotyped, and designed to produce credulity rather than initiative and criticism. If the leaders are interested in their own theology, there will be heresies, and orthodoxy will come to be more and more rigidly defined. Men who are strongly influenced by a creed differ from the average in their power to be moved by something more or less abstract and more or less remote from daily life. If such men control an unpopular government, the result is to make the bulk of the population even more frivolous and thoughtless than it would naturally be – a result which is much promoted by the knowledge that all thought is potentially heretical, and therefore dangerous. The rulers, in a theocracy, are likely to be fanatics; being fanatics, they will be severe; being severe, they will be opposed; being opposed, they will become more severe. Their power-impulses will wear, even to themselves, the cloak of religious zeal, and will therefore be subject to no restraint. Hence the rack and the stake, the Gestapo and the Cheka.

We have seen that monarchy and oligarchy have both merits and demerits. The principal demerit of both is that, sooner or later, the government becomes so indifferent to the desires of ordinary men that there is revolution. Democracy, when firmly established, is a safeguard against this kind of instability. Since civil war is a very grave evil, a form of government which makes it unlikely is to be commended. Now civil war is unlikely where, if it occurred, it would give victory to the previous holders of power. Other things being equal, if power is in the hands of the majority, the government is more likely to win in a civil war than if it represents only a minority. This, so far as it goes, is an argument for democracy; but various recent instances show that it is subject to many limitations.

A government is usually called 'democratic' if a fairly large percentage of the population has a share of political power. The most extreme Greek democracies excluded women and slaves, and America considered itself a democracy before women had the vote. Clearly an oligarchy approaches more nearly to a democracy as the percentage possessed of political power increases. The characteristic features of oligarchy only appear when this percentage is rather small.

In all organisations, but especially in States, the problem of government is twofold. From the point of view of the government, the problem is to secure acquiescence from the governed; from the point of view of the governed, the problem is to make the government take account, not only of its own interests, but also of the interests of those over whom it has power. If either of these problems is completely solved, the other does not arise; if neither is solved, there is revolution. But as a rule a compromise solution is reached. Apart from brute force, the principal factors on the government side are tradition, religion, fear of foreign enemies, and the natural desire of most men to follow a leader. For the protection of the governed, only one method has been hitherto discovered which is in any degree effective, namely, democracy.

Democracy, as a method of government, is subject to some limitations which are essential, and to others which are, in principle, avoidable. The essential limitations arise chiefly from two sources: some decisions must be speedy, and others require expert knowledge. When Great Britain abandoned the gold standard in 1931, both factors were involved: it was absolutely necessary to act quickly, and the questions involved were such as most men could not understand. The democracy, therefore, could only express its opinion retrospectively. War, though less technical than currency, has even more urgency: it is possible to consult Parliament or Congress (though as a rule this is something of a farce, since the issue will have been already decided in fact, if not in form), but it is impossible to consult the electorate.

Owing to these essential limitations, many of the most important matters must be entrusted by the electorate to the Government. Democracy is successful in so far as the Government is obliged to respect public opinion. The Long Parliament decreed that it could not be dissolved without its own consent; what has hindered subsequent Parliaments from doing likewise? The answer is neither simple nor reassuring. In the first place, in the absence of a revolutionary situation, members of the outgoing Parliament were assured of a pleasant life even if they belonged to the defeated party; most of them would be re-elected, and, if they lost the pleasures of government, they would gain the almost equal satisfactions to be obtained by publicly criticising the mistakes of their rivals. And in due course they would return to power. If, on the other hand, they made it impossible for the electorate to get rid of them by constitutional means, they would create a revolutionary situation, which would endanger their property and perhaps their lives. The fate of Strafford and Charles I was a warning against rashness.

All this would be different if a revolutionary situation were already in existence. Suppose a Conservative Parliament had reason to fear that the next election would produce a Communist majority, which would expropriate private property without compensation. In such a case, the party in power might well imitate the Long Parliament, and decree its own perpetuity. It would hardly be restrained from this action by reverence for the principles of democracy; it would be restrained, if at all, only by a doubt as to the loyalty of the armed forces.

The moral is that a democracy, since it is compelled to entrust power to elected representatives, cannot feel any security that, in a revolutionary situation, its representatives will continue to represent its wishes. The wishes of Parliament may, in easily conceivable circumstances, be opposed to those of a majority of the nation. If Parliament, in such circumstances, can rely upon a preponderance of force, it may thwart the majority with impunity.

This is not to say that there is a better form of government than democracy. It is only to say that there are issues as to which men will fight, and when they arise no form of government can prevent civil war. One of the most important purposes of government should be to prevent issues from becoming so acute as to lead to civil war; and from this point of view democracy, where it is habitual, is probably preferable to any other known form of government.

The difficulty of democracy, as a form of government, is that it demands a readiness for compromise. The beaten party must not consider that a principle is involved of such importance as to make it pusillanimous to yield; on the other hand, the majority must not press the advantage to the point at which it provokes a revolt. This requires practice, respect for the law, and the habit of believing that opinions other than one's own may not be a proof of wickedness. What is even more necessary, there must not be a state of acute fear, for, when there is such a state, men look for a leader and submit to him when found, with the result that he probably becomes a dictator. Given these conditions, democracy is capable of being the most stable form of government hitherto devised. In the United States, Great Britain, the Dominions, Scandinavia, and Switzerland, it runs hardly any danger except from without; in France it is becoming more and more firmly established. And in addition to stability, it has the merit of making governments pay some attention to the welfare of their subjects – not, perhaps, as much as might be wished, but very much more than is shown by absolute monarchies, oligarchies, or dictatorships.

Democracy, in a modern great State, has certain disadvantages, not, indeed, as compared with other forms of government over the same area, but inevitably owing to the immense population concerned. In antiquity, the representative system being unknown, the citizens assembled in the marketplace voted personally on each issue. So long as the State was confined to a single city, this gave to each citizen a sense of real power and responsibility, the more so as most of the issues were such as his own experience enabled him to understand. But owing to the absence of an elected legislature, democracy could not extend over a wider area. When Roman citizenship was granted to the inhabitants of other parts of Italy, the new citizens could not, in practice, acquire any share of political power, since this could only be exercised by those who were actually in Rome. The geographical difficulty was overcome, in the modern world, by the practice of choosing representatives. Until very recently, the representative, once chosen, had considerable independent power, since men living at a distance from the capital could not know what was happening soon enough, or in sufficient detail, to be able to express their opinion effectively. Now, however, owing to broadcasting, rapid mobility, newspapers, etc., large countries have become more and more like the City States of antiquity; there is more personal contact (of a sort) between men at the centre and voters at a distance; followers can bring pressure on leaders, and leaders reciprocally can exert influence on followers, to an extent which was impossible in the eighteenth and nineteenth centuries. The result has been to diminish the importance of the representative and increase that of the leader. Parliaments are no longer effective intermediaries between voters and governments. All the dubious propagandist devices formerly confined to election times can now be employed continuously. The Greek City State, with its demagogues, tyrants, body-guards, and exiles, has revived because its methods of propaganda have again become available.

Except when he feels enthusiasm for a leader, the voter in a large democracy has so little sense of power that he often does not think it worth while to use his vote. If he is not a keen propagandist for one of the parties, the vastness of the forces that decide who shall govern makes his own part in them appear completely negligible. In practice, all that he can do, as a rule, is to vote for one or other of two men, whose programmes may not interest him, and may differ very little, and who, he knows, may with impunity abandon their programmes as soon as they are elected. If, on the other hand, there is a leader whom he enthusiastically admires, the psychology involved is that which we considered in connection with monarchy: it is that of the tie between a king and the tribe or sect of his active supporters. Every skilful political agitator or organiser devotes himself to stimulating devotion to an individual. If the individual is a great leader, the result is one-man government; if he is not, the caucus which has secured his election becomes the real power.

This is not true democracy. The question of the preservation of democracy when governmental areas are large is a very difficult one, to which I shall return in a later chapter.

So far, we have been concerned with the forms of government in politics. But the forms which occur in economic organisations are so important and peculiar that they require separate consideration.

In an industrial undertaking, there is, to begin with, a distinction analogous to that between citizens and slaves in antiquity. The citizens are those who have invested capital in the undertaking, while the slaves are the employees. I do not wish to press that analogy. The employee differs from a slave in the fact that he is free to change his job if he can, and in his right to spend his non-working hours as he pleases. The analogy that I wish to bring out is in relation to government. Tyrannies, oligarchies, and democracies differed in their relations to free men; in relation to slaves, they were all alike. Similarly in a capitalist industrial enterprise the power may be divided among investors monarchically, oligarchically, or democratically, but employees, unless they are investors, have no share in it whatever, and are thought to have as little claim as slaves were thought to have in antiquity.

Business corporations exhibit a great variety of oligarchical forms of constitution. I am not thinking, at the moment, of the fact that the employees are excluded from the management; I am thinking only of the shareholders. The best account of this subject known to me is in a book to which I have already alluded, *The Modern Corporation and Private Property*, by Berle and Means. In a chapter called 'The Evolution of Control', they show how oligarchies, often with very small participation in ownership, have acquired the government of vast aggregations of capital. By means of devices concerned with the proxy committee, the management 'can virtually dictate their own successors. Where ownership is sufficiently subdivided, the management can thus become a self-perpetuating body even though its share in the ownership is negligible. The nearest approach to this condition which the present writer has been able to discover elsewhere is the organisation which dominates the Catholic Church. The Pope selects the Cardinals and the College of Cardinals in turn selects the succeeding Pope.'[1] This form of government exists in some of the largest existing corporations, such as the American Telephone and Telegraph Company, and the United States Steel Corporation, with assets (on 1st January, 1930) of four billion and two billion dollars respectively. In the latter, the directors collectively own only 1.4 per cent of the shares; yet the economic power is wholly theirs.

The complexity of the organisation of a business corporation is apt to be greater than that of any political institution. Directors, shareholders, debenture holders, executive staff, and ordinary employees, all have different functions. The government is usually in form an oligarchy, of which the units are shares, not shareholders, and the directors are their chosen representatives. In practice, the directors usually have much more power, as against the shareholders, than belongs to the government of a political oligarchy as against the individual oligarchs. *Per contra*, where trade unionism is well organised, the employees have a considerable voice as to the terms of their employment. In capitalistic enterprises there is a peculiar duality of purpose: on the one hand they exist to provide goods or services for the public,

[1] Op. cit., pp. 87–8.

and on the other hand they aim at providing profits for the shareholders. In political organisations, the politicians are supposed to be aiming at the public good, not only at maximising their own salaries; this pretence is kept up even under despotisms. This is why there is more hypocrisy in politics than in business. But under the combined influence of democracy and socialistic criticism, many important industrial magnates have acquired the art of political humbug, and have learnt to pretend that the public good is their motive for making a fortune. This is another example of the modern tendency to the coalescence of politics and economics.

Something must be said as to the ways in which, in a given institution, the forms of government change. This is a matter as to which history gives no sure guidance. We have seen that, in Egypt and Babylonia, absolute monarchy was fully developed at the period when historical records begin; from anthropological evidence, it may be presumed to have developed out of the authority of chiefs originally limited by a Council of Elders. Throughout Asia (excluding China), absolute monarchy has never, except under European influence, shown any sign of giving way to any other form of government. In Europe, on the contrary, it has never, in historical times, been stable for long periods. In the Middle Ages, the power of kings was limited by that of the feudal nobility, as well as by the municipal autonomy of the more important commercial cities. After the Renaissance, the power of kings increased throughout Europe, but this increase was brought to an end by the rise of the middle class, first in England; then in France and then in the rest of Western Europe. Until the Bolsheviks dismissed the Constituent Assembly at the beginning of 1918 it might have been thought that parliamentary democracy was certain to prevail throughout the civilised world

Movements away from democracy are, however, no new thing. They occurred in many Greek City States, in Rome when the Empire was established, and in the commercial republics of mediaeval Italy. Is it possible to discover any general principles determining the various developments towards or away from democracy?

The two great influences against democracy in the past have been wealth and war. We may take the Medici and Napoleon as illustrating these two. Men whose wealth is obtained by commerce are, as a rule, less harsh and more conciliatory than those whose power is due to ownership of land; they are, therefore, more skilful in buying their way into power, and governing afterwards so as not to rouse violent resentments, than are those whose status is merely hereditary and traditional. The gains made in commerce, for example in Venice or in the towns of the Hanseatic League, were made at the expense of the foreigner, and accordingly aroused no unpopularity at home, such as attaches to the manufacturer who makes his fortune by employing sweated labour. An oligarchy of substantial burghers is therefore the most natural and stable form of government for a predominantly commercial community. And this easily develops into monarchy if one family is much richer than any other.

War operates by a different and more violent psychology. Fear makes men wish for a leader, and a successful general rouses the passionate admiration which is the obverse of fear. Since victory seems, at the moment, the one thing of real importance, the successful general easily persuades his country to entrust him with supreme power. So long as the crisis continues, he is judged indispensable, and when it is over he may have become very difficult to remove.

The modern movements against democracy, though they are connected with a war mentality, are not quite analogous to the case of Napoleon. Broadly speaking, the German and Italian democracies fell, not because a majority was tired of democracy, but because the preponderance of armed force was not on the side of numerical majority. It may seem strange that the civil government should ever be stronger than the commander-in-chief, yet this is the case wherever democracy is firmly rooted in the habits of the nation. Lincoln, in appointing a commander-in-chief, wrote: 'They tell me that you aim at dictatorship. The way to achieve this is to win victories. I look to you for the victories, and I will risk the dictatorship.' He could safely do so, because no American army would have followed a general in an attack upon the civil government. In the seventeenth century, Cromwell's soldiers were quite willing to obey him in dismissing the Long Parliament; in the nineteenth, the Duke of Wellington, if he had ever harboured such a project, could not have got a man to follow him.

Democracy, when it is new, arises from resentment against the previous holders of power; but so long as it is new it is unstable. Men who represent themselves as enemies of the old monarchs or oligarchs may succeed in restoring a monarchical or oligarchical system: Napoleon and Hitler could win public support when the Bourbons and Hohenzollern could not. It is only where democracy has lasted long enough to become traditional that it is stable. Cromwell, Napoleon, and Hitler appeared in the early days of democracy in their respective countries; in view of the first two, the third should be in no way surprising. Nor is there reason to suppose him more permanent than his predecessors.

There are, however, some serious reasons for doubting whether, in the near future, democracy is likely to recover the prestige that it had in the latter half of the nineteenth century. We have been saying that, in order to become stable, it must become traditional. What chance has it of becoming sufficiently established in Eastern Europe and Asia to begin the process of becoming traditional?

Government has at all times been greatly affected by military technique. In the days when Rome was tending towards democracy, Roman armies were composed of Roman citizens; it was the substitution of professional armies that brought about the Empire. The strength of the feudal aristocracy depended upon the impregnability of castles, which ended with the introduction of artillery. The large almost untrained armies of the French Revolution, by defeating the small professional armies opposed to them, showed the importance of popular enthusiasm for the cause, and thereby suggested the military advantages of democracy. We seem now, through the aeroplane, to be returning to the need for forces composed of comparatively few highly trained men. It is to be expected, therefore, that the form of government, in every country exposed to serious war, will be such as airmen will like, which is not likely to be democracy.

But there are certain considerations to be set against this. It may be assumed that the United States, whether a belligerent or not, will be the only victor in the Great War, and it is improbable that the United States will cease to be a democracy. Much of the strength of Fascism is due to its supposed advantages in war, and if these prove to be non-existent democracy may again spread eastward. In the long run, nothing gives a nation such strength in war as the wide diffusion of education and patriotism; and although patriotism may, for the moment, be stimulated by the revivalist methods of Fascism, such methods, as long experience in the religious sphere has proved, inevitably lead in the end to weariness and backsliding. On the whole, therefore, the military arguments point to the survival of democracy where it still exists and its return to the countries in which it is for the moment in eclipse. But it must be admitted that the opposite alternative is by no means impossible.

Chapter 13

Organisations and the Individual

Human beings find it profitable to live in communities, but their desires, unlike those of bees in a hive, remain largely individual; hence arises the difficulty of social life and the need of government. For, on the one hand, government is necessary: without it, only a very small percentage of the population of civilised countries could hope to survive, and that in a state of pitiable destitution. But, on the other hand, government involves inequalities of power, and those who have most power will use it to further their own desires as opposed to those of ordinary citizens. Thus anarchy and despotism are alike disastrous, and some compromise is necessary if human beings are to be happy.

In the present chapter, I wish to consider the organisations concerned with a given individual, not the individuals concerned with a given organisation. This matter is, of course, very different in democratic and in totalitarian States, for in the latter all the organisations concerned, with very few exceptions, are departments of the State. As far as possible, however, I wish to ignore this difference in a preliminary survey.

Organisations, both public and private, affect an individual in two ways. There are those that are designed to facilitate the realisation of his own wishes, or of what are considered to be his interests; and there are those intended to prevent him from thwarting the legitimate interests of others. The distinction is not clear-cut: the police exist to further the interests of honest men, as well as to thwart burglars, but their impact on the lives of burglars is much more emphatic than their contacts with those who abide by the law. I shall return to this distinction presently; for the moment, let us consider the most important points, in the lives of individuals in civilised communities, at which some organisation plays some decisive part.

To begin with birth: the services of a doctor and/or a midwife are considered essential, and although, formerly, a wholly untrained Mrs Gamp was thought sufficient, a certain level of skill, determined by a public authority, is now exacted. Throughout infancy and childhood health is to some extent the concern of the State; the extent of the State's concern in various countries is fairly accurately reflected in the infant and juvenile death-rates. If the parents fail too egregiously in their parental duty, the child can be taken from them by the public authority, and assigned to the care of foster-parents or of an institution. At the age of five or six, the child comes under the education authorities, and thenceforward, for a number of years, is compelled to learn those things that the government thinks every citizen should know. At the end of this process, in the majority of cases, most opinions and mental habits are fixed for life.

Meanwhile, in democratic countries, the child comes under other influences which are not exerted by the State. If the parents are religious or political, they will teach the tenets of a creed or a party. As the child grows older, he becomes increasingly interested in organised amusements, such as cinemas and football matches. If he is rather intelligent, but not very, he may be influenced by the Press. If he goes to a school which is not a State school, he acquires an outlook which is in certain ways peculiar – in England, usually an outlook of social superiority to the herd. Meanwhile he imbibes a moral code which is that of his age and class and nation. The moral code is important, but not easy to define, because precepts are of three not sharply differentiated sorts: first, those which must be really obeyed on pain of general obloquy; secondly, those which must not be *openly* disobeyed; and thirdly, those which are regarded as counsels of perfection, only to be obeyed by saints. Moral codes applicable to the whole population are mainly, though by no means wholly, the result of religious tradition, operating through religious organisations, but capable of surviving their decay for a longer or shorter time. There are also professional codes: things which must not be done by an officer, or a doctor, or a barrister, and so on. Such codes, in modern times, are usually formulated by professional associations. They are very imperative: while the Church and the Army conflicted as to duelling, the Army code prevailed among officers; medical and confessional secrecy prevails even against the law.

As soon as a young man or woman begins to earn money,

various organisations begin to influence his or her activities. The employer is usually an organisation; and there is probably, in addition, a federation of employers. The trade union and the State both control important aspects of the work; and apart from such matters as insurance and Factory Acts, the State can help to decide, by tariffs and by government orders, whether the particular trade that a man has chosen shall prosper or be depressed. The prosperity of an industry may be affected by all kinds of circumstances, such as currency, the international situation, or the ambitions of Japan.

Marriage and duties to children again bring a man into relations with the law, and also with a moral code mainly derived from the Church. If he lives long enough and is sufficiently poor, he may at last enjoy an old age pension; and his death is carefully supervised by the law and the medical profession, to make sure that it has not occurred by his own wish or by anyone else's.

Certain matters remain to be decided by personal initiative. A man can marry to please himself, provided the lady is willing; he probably has a certain liberty of choice, in youth, as to his means of livelihood; his leisure can be spent as he chooses, within the limits of what he can afford; if he is interested in religion or politics, he can join whatever sect or party most attracts him. Except in the matter of marriage, he is still dependent upon organisations even when he has freedom of choice: he cannot, unless he is a very exceptional man, found a religion, create a party, organise a football club, or make his own drinks. What he can do is to choose among ready-made alternatives; but competition tends to make all these alternatives as attractive as possible, within what economic conditions permit.

So far, the effect of the organisations characteristic of civilised societies is to increase a man's liberty as compared with (say) a peasant in a comparatively undeveloped community. Consider the life of a Chinese peasant, as compared with that of an Occidental wage-earner. As a child, it is true, he does not have to go to school, but from a very early age he has to work. He is more likely than not to die in early childhood, from hardship and lack of medical care. If he survives, he has no choice as to his means of livelihood, unless he is prepared to become a soldier or a bandit, or to run the risk of migrating to some large town. Custom deprives him of all but a minimum of freedom as to marriage. Of leisure he has practically none, and if he had it there would be nothing very pleasant to do with it. He lives always on the margin of subsistence, and in times of famine a large part of his family is likely to die of hunger. And hard as life is for the man, it is far harder for the wife and daughters. Even the most depressed of the unemployed, in England, have a life which is almost a paradise in comparison with that of the average Chinese peasant.

To come to another class of organisations, those designed to prevent a man from doing injury to others: the most important of these are the police and the criminal law. In so far as these interfere with crimes of violence, such as murder, robbery, and assault, they increase the freedom and happiness of all but a small minority of exceptionally ferocious individuals. Where the police are not in control, gangs of marauders quickly establish a reign of terror, which makes most of the pleasures of civilised life impossible for all except the gangsters. There is, of course, a danger: it is possible for the police themselves to become gangsters, or at any rate to establish some form of tyranny. This danger is by no means imaginary, but the methods of coping with it are well known. There is also the danger that the police may be used by the holders of power to prevent or obstruct movements in favour of desirable reforms. That this should happen to some extent, seems almost inevitable. It is a part of the fundamental difficulty that the measures which are necessary to prevent anarchy are such as make it more difficult to change the *status quo* when it ought to be changed. In spite of this difficulty, few members of civilised communities would think it possible to dispense wholly with the police.

So far, we have taken no account of war and revolution or the fear of them. These involve the State's instinct of self-preservation, and lead to the most drastic forms of control over individual lives. In almost all Continental countries, there is universal compulsory military service. Everywhere, when war breaks out, every male of military age can be called upon to fight, and every adult can be ordered to do the work that the government thinks most conducive to victory. Those whose activities are thought helpful to the enemy are liable to the death penalty. In time of peace, all governments take steps – some more drastically, others less so – to insure willingness to fight when the moment comes, and loyalty to the national cause at all times. Government action in the matter of revolution varies according to the degree of likelihood of it. Other things being equal, the risk of revolution will be greater where government cares little for the welfare of the citizens. But where as in totalitarian States, the government has a monopoly, not only of physical coercion, but of moral and economic persuasion, it can go further in disregard of citizens than is possible for a less intensive government, since revolutionary sentiment is less easy to propagate and to organise. It is therefore to be expected that, in so far as the State is distinct from the body of the citizens, every increase in its power will make it more indifferent to their welfare.

From the above brief survey it seems to result that, in the main, the effects of organisations, apart from those resulting from governmental self-preservation, are such as to increase individual happiness and well-being. Education, health, productivity of labour, provision against destitution, are matters as to which, in principle, there should be no dispute; and all of them depend upon a very high degree of organisation. But when we come to measures intended to prevent revolution or defeat in war, the matter is different. However necessary such measures may be deemed to be, their effects are unpleasant, and they can only be defended on the ground that revolution or defeat would be still more unpleasant. The difference is perhaps only one of degree. It may be said that vaccination, education, and road-making are unpleasant, but less so than smallpox, ignorance, and impassable morasses. The difference of degree is, however, so great as to amount almost to a difference in kind. Moreover, the unpleasantness of the measures involved in peaceful progress need not be more than temporary. Smallpox could be stamped out, and vaccination would then become unnecessary. Education and road-making could both be made fairly agreeable by the employment of enlightened methods. But every technical advance makes war more painful and more destructive, and the prevention of revolution by totalitarian methods more disastrous to humanity and intelligence.

There is another way of classifying the relations of an individual to different organisations: he may be a customer, a voluntary member, an involuntary member, or an enemy.

The organisations of which man is a customer must be thought by him to minister to his comforts, but they do not add much to his feeling of power. He may, of course, be mistaken in his good opinion of their services: the pills he buys may be useless, the beer may be bad, the race-meeting an occasion for losing money to bookmakers. Nevertheless, even in such cases, he gains *something* from the organisations that he patronises: hope, amusement, and the sense of personal initiative. The prospect of buying a new car gives a man something to think and talk about. On the whole, freedom of choice as to how to spend money is a source of pleasure – affection for one's own furniture, for example, is a very strong and very widespread emotion, which would not exist if the State supplied us with furnished apartments.

The organisations of which man is a voluntary member include political parties, Churches, clubs, friendly societies, enterprises in which he has invested money, and so on. Many of these are faced by enemy organisations belonging to the same categories: rival political parties, dissident Churches, competing business enterprises, and so on. The resulting contests give to those who are interested in them a sense of drama as well as an outlet for power impulses. Except where the State is weak, such contests are kept within bounds by the law, which punishes violence or gross fraud unless it is a secret accomplice. The battles between opposing organisations, when compelled by the authorities to be bloodless, afford, on the whole, a useful outlet for the feelings of pugnacity and love of power which are likely, otherwise, to seek more sinister forms of satisfaction. There is always the danger, if the State is lax or not impartial, that political contests may degenerate into riot, murder, and civil war. But if this danger is averted they are a wholesome element in the life of individuals and communities.

The most important organisation of which a man is an involuntary member is the State. The principle of nationality, so far as it has prevailed, has, however, led to membership of a State being usually in accordance with the will of the citizen, though not due to his will.

> He might have been a Russian,
> A Frenchman, Turk, or Prussian,
> Or perhaps Italian,
> But in spite of all temptations
> To belong to other nations,
> He remains an Englishman.

Most people, given the chance to change their State, would not choose to do so, except when the State represents an alien nationality. Nothing has done more to strengthen the State than the success of the principle of nationality. Where patriotism and citizenship go hand in hand, a man's loyalty to his State usually exceeds his loyalty to voluntary organisations such as Churches and parties.

Loyalty to the State has both positive and negative motives. There is an element which is connected with love of home and family. But this would not take the forms which are taken by loyalty to the State, if it were not reinforced by the twin motives of love of power and fear of foreign aggression. The contests of States, unlike those of political parties, are all-in contests. The whole civilised world was shocked by the kidnapping and murder of the one Lindbergh baby, but such acts, on a vast scale, are to be the commonplaces of the next war, for which we are all preparing, at the cost – in Great Britain – of more than a quarter of our income. No other organisation rouses anything like the loyalty aroused by the national State. And the chief activity of the State is preparation for large-scale homicide. It is loyalty to this organisation for death that causes men to endure the totalitarian State, and to risk the destruction of home and children and our whole civilisation rather than submit to alien rule. Individual psychology and governmental organisation have effected a tragic synthesis, from which we and our children must suffer if we continue powerless to find an issue except through disaster.

Chapter 14

Competition

The nineteenth century, which was keenly aware of the dangers of arbitrary power, had a favourite device for avoiding them, namely competition. The evils of monopoly were still familiar from tradition. The Stuarts, and even Elizabeth, granted profitable monopolies to courtiers, the objection to which was one of the causes of the Civil War. In feudal times, it was common for lords of the manor to insist upon grain being ground in their mills. Continental monarchies, before 1848, abounded in semi-feudal restrictions on freedom of competition. These restrictions were made, not in the interest of either producers or consumers, but for the benefit of monarchs and landowners. In eighteenth-century England, on the contrary, many restrictions survived which were inconvenient both to landowners and to capitalists – for example, laws as to minimum wages, and prohibition of the enclosure of common lands. In England, therefore, until the Corn Law question, landowners and capitalists, on the whole, agreed in advocating *laissez-faire*.

All that was most vigorous in Europe was in favour, also, of free competition in matters of opinion. From 1815 to 1848, Church and State, over the whole of the Continent, were united in opposing the ideas of the French Revolution. The censorship, throughout Germany and Austria, was at once severe and ridiculous. Heine made fun of it in a chapter consisting of the following words:

'The German Censors ....

....

.... idiots ....

In France and Italy, the Napoleonic legend, as well as admiration of the Revolution, was the object of governmental suppression. In Spain and the States of the Church, all liberal thought, even the mildest, was forbidden; the Pope's government still officially believed in sorcery. The principle of nationality was not allowed to be advocated in Italy, Germany, or Austria-Hungary. And everywhere reaction was associated with opposition to the interests of commerce, with maintenance of feudal rights as against the rural population, and with the support of foolish kings and an idle nobility. In these circumstances, *laissez-faire* was the natural expression of energies that were hampered in their legitimate activities.

The freedoms desired by Liberals were achieved in America in the moment of winning independence; in England, in the period from 1824 to 1846; in France in 1871; in Germany by stages from 1848 to 1918; in Italy in the Risorgimento; and even in Russia, for a moment, in the February Revolution. But the result was not quite what Liberals had intended; in industry, it bore more resemblance to the hostile prophecies of Marx. America, with the longest Liberal tradition, was the first to enter the state of trusts, i.e. of monopolies not granted by the State, like those of earlier times, but resulting from the natural operation of competition. American liberalism was outraged, but impotent, and industrial development in other countries gradually followed the lead given by Rockefeller. It was discovered that competition, unless artificially maintained, brings about its own extinction by leading to the complete victory of someone among the competitors.

This, however, is not true of all forms of competition. It is true, broadly speaking, where increase in the size of an organisation means increase of efficiency. There remain, therefore, two questions: first, in what kinds of cases is competition technically wasteful? Secondly, in what cases is it desirable on non-technical grounds?

Technical considerations, broadly speaking, have led to an increase in the optimum size of organisations suitable for dealing with a given matter. In the seventeenth century, roads were dealt with by parishes; now, they are controlled by County Councils largely financed and supervised nationally. Electricity can be best utilised by an authority controlling a considerable area, particularly where there is some important source of power, such as Niagara. Irrigation may demand a work like the Aswan dam, of which the expense is prohibitive unless the area controlled is very large. The economies of large-scale production depend upon control of a market sufficient to absorb an enormous output. And so on.

There are other directions in which the advantages of large areas have not yet been fully utilised. Elementary education might be enlivened and improved by government educational films and by lessons broadcast from the BBC. It would be still better if such films and lessons could be prepared by an international authority, though at present this is a utopian dream. Civil aviation is crippled by not being international. It is obvious that, for most purposes, large States are better than small ones, and that no State can adequately fulfil the primary purpose of protecting the lives of its citizens unless it is world-wide.

There are, however, certain advantages in small areas. They involve less red tape, quicker decisions, and more possibility of adaptation to local needs and customs. The obvious solution is a local government which is not sovereign, but has certain defined powers, and is controlled, on large issues, by the central authority, which should also give financial assistance whenever there is sufficient reason for doing so. This subject, however, would take us into questions of detail which I do not wish to discuss.

The question of competition is more difficult. It has been much debated in the economic sphere, but its importance is at least as great in regard to armed force and propaganda. While the Liberal view was that there should be free competition in business and propaganda, but not in armed force, Italian Fascists and German Nazis have proclaimed the diametrically opposite opinion, that competition is always bad except where it takes the form of national war, in which case it is the noblest of human activities. Marxists decry competition except in the form of the struggle for power between antagonistic classes. Plato, so far as I remember, admires only one kind of competition, namely emulation for honour among comrades in arms, which, he says, is promoted by homosexual love.

In the sphere of production, competition between a multitude of small firms, which characterised the early phase of industrialism, has given place, in the most important branches of production, to competition between trusts each coextensive with at least one State. There is only one important international trust, namely the armament industry, which is exceptional in that orders to one firm are a cause of orders to another: if one country arms, so do others, and therefore the usual motives for competition do not exist. Apart from this peculiar case, competition in business still exists, but it is now merged in the competition between nations, in which war is the ultimate arbiter of success.

The good or evil of modern business competition, therefore, is the same as that of rivalry between States.

There is, however, another form of economic competition which is as fierce as it ever was, I mean the competition for jobs. This begins with scholarship examinations at school, and continues throughout most men's working lives. This form of competition can be mitigated, but cannot be wholly abolished. Even if all actors received the same salary, a man would rather act the part of Hamlet than that of the First Sailor. There are two conditions to be observed: first that the unsuccessful should suffer no avoidable hardship; secondly, that success should, as far as possible, be the reward of some genuine merit, and not of sycophancy or cunning. The second condition has received much less attention from Socialists than it deserves. I shall not, however, pursue this subject, as it would take us too far from our theme.

The most important form of competition, at the present day, is between States, especially those that are called Great Powers. This has become a totalitarian competition, for power, for wealth, for control over men's beliefs, but above all for life itself, since the infliction of the death penalty is the principal means to victory. It is obvious that the only way of ending this competition is the abolition of national sovereignty and national armed forces, and the substitution of a single international government with a monopoly of armed force. The alternative to this measure is the death of a large percentage of the population of civilised countries, and the reduction of the remainder to destitution and semi-barbarism. At present, a vast majority prefer this alternative.

Competition in propaganda, which Liberals, in theory, would leave free, has become connected with the competition between armed States. If you preach Fascism, your most important effect is to strengthen Germany and Italy; if you preach Communism, you are not likely to bring it about, but you may help Russia to win the next war; if you urge the importance of democracy, you will find yourself lending support to the policy of a military alliance with France for the defence of Czechoslovakia. That Russia, Italy, and Germany should have successively abandoned the principle of freedom in propaganda, is not surprising, for the previous adoption of this principle enabled the present governments of those countries to overthrow their predecessors, and its continuance would have made the carrying out of their own policy totally impossible. The world at present is so different from that of the eighteenth and nineteenth centuries that the

Liberal arguments for free competition in propaganda, in so far as they remain valid, need to be carefully re-stated in modern terms. I believe that they retain a large measure of validity, but that they are subject to limitations which it is important to realise.

The doctrine of Liberals, for example of John Stuart Mill in his book *On Liberty*, was far less extreme than is often supposed. Men were to be free in so far as their actions did not injure others, but when others were involved they might, if expedient, be restrained by the action of the State. A man might, say, have been conscientiously convinced that Queen Victoria ought to be assassinated, but Mill would not have allowed him freedom to propagate this opinion. This is an extreme case, but in fact almost any opinion worth either advocating or combating is sure to affect someone adversely. The right of free speech is nugatory unless it includes the right to say things that may have unpleasant consequences to certain individuals or classes. If, therefore, there is to be any scope for freedom in propaganda, it will need for its justification some stronger principle than Mill's.

We may look at this question from the point of view of the government, from that of the average citizen, from that of the ardent innovator, or from that of the philosopher. Let us begin with the point of view of the government.

Governments, as we have already remarked, are threatened by two dangers: revolution, and defeat in war. (In a parliamentary country, the official opposition is to be reckoned as part of the government.) These dangers rouse the instinct of self-preservation, and it is to be expected that governments will do what they can to avert them. From this point of view, the question is: how much freedom of propaganda will produce the greatest degree of stability, both against internal and against external dangers? The answer depends, of course, upon the character of the government and the circumstances of the time. If the government is itself recent and revolutionary, and the population has strong reasons for discontent, freedom is almost sure to bring further revolution. These circumstances existed in France in 1793, in Russia in 1918, and in Germany in 1933, and accordingly in all three cases freedom of propaganda was destroyed by the government. But when the government is traditional, and the economic circumstances of the population are not too desperate, freedom acts as a safety valve and tends to diminish discontent. Although the British Government has done a good deal to hinder

Communist propaganda, that is not the reason for the failure of Communists in Great Britain, and it would have been wise, even from a governmental point of view, to have allowed absolute freedom to their propaganda.

I do not think that a government should ever allow a propaganda urging, say, the assassination of some particular person. For in this case the action recommended may take place even if very few men are converted by the propaganda. It is the duty of the State to protect its citizens' lives unless they have legally incurred the death penalty, and if there is an agitation in favour of someone's assassination it may become very difficult to protect him. The Weimar Republic was too lax in this respect. But I do not think that a stable government ought to prohibit an agitation in favour of making some *class* of persons *legally* liable to the death penalty, for such an agitation would involve no threat to legality.

There can be no good reason, even from a governmental point of view, for interference with opinions which do not involve danger to the existence of the State. If a man holds that the earth is flat, or that the Sabbath should be observed on Saturday, he should be free to do his best to convert people to his way of thinking. The State should not regard itself as the guardian of the Truth in science, metaphysics, or morals. It has done so at most times, and does so at present in Germany, Italy, and Russia. But this is a confession of weakness, from which stable States should be exempt.

Coming now to the average citizen one finds that he takes very little interest in freedom of propaganda except in these circumstances in which it seems to government most dangerous, namely, when it threatens the existence of governments. The government may differ from its subjects in religion or nationality; it may represent the king as against the nobles, the nobles as against the bourgeoisie, or the bourgeoisie as against the poor; it may seem lacking in patriotism, like Charles II and the German governments after the war. In such situations, the average citizen may become interested in an agitation against the government, and will invoke the principle of free speech which his champions are imprisoned. But these are pre-revolutionary situations, and to say that, where they exist, governments should tolerate adverse propaganda, is to say, in effect, that they ought to abdicate. This is often true even from their point of view since by abdicating they lose only their power, whereas if they persist they probably ultimately lose their lives. But few governments have had the wisdom to see this. Nor is it always true when a strong country oppresses a weak one.

> She's the most distressful country
> That ever yet was seen,
> For they're hanging men and women there
> For wearing o' the green.

England was able to pursue this policy towards Ireland for eight centuries, with, in the end, only some loss of money and a considerable loss of prestige. During the eight centuries British policy was successful, since landowners were rich while peasants starved.

Freedom of propaganda, in the cases in which it interests the ordinary citizen, involves either violent revolution or the recognition of a further freedom, namely that of choosing the government. It is bound up with democracy and the right of discontented communities to autonomy; in a word, with the right to achieve peacefully what would otherwise be achieved by revolution. This is an important right, and its recognition is very necessary for the peace of the world; but it goes far beyond the right of free propaganda.

It remains to consider the standpoint of the ardent innovator. We may take as typical the Christian before Constantine, the Protestant in the time of Luther, and the Communist at the present day. Such men have seldom been believers in free speech. They have been willing themselves to suffer martyrdom, but have been equally willing to inflict it. History shows that, in the past, determined men could speak freely in spite of governments. Modern governments, however, are more efficient, and will perhaps succeed in making fundamental innovation impossible. On the other hand, war may cause revolution and even anarchy, leading, perhaps, to some quite new beginning. On this ground some Communists look forward with hope to the next war.

The ardent innovator is, as a rule, a millenarian: he holds that the millennium will have arrived when all men embrace his creed. Though in the present he is revolutionary, in the future he is a conservative: a perfect State is to be reached, and when reached is only to be preserved unchanged. Holding these views, he naturally shrinks from no degree of violence either in seeking the perfect State or in preventing its overthrow: in opposition he is a terrorist; in government, a persecutor. His belief in violence naturally provokes the same belief in his opponents: while they are in power they will persecute him, and when they are in opposition they will plot his assassination. His millennium is not therefore altogether pleasant for everybody; there will be spies, arrests by administrative orders, and concentration camps. But, like Tertullian, he sees no harm in that.

There are, it is true, millenarians of a gentler type. There are those who consider that what is best in a man must come from within, and cannot be imposed by any external authority; this view is exemplified by the Society of Friends. There are those who hold that external influences may be important and beneficial when they take the form of benevolence and wise persuasion, but not when they take the form of prison or execution. Such men may believe in freedom of propaganda in spite of being ardent innovators.

There is another kind of innovator, who has only existed since evolution became fashionable; of this kind Sorel in his syndicalist days may be taken as typical. Such men hold that human life should be a continual progress, not towards a definable goal, not in any sense that can be stated precisely before the progress has been made, but of such a sort that each step, when achieved, is seen to have been an advance. It is better to see than not to see, to have speech than to be without it, and so on; but while all animals were still blind, it was not possible for them to propose the acquisition of sight as the next step in reform. Nevertheless, the fact that it was the next step proves, retrospectively, that a static conservatism would have been a mistake. All innovations, therefore – so it is argued – must be encouraged, since one among them, though we cannot know which, will prove to embody the spirit of evolution.

No doubt there is an element of truth in this view, but it is one that easily develops into a shallow mysticism of progress, and owing to its vagueness it cannot be made a basis for practical politics. The historically important innovators have believed in taking the kingdom of heaven by storm; they have often achieved their kingdom, but it has proved to be not the kingdom of heaven.

I come now to the standpoint of the philosopher as regards freedom of propaganda. Gibbon, describing the tolerant spirit of antiquity, says: 'The various modes of worship, which prevailed in the Roman world, were all considered by the people, as equally true; by the philosopher, as equally false; and by the magistrate, as equally useful.' The philosopher whom I have in mind will not go so far as to say that all prevalent creeds are *equally* false, but he will not allow that any is free from falsehood, or that, if by chance it were, this fortunate fact could be discovered by the faculties of the human mind. To the unphilosophical propagandist, there is his own propaganda, which is that of truth, and the opposite propaganda, which is that of falsehood. If he believes in permitting both, it is only because he fears that his might be the one to suffer prohibition. To the philosophical spectator, the matter is not so simple.

What, to the philosopher, can be the uses of propaganda? He cannot say, like the propagandist: 'Pin-factories exist to manufacture pins, and opinion-factories to manufacture opinions. If the opinions manufactured are as like as two pins, what of that, provided they are good opinions? And if the large-scale production rendered possible by monopoly is cheaper than competing small-scale production, there is the same reason for monopoly in the one case as in the other. Nay, more: a competing opinion-factory does not usually, like a competing pin-factory, manufacture other opinions which may be just as good: it manufactures opinions designed to damage those of my factory, and therefore immensely increases the work required to keep people supplied with my produce. Competing factories, therefore, must be forbidden.' This, I say, the philosopher cannot adopt as his view. He must contend that any useful purpose which is to be served by propaganda must be *not* that of causing an almost certainly erroneous opinion to be dogmatically believed, but, on the contrary, that of promoting judgement, rational doubt, and the power of weighing opposing considerations; and this purpose it can only serve if there is competition among propagandas. He will compare the public to a judge who listens to counsel on either side, and will hold that a monopoly in propaganda is as absurd as if, in a criminal trial, only the prosecution or only the defence were allowed to be heard. So far from desiring uniformity of propaganda, he will advocate that, as far as possible, everybody should hear all sides of every question. Instead of different newspapers, each devoted to the interests of one party and encouraging the dogmatism of its readers, he will advocate a single newspaper, in which all parties are represented.

Freedom of debate, of which the intellectual advantages are obvious, does not necessarily involve competing organisations. The BBC allows controversy. Rival scientific theories can all be represented within the Royal Society. Learned bodies, in general, do not indulge in corporate propaganda, but give opportunities to their members severally to advocate each his own theory. Such discussion within a single organisation pre-supposes a fundamental agreement; no Egyptologist wishes to invoke the military to crush a rival Egyptologist whose theories he dislikes. When a community is in fundamental agreement as to its form of government, free discussion if possible, but where such agreement does not exist, propaganda is felt to be a prelude to the use of force, and those who possess force will naturally aim at a monopoly of propaganda. Freedom of propaganda is possible when the differences are not such as to make peaceable cooperation under one government impossible. Protestants and Catholics could not cooperate politically in the sixteenth century, but in the eighteenth and nineteenth they could; hence in the interval religious toleration became possible. A stable govermental framework is essential to intellectual freedom; but unfortunately it may also be the chief engine of tyranny. The solution of this difficulty depends very largely upon the form of government.

Chapter 15

Power and Moral Codes

Morality, at any rate since the days of the Hebrew prophets, has had two divergent aspects. On the one hand, it has been a social institution analogous to law; on the other hand, it has been a matter for the individual conscience. In the former aspect, it is part of the apparatus of power; in the latter, it is often revolutionary. The kind which is analogous to law is called 'positive' morality; the other kind may be called 'personal'. I wish in this chapter to consider the relations of these two kinds of morality to each other and to power.

Positive morality is older than personal morality, and probably older than law and government. It consists originally of tribal customs, out of which law gradually develops. Consider the extraordinarily elaborate rules as to who may marry whom, which are found among very primitive savages. To us, these seem merely rules, but presumably to those who accept them they have the same moral compulsive force as we feel in our rules against incestuous unions. Their source is obscure, but is no doubt in some sense religious. This part of positive morality appears to have no relation to social inequalities; it neither confers exceptional power nor assumes its existence. There are still moral rules of this sort among civilised people. The Greek Church prohibits the marriage of godparents of the same child, a prohibition which fulfils no social purpose, either good or bad, but has its source solely in theology. It seems probable that many prohibitions which are now accepted on rational grounds were originally superstitious. Murder was objectionable because of the hostility of the ghost, which was not directed only against the murderer, but against his community. The community therefore had an interest in the matter, which they could deal with either by punishment or by ceremonies of purification. Gradually purification came to have a spiritual signification, and to be identified with repentance and absolution; but its original ceremonial character is still recalled by such phrases as 'washed in the blood of the Lamb'.

This aspect of positive morality, important as it is, is not the one with which I wish to deal. I wish to consider those aspects of accepted ethical codes in which they minister to power. One of the purposes – usually in large part unconscious – of a traditional morality is to make the existing social system work. It achieves this purpose, when it is successful, both more cheaply and more effectively than a police force does. But it is liable to be confronted with a revolutionary morality, inspired by the desire for a redistribution of power. I want, in this chapter, to consider, first, the effect of power on moral codes, and then the question whether some other basis can be found for morality.

The most obvious example of power-morality is the inculcation of obedience. It is (or rather was) the duty of children to submit to parents, wives to husbands, servants to masters, subjects to princes, and (in religious matters) laymen to priests; there were also more specialised duties of obedience in armies and religious orders. Each of these duties has a long history, running parallel with that of the institution concerned.

Let us begin with filial piety. There are savages at the present day who, when their parents grow too old for work, sell them to be eaten. At some stage in the development of civilisation, it must have occurred to some man of unusual forethought that he could, while his children were still young, produce in them a state of mind which would lead them to keep him alive in old age; presumably he was a man whose own parents were already disposed of. In creating a party to support his subversive opinion, I doubt whether he appealed merely to motives of prudence; I suspect that he invoked the Rights of Man, the advantages of a mainly frugiferous diet, and the moral blamelessness of the old who have worn themselves out labouring for their children. Probably there was at the moment some emaciated but unusually wise elder, whose advice was felt to be more valuable than his flesh. However this may be, it came to be felt that one's parents should be honoured rather than eaten. To us, the respect for fathers in early civilisations seems excessive, but we have to remember that a very powerful deterent was needed to put an end to the lucrative practice of having them eaten. And so we find the Ten Commandments suggesting that if you fail to honour your father and mother you will die young, the Romans considering patricide the most atrocious of crimes, and Confucius making filial piety the very basis of morality. All this is a device, however instinctive and unconscious, for prolonging parental power beyond the early years when children are helpless. The authority of parents has of course been reinforced by their possession of property, but if filial piety had not existed young men would not have allowed their fathers to retain control of their flocks and herds after they had become feeble.

The same sort of thing happened in regard to the subjection of women. The superior strength of male animals does not, in most cases, lead to a continual subjection of the females, because the males have not a sufficient constancy of purpose. Among human beings, the subjection of women is much more complete at a certain level of civilisation than it is among savages. And the subjection is always reinforced by morality. A man, says St Paul, 'is the image and glory of God: but the woman is the glory of the man. For the man is not of the woman; but the woman of the man. Neither was the man created for the woman; but the woman for the man' (I Corinthians xi, 7–9). It follows that wives ought to obey their husbands, and that unfaithfulness is a worse sin in a wife than in a husband. Christianity, it is true, holds, in theory, that adultery is equally sinful in either sex, since it is a sin against God. But this view has not prevailed in practice, and was not held even theoretically in pre-Christian times. Adultery with a married woman was wicked, because it was an offence against her husband; but female slaves and war-captives were the legitimate property of their master, and no blame attached to intercourse with them. This view was held by pious Christian slave-owners, though not by their wives, even in nineteenth-century America.

The basis of the difference between morality for men and morality for women was obviously the superior power of men. Originally the superiority was only physical, but from this basis it gradually extended to economics, politics, and religion. The great advantage of morality over the police appears very clearly in this case, for women, until quite recently, genuinely believed the moral precepts which embodied male domination, and therefore required much less compulsion than would otherwise have been necessary.

The code of Hammurabi gives an interesting illustration of the unimportance of women in the eyes of the legislator. If a man strikes the daughter of a gentleman when she is pregnant, and she dies in consequence, it is decreed that the daughter of the striker shall be put to death. As between the gentleman and the striker, this is just; the daughter who is executed is merely a possession of the latter, and has no claim to life on her own account. And in killing the gentleman's daughter the striker is guilty of an offence, not against her, but against the gentleman. The daughters had no rights because they had no power.

Kings, until George I, were objects of religious veneration.

> There's such divinity doth hedge a king,
> That treason can but peep the thing it would,
> Acts little of his will.

The word 'treason', even in republics, has still a flavour of impiety. In England, government profits much by the tradition of royalty. Victorian statesmen, even Mr Gladstone, felt it their duty to the Queen to see to it that she was never left without a Prime Minister. The duty of obedience to authority is still felt by many as a duty towards the sovereign. This is a decaying sentiment, but as it decays government becomes less stable, and dictatorships of the Right or the Left become more possible.

Bagehot's *English Constitution* – a book still well worth reading – begins the discussion of the monarchy as follows:

'The use of the Queen, in a dignified capacity, is incalculable. Without her in England, the present English Government would fail and pass away. Most people when they read that the Queen walked on the slopes at Windsor – that the Prince of Wales went to the Derby – have imagined that too much thought and prominence were given to little things. But they have been in error; and it is nice to trace how the actions of a retired widow and an unemployed youth became of such importance.

'The best reason why Monarchy is a strong government is, that it is an intelligible government. The mass of mankind understand it, and they hardly anywhere in the world understand any other. It is often said that men are ruled by their imaginations; but it would be truer to say that they are governed by the weakness of their imaginations.'

This is both true and important. Monarchy makes social cohesion easy, first, because it is not so difficult to feel loyalty to an individual as to an abstraction, and secondly, because kingship, in its long history, has accumulated sentiments of veneration

which no new institution can inspire. Where hereditary monarchy has been abolished it has usually been succeeded, after a
longer or short time, by some other form of one-man rule: tyranny in Greece, the Empire in Rome, Cromwell in England, the
Napoleons in France, Stalin and Hitler in our own day. Such
men inherit a part of the feelings formerly attached to royalty. It
is amusing to note, in the confessions of the accused in Russian
trials, the acceptance of a morality of submission to the ruler
such as would be appropriate in the most ancient and traditional
of absolute monarchies. But a new dictator, unless he is a very
extraordinary man, can hardly inspire *quite* the same religious
veneration as hereditary monarchs enjoyed in the past.

In the case of kingship, the religious element, as we have seen,
has often been carried so far as to interfere with power. Even
then, however, it has helped to give stability to the social system
of which the king is a symbol. This has happened in many semi-
civilised countries, in Japan, and in England. In England, the
doctrine that the king can do no wrong has been used as a
weapon for depriving him of power, but it has enabled his Ministers to have more power than they would have if he did not exist.
Wherever there is a traditional monarchy, rebellion against the
government is an offence against the king, and is regarded by the
orthodox as a sin and an impiety. Kingship acts therefore,
broadly speaking, as a force on the side of the *status quo*, whatever that may be. Its most useful function, historically, has been
the creation of a widely diffused sentiment favourable to social
cohesion. Men are so little gregarious by nature that anarchy is a
constant danger, which kingship has done much to prevent.
Against this merit, however, must be set the demerit of per-
petuating ancient evils and increasing the forces opposed to desirable change. This demerit has, in modern times, caused
monarchy to disappear over the greater part of the earth's surface.

The power of priests is more obviously connected with morals
than any other form of power. In Christian countries, virtue consists in obedience to the will of God, and it is priests who know
what the will of God commands. The precept that we ought to
obey God rather than man is, as we saw, capable of being revolutionary; it is so in two sets of circumstances, one, when the
State is in opposition to the Church, the other, when it is held
that God speaks directly to each individual conscience. The
former state of affairs existed before Constantine, the latter among
the Anabaptists and Independents. But in non-revolutionary

periods, when there is an established and traditional Church, it is accepted by positive morality as the intermediary between God and the individual conscience. So long as this acceptance continues, its power is very great, and rebellion against the Church is thought more wicked than any other kind. The Church has its difficulties nonetheless, for if it uses its power too flagrantly men begin to doubt whether it is interpreting the will of God correctly; and when this doubt becomes common, the whole ecclesiastical edifice crumbles, as it did in Teutonic countries at the Reformation.

In the case of the Church, the relation between power and morals is, to some extent, the opposite of what it is in the cases we have hitherto considered. Positive morality enjoins submission to parents, husbands, and kings, because they are powerful; but the Church is powerful because of its moral authority. This, however, is only true up to a point. Where the Church is secure, a morality of submission to the Church grows up, just as a morality of submission to parents, husbands, and kings has grown up. And a revolutionary rejection of this morality of submission also grows up in the same way. Heresy and schism are specially abhorrent to the Church, and are therefore essential elements in revolutionary programmes. There are, however, more complicated results of opposition to priestly power. The Church being the official guardian of the moral code, its opponents are likely to revolt in morals as well as in doctrine and government. They may revolt, like the Puritans, into greater strictness, or, like the French Revolutionaries, into greater laxity; but in either case morals come to be a private matter, not, as before, the subject of official decisions by a public body.

It must not be supposed that personal morality is in general worse than official priestly morality, even when it is less severe. There is some evidence that when, in the sixth century B.C., Greek sentiment was becoming strongly averse from human sacrifice, the oracle at Delphi tried to retard this humanitarian reform, and to keep alive the old rigid practices. Similarly in our own day, when the State and public opinion consider it permissible to marry one's deceased wife's sister, the Church, in so far as it has power, maintains the old prohibition.

Morality, where the Church has lost power, has not become genuinely personal except for a few exceptional people. For the majority, it is represented by public opinion, both that of neighbours in general, and that of powerful groups such as employers.

From the point of view of the sinner, the change may be slight, and may also be for the worse. Where the individual gains is not as sinner, but as judge: he becomes part of an informal democratic tribunal, whereas, where the Church is strong, he must accept the rulings of Authority. The Protestant whose moral feelings are strong usurps the ethical functions of the priest, and acquires a quasi-governmental attitude towards other people's virtues and vices, especially the latter:

> Ye've naught to do but mark and tell
> Your neighbours' faults and folly.

This is not anarchy; it is democracy.

The thesis that the moral code is an expression of power is, as we have seen, not wholly true. From the exogamous rules of savages onward, there are, at all stages of civilisation, ethical principles which have no visible relation to power – among ourselves, the condemnation of homosexuality may serve as an example. The Marxist thesis, that the moral code is an expression of *economic* power, is even less adequate than the thesis that it is an expression of power in general. Nevertheless, the Marxist thesis is true in a very great many instances. For example: in the Middle Ages, when the most powerful of the laity were landowners, when bishoprics and monastic orders derived their income from land, and when the only investors of money were Jews, the Church unhesitatingly condemned 'usury', i.e. all lending of money at interest. This was a debtor's morality. With the rise of the rich merchant class, it became impossible to maintain the old prohibition: it was relaxed first by Calvin, whose clientèle was mainly urban and prosperous, then by the other Protestants, and last of all by the Catholic Church.[1] Creditor's morality became the fashion, and non-payment of debts a heinous sin. The Society of Friends, practically if not theoretically, excluded bankrupts until very recently.

The moral code towards enemies is a matter as to which different ages have differed greatly, largely because the profitable uses of power have differed. On this subject, let us first hear the Old Testament.

'When the Lord thy God shall bring thee into the land whither thou goest to possess it, and hath cast out many nations before

[1] On this subject, cf. R. H. Tawney, *Religion and the Rise of Capitalism*.

thee, the Hittites, and the Girgashites, and the Amorites, and the Canaanites, and the Perizzites, and the Hivites and the Jebusites, seven nations greater and mightier than thou;

'And when the Lord thy God shall deliver them before thee; thou shalt smite them, and utterly destroy them; thou shalt make no covenant with them, nor show mercy unto them:

'Neither shalt thou make marriages with them; thy daughter shalt thou not give unto his son, nor his daughter shalt thou take unto thy son.

For they will turn away thy son from following me, that they may serve other gods: so will the anger of the Lord be kindled against you, and destroy thee suddenly.'

If they do all this, 'there shall not be male or female barren among you, or among your cattle'.[1]

As regards these seven nations, we are told in a later chapter even more explicitly:

'Thou shalt save alive nothing that breatheth . . . that they teach you not to do after all their abominations' (xx. 16, 18).

But towards 'cities which are very far off from thee, and which are not of these nations' it is permissible to be more merciful:

'Thou shall smite every male thereof with the edge of the sword: but the women, and the little ones, and the cattle, and all that is in the city, even all the spoil thereof, shalt thou take unto thyself' (ibid., 13–15).

It will be remembered that when Saul smote the Amalekites he got into trouble for being insufficiently thorough:

'And he took Agag the king of the Amalekites alive and utterly destroyed all the people with the edge of the sword.

'But Saul and the people spared Agag, and the best of the sheep, and of the oxen, and of the fatlings, and the lambs, and all that was good, and would not utterly destroy them: but everything that was vile and refuse, that they destroyed utterly.

'Then came the word of the Lord unto Samuel, saying,

It repenteth me that I have set up Saul to be king: for he is turned back from following me, and hath not performed my commandments.'[2]

---

[1] Deuteronomy, vii, 1–4 and 14.
[2] I Samuel, xv, 8–11.

It is obvious in these passages that the interests of the children of Israel were to prevail completely when they came into conflict with those of the Gentiles, but that internally the interests of religion, i.e. of the priests, were to prevail over the economic interests of the laity. The word of the Lord came unto Samuel, but it was the word of Samuel that came unto Saul, and the word was: 'What meaneth then this bleating of sheep in mine ears, and the lowing of oxen which I hear?' To which Saul could only reply by confessing his sin.

The Jews, from their horror of idolatry – of which the microbes apparently lurked even in sheep and cows – were led to exceptional thoroughness in the extermination of the vanquished. But no nation of antiquity recognised any legal or moral limits to what might be done with defeated populations. It was customary to exterminate some and sell the rest into slavery. Some Greeks – for instance, Euripides in the *Trojan Women* – tried to create a sentiment against this practice, but without success. The vanquished, having no power, had no claim to mercy. This view was not abandoned, even in theory, until the coming of Christianity.

Duty to enemies is a difficult conception. Clemency was recognised as a virtue in antiquity, but only when it was successful, that is to say, when it turned enemies into friends; otherwise, it was condemned as a weakness. When fear had been aroused, no one expected magnanimity: the Romans showed none towards Hannibal or the followers of Spartacus. In the days of chivalry, a knight was expected to show courtesy to a knightly captive. But the conflicts of knights were not very serious; not the faintest mercy was shown to the Albigenses. In our day, almost equal ferocity has been shown towards the victims of the white terrors in Finland, Hungary, Germany, and Spain, and hardly any protests have been aroused except among political opponents. The terror in Russia, likewise, has been condoned by most of the Left. Now, as in the days of the Old Testament, no duty to enemies is acknowledged in practice when they are sufficiently formidable to arouse fear. Positive morality, in effect, is still only operative within the social group concerned, and is therefore still, in effect, a department of government. Nothing short of a world government will cause people of pugnacious disposition to admit, except as a counsel of perfection, that moral obligations are not confined to a section of the human race.

I have been concerned hitherto in this chapter with positive morality, and, as has become evident, it is not enough. Broadly speaking, it is on the side of the powers that be, it does not allow a place for revolution, it does nothing to mitigate the fierceness of strife, and it can find no place for the prophet who proclaims some new moral insight. Certain difficult questions of theory are involved, but before considering them let us remind ourselves of some of the things that only opposition to positive morality could achieve.

The world owes something to the Gospels, though not so much as it would if they had had more influence. It owes something to those who denounced slavery and the subjection of women. We may hope that in time it will owe something to those who denounce war and economic injustice. In the eighteenth and nineteenth centuries, it owed much to the apostles of tolerance; perhaps it will again in some happier age than ours. Revolutions against the mediaeval Church, the Renaissance monarchies, and the present power of plutocracy, are necessary for the avoidance of stagnation. Admitting, as we must, that mankind needs revolution and individual morality, the problem is to find a place for these things without plunging the world into anarchy.

There are two questions to be considered: first, what is the wisest attitude for positive morality, from its own standpoint, to take to personal morality? Second, what degree of respect does personal morality owe to positive morality? But before discussing either of these, something must be said as to what is meant by personal morality.

Personal morality may be considered as a historical phenomenon, or from the standpoint of the philosopher. Let us begin with the former.

Almost every individual that has ever existed, so far as history is aware, has had a profound horror of certain kinds of acts. As a rule, these acts are held in abhorrence not only by one individual, but by a whole tribe or nation or sect or class. Sometimes the origin of the abhorrence is unknown, sometimes it can be traced to a historical personage who was a mortal innovator. We know why Mohammedans will not make images of animals or human beings; it is because the Prophet forbade them to do so. We know why orthodox Jews will not eat hare; it is because the Mosaic Law declares that the hare is unclean. Such prohibitions, when accepted, belong to positive morality; but in their origin, at any rate when their origin is known, they belonged to private morality.

Morality, for us, however, has come to mean something more than ritual precepts, whether positive or negative. In the form in which it is familiar to us it is not primitive, but appears to have a number of independent sources – Chinese sages, Indian Buddhists, Hebrew prophets, and Greek philosophers. These men, whose importance in history it is difficult to overestimate, all lived within a few centuries of each other, and all shared certain characteristics which marked them out from their predecessors. Lao-Tse and Chung-Tse deliver the doctrine of the Tao as what they know of their own knowledge, not through tradition or the wisdom of others; and the doctrine consists not of specific duties, but of a way of life, a manner of thinking and feeling, from which it will become plain, without the need for rules, what must be done on each occasion. The same may be said of the early Buddhists. The Hebrew prophets, at their best, transcend the Law, and advocate a new and more inward kind of virtue, recommended not by tradition, but by the words 'thus saith the Lord'. Socrates acts as his daemon commands, not as the legally constituted authorities desire; he is prepared to suffer martyrdom rather than be untrue to the inner voice. All these men were rebels in their day, and all have come to be honoured. Something of what was new in them has come to be taken as a matter of course. But it is not altogether easy to say what this something is.

The minimum that must be accepted by any thoughtful person who either adheres to a religion having a historical origin, or thinks that some such religion was an improvement on what went before, is this: that a way of life which was in some sense better than some previous way of life was first advocated by some individual or set of individuals, in opposition to the teaching of State and Church in their day. It follows that it cannot always be wrong for an individual to set himself up in moral questions, even against the judgement of all mankind up to his day. In science, every one now admits the corresponding doctrine; but in science the ways of testing a new doctrine are known, and it soon comes to be generally accepted, or else rejected on other grounds than tradition. In ethics, no such obvious ways exist by which a new doctrine can be tested. A prophet may preface his teaching 'thus saith the Lord', which is sufficient for him; but how are other people to know that he has had a genuine revelation? Deuteronomy, oddly enough, proposes the same test as is often held to be conclusive in science, namely success in prediction: 'And if thou say in thine heart, How shall we know the word which the Lord hath not spoken? When a prophet speaketh in the name of the Lord, if the thing follow not, nor come to pass, that is the thing which the Lord hath not spoken, but the prophet hath spoken it presumptuously.'[1] But the modern mind can hardly accept this test of an ethical doctrine.

We must face the question: What is meant by an ethical doctrine, and in what ways, if any, can it be tested?

Historically, ethics is connected with religion. For most men, authority has sufficed: what is laid down as right or wrong by the Bible or the Church *is* right or wrong. But certain individuals have, from time to time, been divinely inspired: they have known what was right or wrong because God spoke directly to them. These individuals, according to orthodox opinion, all lived a long time ago, and if a modern man professes to be one of them it is best to put him in an asylum, unless, indeed, the Church sanctions his pronouncements. This, however, is merely the usual situation of the rebel become dictator and does not help us to decide what are the legitimate functions of rebels.

Can we translate ethics into non-theological terms? Victorian freethinkers had no doubt that this was possible. The utilitarians, for instance, were highly moral men, and were convinced that their morality had a rational basis. The matter is, however, rather more difficult than it appeared to them.

Let us consider a question suggested by the mention of the utilitarians, namely: can a rule of conduct ever be a self-subsistent proposition of ethics, or must it always be deduced from the good or bad effects of the conduct in question? The traditional view is that certain kinds of acts are sinful, and certain others virtuous, independently of their effects. Other kinds of acts are ethically neutral, and may be judged by their results. Whether euthanasia or marriage with a deceased wife's sister should be legalised is an ethical question, but the gold standard is not. There are two definitions of 'ethical' questions, either of which will cover the cases to which this adjective is applied. A question is 'ethical' (1) if it interested the ancient Hebrews, (2) if it is one on which the Archbishop of Canterbury is the official expert. It is obvious that this common use of the word 'ethical' is wholly indefensible.

Nevertheless, I find, speaking personally, that there are kinds

[1] Deuteronomy, xviii, 21, 22.

of conduct against which I feel a repugnance which seems to me to be moral, but to be not obviously based upon an estimate of consequences. I am informed by many people that the preservation of democracy, which I think important, can only be secured by gassing immense numbers of children and doing a number of other horrible things. I find that, at this point, I cannot acquiesce in the use of such means. I tell myself that they will not secure the end, or that, if they do, they will incidentally have other effects so evil as to outweigh any good that democracy might do. I am not quite sure how far this argument is honest: I think I should refuse to use such means even if I were persuaded that they would secure the end and that no others would. *Per contra,* psychological imagination assures me that nothing that I should think good can possibly be achieved by such means. On the whole, I think that, speaking philosophically, all acts ought to be judged by their effects; but as this is difficult and uncertain and takes time, it is desirable, in practice, that some kinds of acts should be condemned and others praised without waiting to investigate consequences. I should say, therefore, with the utilitarians, that the right act, in any given circumstances, is that which, on the data, will probably produce the greatest balance of good over evil of all the acts that are possible; but that the performance of such acts may be promoted by the existence of a moral code.

Accepting this view, ethics is reduced to defining 'good' and 'bad', not as means, but as ends in themselves. The utilitarian says that the good is pleasure and the bad is pain. But if someone disagrees with him, what arguments can he produce?

Consider various views as to the ends of life. One man says 'the good is pleasure'; another, 'the good is pleasure for Aryans and pain for Jews'; another, 'the good is to praise God and glorify Him forever'. What are these three men asserting, and what methods exist by which they can convince each other? They cannot, as men of science do, appeal to facts: no facts are relevant to the dispute. Their difference is in the realm of desire, not in the realm of statements about matters of fact. I do not assert that when I say 'this is good' I mean 'I desire this'; it is only a particular kind of desire that leads me to call a thing good. The desire must be in some degree impersonal; it must have to do with the sort of world that would content me, not only with my personal circumstances. A king might say: 'Monarchy is good, and I am glad I am a monarch.' The first part of this statement is indubitably ethical, but his pleasure in being a monarch only becomes ethical if a survey persuades him that no one else would make such a good king.

I have suggested on a former occasion (in *Religion and Science*) that a judgement of intrinsic value is to be interpreted, not as an assertion, but as an expression of desire concerning the desires of mankind. When I say 'hatred is bad', I am really saying: 'Would that no one felt hatred.' I make no assertion; I merely express a certain type of wish. The hearer can gather that I feel this wish but that is the only *fact* that he can gather, and that is a fact of psychology. There are no facts of ethics.

The great ethical innovators have not been men who *knew* more than others; they have been men who *desired* more, or, to be more accurate, men whose desires were more impersonal and of larger scope than those of average men. Most men desire their own happiness; a considerable percentage desire the happiness of their children; not a few desire the happiness of their nation; some, genuinely and strongly, desire the happiness of all mankind. These men, seeing that many others have no such feeling, and that this is an obstacle to universal felicity, wish that others felt as they do; this wish can be expressed in the words 'happiness is good'.

All great moralists, from Buddha and the Stoics down to recent times, treated the good as something to be, if possible, enjoyed by all men equally. They did not think of themselves as princes or Jews or Greeks; they thought of themselves merely as human beings. Their ethic had always a twofold source: on the one hand, they valued certain elements in their own lives; on the other hand, sympathy made them desire for others what they desired for themselves. Sympathy is the universalising force in ethics; I mean sympathy as an emotion, not as a theoretical principle. Sympathy is in some degree instinctive: a child may be made unhappy by another child's cry. But limitations of sympathy are also natural. The cat has no sympathy for the mouse; the Romans had no sympathy for any animals except elephants; the Nazis have none for Jews, and Stalin had none for kulaks. Where there is limitation of sympathy there is a corresponding limitation in the conception of the good: the good becomes something to be enjoyed only by the magnanimous man, or only by the superman, or the Aryan, or the proletarian, or the Christadelphian. All these are cat-and-mouse ethics.

The refutation of a cat-and-mouse ethic, where it is possible, is practical, not theoretical. Two adepts at such an ethic, like quarrelsome little boys, each begin: 'Let's play I'm the cat and you're the mouse.' 'No, no,' they each retort, 'you shan't be the cat, I will.' And so, more often than not, they become the Kilkenny cats. But if one of them succeeds completely, he may establish his ethic; we then get Kipling and the White Man's Burden, or the Nordic Race, or some such creed of inequality. Such creeds, inevitably, appeal only to the cat, not to the mouse; they are imposed on the mouse by naked power.

Ethical controversies are very often as to means, not ends. Slavery may be attacked by the argument that it is uneconomic; the subjection of woman may be criticised by maintaining that the conversation of free women is more interesting; persecution may be deplored on the gound (wholly fallacious, incidentally) that the religious convictions produced by it are not genuine. Behind such arguments, however, there is generally a difference as to ends. Sometimes, as in Nietzsche's criticism of Christianity, the difference of ends becomes nakedly apparent. In Christian ethics, all men count alike; for Nietzsche, the majority are only a means to the hero. Controversies as to ends cannot be conducted, like scientific controversies, by appeals to facts; they must be conducted by an attempt to change men's feelings. The Christian may endeavour to rouse sympathy, the Nietzschean may stimulate pride. Economic and military power may reinforce propaganda. The contest is, in short, an ordinary contest for power. Any creed, even one which teaches universal equality, may be a means to the domination of a section; this happened, for instance, when the French Revolution set to work to spread democracy by force of arms.

Power is the means, in ethical contests as in those of politics. But with the ethical systems that have had most influence in the past, power is not the end. Although men hate one another, exploit one another, and torture one another, they have, until recently, given their reverence to those who preached a different way of life. The great religions that aimed at universality replacing the tribal and national cults of earlier times, considered men as men, not as Jew or Gentile, bond or free. Their founders were men whose sympathy was universal, and who were felt, on this account, to be possessed of a wisdom surpassing that of temporary and passionate despots. The result was not all that the founders could have wished. At an *auto-da-fé*, the mob had to be prevented by the police from attacking the victims, and was furious if one whom it had hoped to see burnt alive succeeded, by a tardy recantation, in winning the privilege of being strangled first and burnt afterwards. Nevertheless, the principle of universal sympathy conquered first one province, then another. It is the analogue, in the realm of feeling, of impersonal curiosity in the realm of intellect; both alike are essential elements in mental growth. I do not think that the return to a tribal or aristocratic ethic can be of long duration; the whole history of man since the time of Buddha points in the opposite direction. However passionately power may be desired, it is not power that is thought good in moments of reflective meditation. This is proved by the characters of the men whom mankind have thought most nearly divine.

The traditional moral rules that we considered at the beginning of this chapter – filial piety, wifely submission, loyalty to kings, and so on – have all decayed completely or partially. They may be succeeded, as in the Renaissance, by an absence of moral restraint, or, as in the Reformation, by a new code in many ways more strict than those that have become obsolete. Loyalty to the State plays a much larger part in positive morality in our time than it did formerly; this, of course, is the natural result of the increase in the power of the State. The parts of morals that are concerned with other groups, such as the family and the Church, have less control than they used to have; but I do not see any evidence that, on the balance, moral principles or moral sentiments have less influence over man's actions now than in the eighteenth century or the Middle Ages.

Let us end this chapter with a summary analysis. The moral codes of primitive societies are generally believed, in those societies, to have a supernatural origin; in part, we can see no reason for this belief, but to a considerable extent it represents the balance of power in the community concerned: the gods consider submission to the powerful a duty, but the powerful must not be so ruthless as to rouse rebellion. Under the influence of prophets and sages, however, a new morality arises, sometimes side by side with the old one, sometimes in place of it. Prophets and sages, with few exceptions, have valued things other than power – wisdom, justice, or universal love, for example – and have persuaded large sections of mankind that these are aims more worthy to be pursued than personal success. Those who suffer by some part of the social system which the prophet or sage wishes to alter have personal reasons for supporting his opinion; it is the union of their self-seeking with his impersonal ethic that makes the resulting revolutionary movement irresistible.

We can now arrive at some conclusion as to the place of rebellion in social life. Rebellion is of two sorts: it may be purely personal, or it may be inspired by desire for a different kind of community from that in which the rebel finds himself. In the latter case, his desire can be shared by others; in many instances, it has been shared by all except a small minority who profited by the existing system. This type of rebel is constructive, not anarchic; even if his movement leads to temporary anarchy, it is intended to give rise, in the end, to a new stable community. It is the impersonal character of his aims that distinguishes him from the anarchic rebel. Only the event can decide, for the general public, whether a rebellion will come to be thought justified; when it is thought to have been justified, previously existing authority would have been wise, from its own point of view, in not offering a desperate resistance. An individual may perceive a way of life, or a method of social organisation, by which more of the desires of mankind could be satisfied than under the existing method. If he perceives truly, and can persuade men to adopt his reform, he is justified. Without rebellion, mankind would stagnate, and injustice would be irremediable. The man who refuses to obey authority has, therefore, in certain circumstances, a legitimate function, provided his disobedience has motives which are social rather than personal. But the matter is one as to which, by its very nature, it is impossible to lay down rules.

Chapter 16

Power Philosophies

My purpose, in this chapter, is to consider certain philosophies which are inspired mainly by love of power. I do not mean that power is their subject-matter, but that it is the philosopher's conscious or unconscious motive in his metaphysics and in his ethical judgements.

Our beliefs result from the combination, in varying degrees, of desire with observation. In some, the part of the one factor is very slight; in others, that of the other. What can be strictly established by empirical evidence is very little, and when our beliefs go beyond this, desire plays a part in their genesis. On the other hand, few beliefs long survive definite conclusive evidence of their falsity, though they may survive for many ages when there is no evidence either for or against them.

Philosophies are more unified than life. In life, we have many desires, but a philosophy is usually inspired by some one dominant desire which gives it coherence.

> Zu fragmentarisch ist Welt and Leben.
> Ich will mich zum deutschen Professor begeben,
> Derweiss das Leben zusammenzusetzen,
> Und er macht ein verständig System daraus.[1]

Various desires have dominated the work of philosophers. There is the desire to know, and what is by no means the same thing, the desire to prove that the world is knowable. There is the desire for happiness, the desire for virtue, and – a synthesis of these two – the desire for salvation. There is the desire for the sense of union with God or with other human beings. There is the desire for beauty, the desire for enjoyment, and finally, the desire for power.

The great religions aim at virtue, but usually also at something

[1] The world and life are too fragmentary. I will betake myself to the German Professor; he knows how to synthesise life and he makes an intelligible system out of it.

more. Christianity and Buddhism seek salvation, and, in their more mystical forms, union with God or with the universe. Empirical philosophies seek truth, while idealist philosophies, from Descartes to Kant, seek certainty; practically all the great philosophers, down to Kant (inclusive) are concerned mainly with desires belonging to the cognitive part of human nature. The philosophy of Bentham and the Manchester School considers pleasure the end, and wealth the principal means. The power philosophies of modern times have arisen largely as a reaction against 'Manchesterismus', and as a protest against the view that the purpose of life is a series of pleasures – an aim which is condemned as both too fragmentary and insufficiently active.

Human life being a perpetual interaction between volition and uncontrollable facts, the philosopher who is guided by his power impulses seeks to minimise or decry the part played by facts that are not the result of our own will. I am thinking now not merely of men who glorify naked power, like Machiavelli and Thrasymachus in the *Republic*; I am thinking of men who invent theories which veil their own love of power beneath a garment of metaphysics or ethics. The first of such philosophers in modern times, and also the most thorough-going, is Fichte.

The philosophy of Fichte starts from the ego, as the sole existent in the world. The ego exists because it posits itself. Although nothing else exists, the ego one day gets a little knock (*ein kleiner Anstoss*), as a result of which it posits the non-ego. It then proceeds to various emanations, not unlike those of Gnostic Theology; but whereas the Gnostics attributed the emanations to God, and thought humbly of themselves, Fichte considers the distinction between God and the ego unnecessary. When the ego has done with metaphysics, it proceeds to posit that the Germans are good and the French are bad, and that it is therefore the duty of the Germans to fight Napoleon. Both the Germans and the French, of course, are only emanations of Fichte, but the Germans are a higher emanation, that is to say, they are nearer to the one ultimate reality, which is Fichte's ego. Alexander and Augustus asserted that they were gods, and compelled others to pretend agreement; Fichte, not being in control of the government, lost his job on a charge of atheism, since he could not well proclaim his own divinity.

It is obvious that a metaphysic such as Fichte's leaves no place for social duties, since the outer world is merely a product of my dream. The only imaginable ethic compatible with this philosophy is that of self-development. Illogically, however, a man may consider his family and his nation more intimately a part of his ego than other human beings, and therefore more to be valued. Belief in race and nationalism is thus a psychologically natural outcome of a solipsistic philosophy – all the more since love of power obviously inspires the theory, and power can only be achieved with the help of others.

All this is known as 'idealism', and is considered morally nobler than a philosophy which admits the reality of the external world.

The reality of what is independent of my own will is embodied, for philosophy, in the conception of 'truth'. The truth of my beliefs, in the view of common sense, does not depend, in most cases, upon anything that I can do. It is true that if I believe I shall eat my breakfast tomorrow, my belief, if true, is so partly in virtue of my own future volitions; but if I believe that Caesar was murdered on the Ides of March, what makes my belief true lies wholly outside the power of my will. Philosophies inspired by love of power find this situation unpleasant, and therefore set to work, in various ways, to undermine the commonsense conception of facts as the sources of truth or falsehood in beliefs. Hegelians maintain that truth does not consist in agreement with fact, but in the mutual consistency of the whole system of our beliefs. All your beliefs are true if, like the events in a good novel, they all fit together; there is, in fact, no difference between truth for the novelist and truth for the historian. This gives freedom to creative fancy, which it liberates from the shackles of the supposed 'real' world.

Pragmatism, in some of its forms, is a power-philosophy. For pragmatism, a belief is 'true' if its consequences are pleasant. Now human beings can make the consequences of a belief pleasant or unpleasant. Belief in the superior merit of a dictator has pleasanter consequences than disbelief, if you live under his government. Wherever there is effective persecution, the official creed is 'true' in the pragmatist sense. The pragmatist philosophy, therefore, gives to those in power a metaphysical omnipotence which a more pedestrian philosophy would deny to them. I do not suggest that most pragmatists admit these consequences of their philosophy; I say only that they are consequences, and that the pragmatist's attack on the common view of truth is an outcome of love of power, though perhaps more of power over inanimate nature than of power over other human beings.

Bergson's Creative Evolution is a power-philosophy, which has been developed fantastically in the last Act of Bernard Shaw's *Back to Methuselah*. Bergson holds that the intellect is to be condemned as unduly passive and merely contemplative, and that we only see truly during vigorous action such as a cavalry charge. He believes that animals acquired eyes because they felt that it would be pleasant to be able to see; their intellects would not have been able to think about seeing, since they were blind, but intuition was able to perform this miracle. All evolution, according to him, is due to desire, and there is no limit to what can be achieved if desire is sufficiently passionate. The groping attempts of bio-chemists to understand the mechanism of life are futile, since life is not mechanical, and its development is always such as the intellect is inherently incapable of imagining in advance; it is only in action that life can be understood. It follows that men should be passionate and irrational; fortunately for Bergson's happiness, they usually are.

Some philosophers do not allow their power impulses to dominate their metaphysics, but give them free rein in ethics. Of these, the most important is Nietzsche, who rejects Christian morality as that of slaves, and supplies in its place a morality suitable to heroic rulers. This is, of course, not essentially new. Something of it is to be found in Heraclitus, something in Plato, much in the Renaissance. But in Nietzsche it is worked out, and set up in conscious opposition to the teaching of the New Testament. In his view, the herd have no value on their own account, but only as means to the greatness of the hero, who has a right to inflict injury upon them if thereby he can further his own self-development. In practice, aristocracies have always acted in a manner which only some such ethic could justify; but Christian theory has held that in the sight of God all men are equal. Democracy can appeal to Christian teaching for support; but for aristocracy the best ethic is Nietzsche's. 'If there were gods, how could I bear to be not a god? *Therefore* there are no gods.' So says Nietzsche's Zarathustra. God must be dethroned to make room for earthly tyrants.

The love of power is a part of normal human nature, but power-philosophies are, in a certain precise sense, insane. The existence of the external world, both that of matter and that of other human beings, is a datum, which may be humiliating to a certain kind of pride, but can only be denied by a madman. Men who allow their love of power to give them a distorted view of the world are to be found in every asylum: one man will think he is the Governor of the Bank of England, another will think he is the King, and yet another will think he is God. Highly similar delusions, if expressed by educated men in obscure language, lead to professorships of philosophy; and if expressed by emotional men in eloquent language, lead to dictatorships. *Certified* lunatics are shut up because of their proneness to violence when their pretensions are questioned; the *uncertified* variety are given the control of powerful armies, and can inflict death and disaster upon all sane men within their reach. The success of insanity, in literature, in philosophy, and in politics, is one of the peculiarities of our age, and the successful form of insanity proceeds almost entirely from impulses towards power.

To understand this situation, we must consider the relation of power philosophies to social life, which is more complex than might have been expected.

Let us begin with solipsism. When Fichte maintains that everything starts from the ego, the reader does not say: 'Everything start from Johann Gottlieb Fichte! How absurd! Why, I never heard of him till a few days ago. And how about the times before he was born? Does he really imagine that he invented them? What ridiculous conceit!' This, I repeat, is what the reader does *not* say; he substitutes himself for Fichte, and finds the argument not unplausible. 'After all,' he thinks, 'what do I know of past times? Only that *I* have had certain experiences which I chose to interpret as related to a period before I was born. And what do I know of places I have never seen? Only that *I* have seen them on the map, have read of them, or have heard tell of them. I know only my own experience; the rest is doubtful inference. If I choose to put myself in the place of God, and say that the world is my creation, nothing can prove to me that I am mistaken.' Fichte maintains that there is only Fichte, and John Smith, reading the argument, concludes that there is only John Smith, without ever noticing that this is not what Fichte says.

In this way it is possible for solipsism to become the basis for a certain kind of social life. A collection of lunatics, each of whom thinks he is God, may learn to behave politely to one another. But the politeness will only last as long as each God finds his omnipotence not thwarted by any of the other divinities. If Mr A thinks he is God, he may tolerate the pretensions of others so long as their acts minister to his purposes. But if Mr B ventures to thwart him, and to provide evidence that he is not omnipotent,

Mr A's wrath will be kindled, and he will perceive that Mr B is Satan or one of his ministers. Mr B, of course, will take the same view of Mr A. Each will form a party, and there will be war – theological war, bitter, cruel, and mad. For 'Mr A' read Hitler, for 'Mr B' read Stalin, and you have a picture of the modern world. 'I am Wotan!' says Hitler. 'I am Dialectical Materialism!' says Stalin. And since the claim of each is supported by vast resources in the way of armies, aeroplanes, poison gases, and innocent enthusiasts, the madness of both remains unnoticed.

Take, next, Nietzsche's cult of the hero, to whom the 'bungled and botched' are to be sacrificed. The admiring reader is, of course, convinced that he himself is a hero, whereas that rascal so-and-so, who has got ahead of him by unscrupulous intrigues, is one of the bungled and botched. It follows that Nietzsche's philosophy is excellent. But if so-and-so also reads it, and also admires it, how is it to be decided which is the hero? Obviously only by war. And when one of the two has achieved victory, he will have to keep on proving his right to the title of hero by remaining in power. In order to do this, he must create a vigorous secret police; he will live in fear of assassination, every one else will be terrified of delation, and the cult of heroism will end by producing a nation of trembling poltroons.

The same sort of troubles arise with the pragmatist theory that a belief is true if the consequences are pleasant. Pleasant to whom? Belief in Stalin is pleasant for him, but unpleasant for Trotsky. Belief in Hitler is pleasant for the Nazis, but unpleasant for those whom they put in concentration camps. Nothing but naked force can decide the question: who is to enjoy the pleasant consequences which prove that a belief is true?

Power philosophies, when account is taken of their social consequences, are self-refuting. The belief that I am God, if no one shares it, leads to my being shut up; if others share it, it leads to a war in which I probably perish. The cult of the hero produces a nation of cowards. Belief in pragmatism, if widespread, leads to the rule of naked force, which is unpleasant; therefore, by its own criterion, belief in pragmatism is false. If social life is to satisfy social desires, it must be based upon some philosophy not derived from the love of power.

Chapter 17

The Ethics of Power

We have been concerned so much, in the preceding pages, with the evils connected with power, that it might seem natural to draw an ascetic conclusion, and to urge, as the best manner of life for the individual, a complete renunciation of all attempts to influence others, whether for good or evil. Ever since Lao-Tse, this view has had advocates who were both eloquent and wise; it has been held by many mystics, by the quietists, and by those who valued personal holiness, conceived as a state of mind rather than as an activity. I cannot agree with these men, although I admit that some of them have been highly beneficent. But they have been so because, though they believed that they had renounced power, they had, in fact, renounced it only in certain forms; if they had renounced it completely, they would not have proclaimed their doctrines, and would not have been beneficent. They renounced coercive power, but not the power that rests upon persuasion.

Love of power, in its widest sense, is the desire to be able to produce intended effects upon the outer world, whether human or non-human. This desire is an essential part of human nature, and in energetic men it is a very large and important part. Every desire, if it cannot be instantly gratified, brings about a wish for the ability to gratify it, and therefore some form of the love of power. This is true of the best desires as well as the worst. If you love your neighbour, you will wish for power to make him happy. To condemn *all* love of power, therefore, is to condemn love of your neighbour.

There is, however, a great difference between power desired as a means and power desired as an end in itself. The man who desires power as a means has first some other desire, and is then led to wish that he were in a position to achieve it. The man who desires power as an end will choose his objective by the possibility of securing it. In politics, for example, one man wishes to see certain measures enacted, and is thus led to take part in public affairs while another man, wishing only for personal success, adopts whatever programme seems most likely to lead to this result.

Christ's third temptation in the wilderness illustrates this distinction. He is offered all the kingdoms of the earth if He will fall down and worship Satan; that is to say, He is offered power to achieve certain objects, but not those that He has in view. This temptation is one to which almost every modern man is exposed, sometimes in a gross form, sometimes in a very subtle one. He may, though a Socialist, accept a position on a Conservative newspaper; this is a comparatively gross form. He may despair of the achievement of Socialism by peaceful means, and become a Communist, not because he thinks that what he wants will be achieved in this way, but because he thinks that *something* will be achieved. To advocate unsuccessfully what he wants seems to him more futile than to advocate successfully what he does not want. But if his wants, other than personal success, are strong and definite, there will be no satisfaction to his sense of power unless *those* wants are satisfied, and to change his objects for the sake of success will seem to him an act of apostasy which might be described as worshipping Satan.

Love of power, if it is to be beneficent, must be bound up with some end other than power. I do not mean that there must be *no* love of power for its own sake, for this motive is sure to arise in the course of an active career; I mean that the desire for some other end must be so strong that power is unsatisfying unless it ministers to this end.

It is not enough that there should be a purpose other than power; it is necessary that this purpose should be one which, if achieved, will help to satisfy the desires of others. If you aim at discovery, or artistic creation, or the invention of a labour-saving machine, or the reconciliation of groups hitherto at enmity with each other, your success, if you succeed, is likely to be a cause of satisfactions to others besides yourself. This is the second condition that love of power must fulfil if it is to be beneficent: it must be linked to some purpose which is, broadly speaking, in harmony with the desires of the other people who will be affected if the purpose is realised.

There is a third condition, somewhat more difficult to formulate. The means of realising your purpose must not be such as will incidentally have bad effects outweighing the excellence of the end to be achieved. Every man's character and desires undergo perpetual modification as a result of what he does and what he suffers. Violence and injustice breed violence and injustice; both in those who inflict them and in their victims. Defeat, if it is incomplete, breeds rage and hatred, while if it is complete it breeds apathy and inaction. Victory by force produces ruthlessness and contempt for the vanquished, however exalted may have been the original motives for war. All these considerations, while they do not prove that no good purpose can ever be achieved by force, do show that force is very dangerous, and that when there is very much of it any original good purpose is likely to be lost sight of before the end of the strife.

The existence of civilised communities, however, is impossible without some element of force, since there are criminals and men of anti-social ambitions who, if unchecked, would soon cause a reversion to anarchy and barbarism. Where force is unavoidable, it should be exerted by the constituted authority in accordance with the will of the community as expressed in the criminal law. There are, however, two difficulties at this point; first, that the most important uses of force are between different States, where there is no common government and no effectively acknowledged law or judicial authority; second, that the concentration of force in the hands of the government enables it, to some extent, to tyrannise over the rest of the community. Each of these difficulties I shall consider in the next chapter. In the present chapter I am considering power in relation to individual morality, not in relation to the government.

Love of power, like lust, is such a strong motive that it influences most men's actions more than they think it should. It may therefore be argued that the ethic which will produce the best consequences will be one more hostile to love of power than reason can justify: since men are pretty sure to sin against their own code in the direction of the pursuit of power, their acts, it may be said, will be about right if their code is somewhat too severe. A man who is propounding an ethical doctrine can, however, hardly allow himself to be influenced by such considerations, since, if he does, he is obliged to lie consciously in the interests of virtue. The desire to be edifying rather than truthful is the bane of preachers and educators; and whatever may be said in its favour theoretically, it is in practice unmitigatedly harmful. We must admit that men have acted badly from love of power, and will continue to do so; but we ought not, on this account, to maintain that love of power is undesirable in forms and circumstances in which we believe it to be beneficial or at least innocuous.

The forms that a man's love of power will take depend upon his temperament, his opportunities, and his skill; his temperament, moreover, is largely moulded by his circumstances. To turn an individual's love of power into specified channels is, therefore, a matter of providing him with the right circumstances, the right opportunities, and the appropriate type of skill. This leaves out of account the question of congenital disposition, which, in so far as it is amenable to treatment, is a matter for eugenics; but it is probably only a small percentage of the population that cannot be led, by the above means, to choose some useful form of activity.

To begin with circumstances as affecting temperament: the source of cruel impulses is usually to be found either in an unfortunate childhood, or in experiences, such as those of civil war, in which suffering and death are frequently seen and inflicted; absence of any legitimate outlet for energy in adolescence and early youth may have the same effect. I believe that few men are cruel if they have had a wise early education, have not lived among scenes of violence, and have not had undue difficulty in finding a career. Given these conditions, most men's love of power will prefer, if it can, to find a beneficent or at least harmless outlet.

The question of opportunity has both a positive and a negative aspect: it is important that there shall not be opportunity for the career of a pirate, or a brigand, or a dictator, as well as that there should be opportunity for a less destructive profession. There must be a strong government, to prevent crime, and a wise economic system, both to prevent the possibility of legal forms of brigandage, and to offer attractive careers to as many young people as possible. This is much easier in a community which is growing richer than in one which is growing poorer. Nothing improves the moral level of a community as much as an increase of wealth, and nothing lowers it so much as a diminution of wealth. The harshness of the general outlook from the Rhine to the Pacific at the present day is very largely due to the fact that so many people are poorer than their parents were.

The importance of skill in determining the form taken by love of power is very great. Destruction, broadly speaking, apart from certain forms of modern war, requires very little skill, whereas construction always requires some, and in the highest forms requires a great deal. Most men who have acquired a difficult type of skill enjoy exercising it, and prefer this activity to easier ones; this is because the difficult kind of skill, other things being equal, is more satisfying to love of power. The man who has learnt to throw bombs from an aeroplane will prefer this to the humdrum occupations that will be open to him in peace time; but the man who has learnt (say) to combat yellow fever will prefer this to the work of an army surgeon in war time. Modern war involves a very great deal of skill, and this helps to make it attractive to various kinds of experts. Much scientific skill is needed equally in peace and in war; there is no way by which a scientific pacifist can make sure that his discoveries or inventions will not be used to increase the destruction in the next struggle. Nevertheless, there is, speaking broadly, a distinction between the kinds of skill that find most scope in peace and those that find most scope in war. In so far as such a distinction exists, a man's love of power will incline him to peace if his skill is of the former kind, and to war if it is of the latter. In such ways, technical training can do much to determine what form love of power shall take.

It is not altogether true that persuasion is one thing and force is another. Many forms of persuasion – even many of which everybody approves – are really a kind of force. Consider what we do to our children. We do not say to them: 'Some people think the earth is round, and others think it is flat; when you grow up, you can, if you like, examine the evidence and form your own conclusion.' Instead of this we say: 'The earth *is* round.' By the time our children are old enough to examine the evidence, our propaganda has closed their minds, and the most persuasive arguments of the Flat Earth Society make no impression. The same applies to the moral precepts that we consider really important, such as 'don't pick your nose' or 'don't eat peas with a knife'. There may, for aught I know, be admirable reasons for eating peas with a knife, but the hypnotic effect of early persuasion has made me completely incapable of appreciating them.

The ethics of power cannot consist in distinguishing some kinds of power as legitimate and others as illegitimate. As we have just seen, we all approve, in certain cases, of a kind of persuasion which is essentially a use of force. Almost everybody would approve of physical violence, even killing, in easily imagined conditions. Suppose you had come upon Guy Fawkes in the very act of firing the train, and suppose you could only have prevented the disaster by shooting him; most pacifists, even, would admit that you would have done right to shoot. The attempt to deal with the question by abstract general principles, praising acts of one type and blaming acts of another, is futile; we must judge the exercise of power by its effects, and we must therefore first make up our minds as to what effects we desire.

For my part, I consider that whatever is good or bad is embodied in individuals, not primarily in communities. Some philosophies which could be used to support the corporative State – notably the philosophy of Hegel – attribute ethical qualities to communities as such, so that a State may be admirable though most of its citizens are wretched. I think that such philosophies are tricks for justifying the privileges of the holders of power, and that, whatever our *politics* may be, there can be no valid argument for an undemocratic *ethic*. I mean by an undemocratic ethic one which singles out a certain portion of mankind and says 'these men are to enjoy the good things, and the rest are merely to minister to them'. I should reject such an ethic in any case, but it has, as we saw in the last chapter, the disadvantage of being self-refuting, since it is very unlikely that, in practice, the supermen will be able to live the kind of life that the aristocratic theorist imagines for them.

Some objects of desire are such as can, logically, be enjoyed by all, while others must, by their very nature, be confined to a portion of the community. All might – with a little rational co-operation – be fairly well off, but it is impossible for all to enjoy a pleasure of being richer than their neighbours. All can enjoy a certain degree of self-direction, but it is impossible for all to be dictators over others. Perhaps in time there will be a population, in which everybody is fairly intelligent, but it is not possible for all to secure the rewards bestowed on *exceptional* intelligence. And so on.

Social cooperation is possible in regard to the good things that are capable of being universal – adequate material well-being, health, intelligence, and every form of happiness which does not consist in superiority to others. But the forms of happiness which consist of victory in a competition cannot be universal. The former kind of happiness is promoted by friendly feeling, the latter (and its correlative unhappiness) by unfriendly feeling. Unfriendly feeling can wholly inhibit the rational pursuit of happiness; it does so at present in what concerns the economic relations of nations. Given a population in which friendly feelings preponderate, there will be no clash between the interests of different individuals or different groups; the clashes which at present exist are caused by unfriendly feeling, which they in turn intensify. England and Scotland fought each other for centuries; at last, by an accident of inheritance, they came to have the same king, and the wars ceased. Everybody was happier in consequence, even Dr Johnson, whose jests doubtless afforded him more pleasure than he would have derived from victorious battles.

We can now arrive at certain conclusions on the subject of the ethics of power.

The ultimate aim of those who have power (and we all have some) should be to promote social cooperation, not in one group as against another, but in the whole human race. The chief obstacle to this end at present is the existence of feelings of unfriendliness and desire for superiority. Such feelings can be diminished either directly by religion and morality, or indirectly by removing the political and economic circumstances for power between States and the connected competition for wealth between large national industries. Both methods are needed: they are not alternatives, but supplement each other.

The Great War, and its aftermath of dictatorships, has caused many to underestimate all forms of power except military and governmental force. This is a short-sighted and unhistorical view. If I had to select four men who have had more power than any others, I should mention Buddha and Christ, Pythagoras and Galileo. No one of these four had the support of the State until after his propaganda had achieved a great measure of success. No one of the four had much success in his own lifetime. No one of the four would have affected human life as he has done if power had been his *primary* object. No one of the four sought the kind of power that enslaves others, but the kind that sets them free – in the case of the first two, by showing how to master the desires that lead to strife, and thence to defeat slavery and subjection; in the case of the second two, by pointing the way towards control of natural forces. It is not ultimately by violence that men are ruled, but by the wisdom of those who appeal to the common desires of mankind, for happiness, for inward and outward peace, and for the understanding of the world in which, by no choice of our own, we have to live.

Chapter 18

The Taming of Power

'In passing by the side of Mount Thai, Confucius came on a woman who was weeping bitterly by a grave. The Master pressed forward and drove quickly to her, then he sent Tze-lu to question her. "Your wailing," said he, "is that of one who has suffered sorrow on sorrow." She replied, "That is so. Once my husband's father was killed here by a tiger. My husband was also killed, and now my son has died in the same way." The Master said, "Why do you not leave this place?" the answer was "There is no oppressive government here." The Master then said, "Remember this, my children: oppressive government is more terrible than tigers." '

The subject of the present chapter is the problem of insuring that government shall be *less* terrible than tigers.

The problem of the taming of power is, as the above quotation shows, a very ancient one. The Taoists thought it insoluble, and advocated anarchism; the Confucians trusted to a certain ethical and governmental training which should turn the holders of power into sages endowed with moderation and benevolence. At the same period, in Greece, democracy, oligarchy, and tyranny were contending for mastery; democracy was intended to check abuses of power, but was perpetually defeating itself by falling a victim to the temporary popularity of some demagogue. Plato, like Confucius, sought the solution in a government of men trained to wisdom. This view has been revived by Mr and Mrs Sidney Webb, who admire an oligarchy in which power is confined to those who have the 'vocation of leadership'. In the interval between Plato and the Webbs, the world has tried military autocracy, theocracy, hereditary monarchy, oligarchy, democracy, and the Rule of the Saints – the last of these, after the failure of Cromwell's experiment, having been revived in our day by Lenin and Hitler. All this suggests that our problem has not yet been solved.

To anyone who studies history or human nature, it must be evident that democracy, while not a complete solution, is an essential part of the solution. The complete solution is not to be found by confining ourselves to political conditions; we must take account also of economics, of propaganda, and of psychology as affected by circumstances and education. Our subject thus divides itself into four parts: (I) political conditions, (II) economic conditions, (III) propaganda conditions, and (IV) psychological and educational conditions. Let us take these in succession.

I

The merits of democracy are negative: it does not insure good government, but it prevents certain evils. Until women began to take part in political affairs, married women had no control over their own property, or even over their own earnings; a charwoman with a drunken husband had no redress if he prevented her from using her wages for support of her children. The oligarchical Parliament of the eighteenth and early nineteenth centuries used its legislative power to increase the wealth of the rich by depressing the condition of both rural and urban lábour. Only democracy has prevented the law from making trade unionism impossible. But for democracy, Western America, Australia, and New Zealand would be inhabited by a semi-servile yellow population governed by a small white aristocracy. The evils of slavery and serfdom are familiar, and wherever a minority has a secure monopoly of political power, the majority is likely to sink, sooner or later, into either slavery or serfdom. All history slows that, as might be expected, minorities cannot be trusted to care for the interests of majorities.

There is a tendency, as strong now as at any former time, to suppose that an oligarchy is admirable if it consists of 'good' men. The government of the Roman Empire was 'bad' until Constantine, and then it became 'good'. In the Book of Kings, there were those who did right in the sight of the Lord, and those who did evil. In English history as taught to children, there are 'good' kings and 'bad' kings. An oligarchy of Jews is 'bad', but one of Nazis is 'good'. The aligarchy of Tsarist aristocrats was 'bad', but that of the Communist Party is 'good'.

This attitude is unworthy of grown-up people. A child is 'good' when it obeys orders and 'naughty' when it does not. When it grows up and becomes a political leader, it retains the ideas of the nursery, and defines the 'good' as those who obey its orders and the 'bad' as those who defy it. Consequently our own political party consists of 'good' men, and the opposite party consists of 'bad' men. 'Good' government is government by our group, 'bad' government that by the other group. The Montagues are 'good', the Capulets 'bad', or vice versa.

Such a point of view, if taken seriously, makes social life impossible. Only force can decide which group is 'good' and which 'bad', and the decision, when made, may at any moment be upset by an insurrection. Neither group, if it attains power, will care for the interests of the other, except in so far as it is controlled by the fear of rousing rebellion. Social life, if it is to be anything better than tyranny, demands a certain impartiality. But since, in many matters, collective action is necessary, the only practicable form of impartiality, in such matters, is the rule of the majority.

Democracy, however, though necessary, is by no means the only political condition required for the taming of power. It is possible, in a democracy, for the majority to exercise a brutal and wholly unnecessary tyranny over a minority. In the period from 1885 to 1922, the government of the United Kingdom was (except for the exclusion of women) democratic, but that did not prevent the oppression of Ireland. Not only a national, but a religious or political minority may be persecuted. The safeguarding of minorities, so far as is compatible with orderly government, is an essential part of the taming of power.

This requires a consideration of the matters as to which the community must act as a whole, and those as to which uniformity is unnecessary. The most obvious questions as to which a collective decision is imperative are those that are essentially geographical. Roads, railways, sewers, gas mains, and so on, must take one course and not another. Sanitary precautions, say against plague or rabies, are geographical: it would not do for Christian Scientists to announce that they will take no precautions against infection, because they might infect others. War is a geographical phenomenon, unless it is civil war, and even then it soon happens that one area is dominated by one side, and another by the other.

Where there is a geographically concentrated minority, such as the Irish before 1922, it is possible to solve a great many problems by devolution. But when the minority is distributed throughout the area concerned, this method is largely inapplicable. Where Christian and Mohammedan populations live side by side, they have, it is true, different marriage laws, but except where religion is concerned they all have to submit to one government. It has been gradually discovered that theological uniformity is not necessary to a State, and that Protestants and Catholics can live peaceably together under one government. But this was not the case during the first 130 years after the Reformation.

The question of the degree of liberty that is compatible with order is one that cannot be settled in the abstract. The only thing that can be said in the abstract is that, where there is no technical reason for a collective decision, there should be some strong reason connected with public order if freedom is to be interfered with. In the reign of Elizabeth, when Roman Catholics wished to deprive her of the throne, it is not surprising that the government viewed them with disfavour. Similarly in the Low Countries, where Protestants were in revolt against Spain, it was to be expected that the Spaniards would persecute them. Nowadays theological questions have not the same political importance. Even political differences, if they do not go too deep, are no reason for persecution. Conservatives, Liberals, and Labour people can all live peaceably side by side, because they do not wish to alter the Constitution by force; but Fascists and Communists are more difficult to assimilate. Where there is democracy, attempts of a minority to seize power by force, and incitements to such attempts, may reasonably be forbidden, on the ground that a law-abiding majority has a right to a quiet life if it can secure it. But there should be toleration of all propaganda not involving incitement to break the law, and the law should be as tolerant as is compatible with technical efficiency and the maintenance of order. I shall return to this subject under the head of psychology.

From the point of view of the taming of power, very difficult questions arise as to the best size of a governmental unit. In a great modern State, even when it is a democracy, the ordinary citizen has very little sense of political power; he does not decide what are to be the issues in an election, they probably concern matters remote from his daily life and almost wholly outside his experience, and his vote makes so small a contribution to the total as to seem to himself negligible. In the ancient City State these evils were much less; so they are, at present, in local government. It might have been expected that the public would take more interest in local than in national questions, but this is not the case; on the contrary, the larger the area concerned, the greater the percentage of the electorate that takes the trouble to vote. This is partly because more money is spent on propaganda in important elections, partly because the issues are in themselves more exciting. The most exciting issues are those involving war and relations to possible enemies. I remember an old yokel in January 1910, who told me he was going to vote Conservative (which was against his economic interests), because he had been persuaded that if the Liberals were victorious the Germans would be in the country within a week. It is not to be supposed that he ever voted in Parish Council elections, though in them he might have had some understanding of the issues; these issues failed to move him because they were not such as to generate mass hysteria or the myths upon which it feeds.

There is thus a dilemma: democracy gives a man a feeling that he has an effective share in political power when the group concerned is small, but not when it is large; on the other hand, the issue is likely to strike him as important when the group concerned is large, but not when it is small.

To some extent this difficulty is avoided when a constituency is vocational, not geographical; a really effective democracy is possible, for example, in a trade union. Each branch can meet to discuss a vexed question of policy; the members have a similarity of interest and experience, and this makes fruitful discussion possible. The final decision of the whole union may, therefore, be one in which a large percentage of members feel they have had a part.

This method, however, has obvious limitations. Many questions are so essentially geographical that a geographical constituency is unavoidable. Public bodies affect our lives at so many points that a busy man who is not a politician cannot take action about most of the local or national issues that concern him. The best solution would probably be an extension of the method of the trade union official, who is elected to represent a certain interest. At present, many interests have no such representative. Democracy, if it is to exist psychologically as well as politically, demands organisation of the various interests, and their representation, in political bargaining, by men who enjoy whatever influence is justified by the numbers and enthusiasm of their constituents. I do not mean that these representatives should be a substitute for Parliament, but that they should be the channel by which Parliament is made aware of the wishes of various groups of citizens.

A federal system is desirable whenever the local interests and sentiments of the constituent units are stronger than the interests and sentiments connected with the federation. If there were ever an international government, it would obviously have to be a federation of national governments, with strictly defined powers. There are already international authorities for certain purposes, e.g. postage, but these are purposes which do not interest the public so much as do those dealt with by national governments. Where this condition is absent, the federal government tends to encroach upon the governments of the several units. In the United States, the federal government has gained at the expense of the States ever since the Constitution was first enacted. The same tendency existed in Germany from 1871 to 1918. Even a federal government of the world, if it found itself involved in a civil war on the question of secession, as might well happen, would, if victorious, be immeasurably strengthened as against the various national governments. Thus the efficacy of federation, as a method, has very definite limits; but within these limits it is desirable and important.

Very large governmental areas are, it would seem, quite unavoidable in the modern world; indeed, for some of the most important purposes, especially peace and war, the whole world is the only adequate area. The psychological disadvantages of large areas – especially the sense of impotence in the average voter, and his ignorance as to most of the issues – must be admitted, and minimised as far as possible, partly, as suggested above, by the organisation of separate interests, and partly by federation or devolution. Some subjection of the individual is an inevitable consequence of increasing social organisation. But if the danger of war were eliminated, local questions would be much more concerned than at present with questions as to which they could have both knowledge and an effective voice. For it is the fear of war, more than anything else, which compels men to direct their attention to distant countries and to the external activities of their own government.

Where democracy exists, there is still need to safeguard individuals and minorities against tyranny, both because tyranny is undesirable in itself, and because it is likely to lead to breaches of order. Montesquieu's advocacy of the separation of legislative, executive, and judiciary, the traditional English belief in checks and balances, Bentham's political doctrines and the whole of nineteenth-century liberalism, were designed to prevent the arbitrary exercise of power. But such methods have come to be considered incompatible with efficiency. No doubt the separation of the War Office and the Horse Guards was a safeguard against military dictatorship, but it had disastrous results in the Crimean War. When, in former times, the legislature and the executive disagreed, the result was a highly inconvenient deadlock; now in England, efficiency is secured by uniting both powers, to all intents and purposes, in the Cabinet. The eighteenth and nineteenth century methods of preventing arbitrary power no longer suit our circumstances, and such new methods as exist are not yet very effective. There is need of associations to safeguard this or that form of liberty, and to bring swift criticism to bear upon officials, police, magistrates, and judges who exceed their powers. There is need also of a certain political balance in every important branch of the public service. For example, there is danger to democracy in the fact that average opinion in the police and the air force is far more reactionary than in the country at large.

In every democracy, individuals and organisations which are intended to have only certain well-defined executive functions are likely, if unchecked, to acquire a very undesirable independent power. This is especially true of the police. The evils resulting from an insufficiently supervised police force are very forcibly set forth, as regards the United States, in *Our Lawless Police*, by Ernest Jerome Hopkins. The gist of the matter is that a policeman is promoted for action leading to the conviction of a criminal, that the Courts accept confession as evidence of guilt, and that, in consequence, it is to the interest of individual officers to torture arrested persons until they confess. This evil exists in all countries in a greater or less degree. In India it is rampant. The desire to obtain a confession was the basis of the tortures of the Inquisition. In Old China, torture of suspected persons was habitual, because a humanitarian Emperor has decreed that no man should be condemned except on his own confession. For the taming of the power of the police, one essential is that a confession shall never, in any circumstances, be accepted as evidence.

This reform, however, though necessary, is by no means sufficient. The police system of all countries is based upon the assumption that the collection of evidence against a suspected criminal is a matter of public interest but that the collection of evidence in his favour is his private concern. It is often said to be more important that the innocent should be acquitted than that the guilty should be condemned, but everywhere it is the duty of the police to seek evidence of guilt, not of innocence. Suppose you are unjustly accused of murder, and there is a good *prima facie* case against you. The whole of the resources of the State are set in motion to seek out possible witnesses against you, and the ablest lawyers are employed by the State to create prejudice against you in the minds of the jury. You, meanwhile, must spend your private fortune collecting evidence of your innocence, with no public organisation to help you. If you plead poverty, you will be allotted Counsel, but probably not so able a man as the public prosecutor. If you succeed in securing an acquittal, you can only escape bankruptcy by means of the cinemas and the Sunday Press. But it is only too likely that you will be unjustly convicted.

If law-abiding citizens are to be protected against unjust persecution by the police, there must be two police forces and two Scotland Yards, one designed, as at present, to prove guilt, the other to prove innocence; and in addition to the public prosecutor there must be a public defender, of equal legal eminence. This is obvious as soon as it is admitted that the acquittal of the innocent is no less a public interest than the condemnation of the guilty. The defending police force should, moreover, become the prosecuting police force where one class of crimes is concerned, namely crimes committed by the prosecuting police in the execution of their 'duty'. By this means, but by no other (so far as I can see), the present oppressive power of the police could be mitigated.

II

I come now to the economic conditions required in order to minimise arbitrary power. This subject is of great importance, both on its own account, and because there has been a very great deal of confusion of thought in relation to it.

Political democracy, while it solves a part of our problem, does not by any means solve the whole. Marx pointed out that there could be no real equalisation of power through politics alone, while economic power remained monarchical or oligarchic. It followed that economic power must be in the hands of the State, and that the State must be democratic. Those who profess, at the present day, to be Marx's followers, have kept only the half of his doctrine, and have thrown over the demand that the State should be democratic. They have thus concentrated both economic and political power in the hands of an oligarchy, which has become, in consequence, more powerful and more able to exercise tyranny than any oligarchy of former times.

Both old-fashioned democracy and new-fashioned Marxism have aimed at the taming of power. The former failed because it was only political, the latter because it was only economic. Without a combination of both, nothing approaching to a solution of the problem is possible.

The arguments in favour of State ownership of land and the large economic organisations are partly technical, partly political. The technical arguments have not been much stressed except by the Fabian Society, and to some extent in America in connection with such matters as the Tennessee Valley Authority. Nevertheless they are very strong, especially in connection with electricity and water power, and cause even Conservative governments to introduce measures which, from a technical point of view, are socialistic. We have seen how, as a result of modern technique, organisations tend to grow and to coalesce and to increase their scope; the inevitable consequence is that the political State must either increasingly take over economic functions, or partially abdicate in favour of vast private enterprises which are sufficiently powerful to defy or control it. If the State does not acquire supremacy over such enterprises, it becomes their puppet, and they become the real State. In one way or another, wherever modern technique exists, economic and political power must become unified. This movement towards unification has the irresistible impersonal character which Marx attributed to the development that he prophesied. But it has nothing to do with the class war or the wrongs of the proletariat.

Socialism as a political movement has aimed at furthering the interests of industrial wage-earners; its technical advantages have been kept comparatively in the background. The belief is that the economic power of the private capitalist enables him to oppress the wage-earner, and that, since the wage-earner cannot, like the handicraftsman of former times, individually own his means of production, the only way of emancipating him is collective ownership by the whole body of workers. It is argued that, if the private capitalist were expropriated, the whole body of the workers would constitute the State; and that, consequently, the problem of economic power can be solved completely by State ownership of land and capital, and in no other way. This is a proposal for the taming of economic power, and therefore comes within the purview of our present discussion.

Before examining the argument, I wish to say unequivocally that I consider it valid, provided it is adequately safeguarded and amplified. *Per contra*, in the absence of such safeguarding and amplifying I consider it very dangerous, and likely to mislead those who seek liberation from economic tyranny so completely that they will find they have inadvertently established a new tyranny at once economic and political, more drastic and more terrible than any previously known.

In the first place, 'ownership' is not the same thing as 'control'. If, say, a railway is owned by the State, and the State is considered to be the whole body of the citizens, that does not insure, of itself, that the average citizen will have any power over the railway. Let us revert, for a moment, to what Messrs Berle and Means say about ownership and control in large American corporations. They point out that, in the majority of such corporations, all the directors together usually own only about one or two per cent of the stock, and yet, in effect, have complete control:

'In the election of the board the stock holder ordinarily has three alternatives. He can refrain from voting, he can attend the annual meeting and personally vote his stock, or he can sign a proxy transferring his voting power to certain individuals selected by the management of the corporation, the proxy committee. As his personal vote will count for little or nothing at the meeting unless he has a very large block of stock, the stock holder is practically reduced to the alternative of not voting at all or else of *handing over his vote to individuals over whom he has no control and in whose selection he did not participate*. In neither case will he be able to exercise any measure of control. Rather, control will tend to be in the hands of those who select the proxy committee. ... Since the proxy committee is appointed by the existing management, the latter can virtually dictate their own successors.'[1]

The helpless individuals described in the above passage are, it

[1] Op. cit., pp. 86-7.

should be noted, not proletarians, but capitalists. They are part owners of the corporation concerned, in the sense that they have legal rights which may, with luck, bring them in a certain income; but owing to their lack of control, the income is very precarious. When I first visited the United States in 1896, I was struck by the enormous number of railways that were bankrupt; on inquiry, I found that this was not due to incompetence on the part of the directors, but to skill: the investments of ordinary shareholders had been transferred, by one device or another, to other companies in which the directors had a large interest. This was a crude method, and nowadays matters are usually managed in a more decorous fashion, but the principle remains the same. In any large corporation, power is necessarily less diffused than ownership, and carries with it advantages which, though at first political, can be made sources of wealth to an indefinite extent. The humble investor can be politely and legally robbed; the only limit is that he must not have such bitter experiences as to lead him to keep his future savings in a stocking.

The situation is in no way essentially different when the State takes the place of a corporation; indeed, since it is the size of the corporation that causes the helplessness of the average shareholder, the average citizen is likely to be still more helpless as against the State. A battleship is public property, but if, on this ground, you try to exercise rights of ownership, you will be soon put in your place. You have a remedy, it is true: at the next General Election, you can vote for a candidate who favours a reduction in the Navy Estimates, if you can find one; or you can write to the papers to urge that sailors should be more polite to sightseers. But more than this you cannot do.

But, it is said, the battleship belongs to a capitalist State, and when it belongs to a workers' State everything will be different. This view seems to me to show a failure to grasp the fact that economic power is now a matter of government rather than ownership. If the United States Steel Corporation, say, were taken over by the United States Government, it would still need men to manage it; they would either be the same men who now manage it, or men with similar abilities and a similar outlook. The attitude which they now have towards the shareholders they would then have towards the citizens. True, they would be subject to the government, but unless it was democratic and responsible to public opinion, it would have a point of view closely similar to that of the officials.

Marxists, having retained, as a result of the authority of Marx and Engels, many ways of thinking that belong to the forties of last century, still conceive of businesses as if they belonged to individual capitalists, and have not learnt the lessons to be derived from the separation of ownership and control. The important person is the man who has control of economic power, not the man who has a fraction of the nominal ownership. The Prime Minister does not own No 10 Downing Street, and Bishops do not own their palaces; but it would be absurd to pretend, on this account, that they are no better off as regards housing than the average wage-earner. Under any form of socialism which is not democratic, those who control economic power can, without 'owning' anything, have palatial official residences, the use of the best cars, a princely entertainment allowance, holidays at the public expense in official holiday resorts, and so on and so on. And why should they have any more concern for the ordinary worker than those in control have now? There can be no reason why they should have, unless the ordinary worker has power to deprive them of their positions. Moreover the subordination of the small investor in existing large corporations shows how easy it is for the official to overpower the democracy, even when the 'democracy' consists of capitalists.

Not only, therefore, is democracy essential if State ownership and control of economic enterprises is to be in any degree advantageous to the average citizen, but it will have to be an effective democracy, and this will be more difficult to secure than it is at present, since the official class will, unless very carefully supervised, combine the powers at present possessed by the government and the men in control of industry and finance, and since the means of agitating against the government will have to be supplied by the government itself, as the sole owner of halls, paper, and all the other essentials of propaganda.

While, therefore, public ownership and control of all large-scale industry and finance is a *necessary* condition for the taming of power, it is far from being a *sufficient* condition. It needs to be supplemented by a democracy more thorough-going, more carefully safeguarded against official tyranny, and with more deliberate provision for freedom of propaganda, than any purely political democracy that has ever existed.

The dangers of State Socialism divorced from democracy have been illustrated by the course of events in the USSR. There are those whose attitude to Russia is one of religious faith; to them, it is impious even to examine the evidence that all is not well in that country. But the testimony of former enthusiasts is becoming more and more convincing to those whose minds are open to reason on the subject. The arguments from history and psychology with which we have been concerned in previous chapters have shown how rash it is to expect irresponsible power to be benevolent. What actually happens, as regards power, is summed up by Eugene Lyons in the following words:

'Absolutism at the top implies hundred of thousands, even millions, of large and small autocrats in a state that monopolises all means of life and expression, work and pleasure, rewards and punishments. A centralised autocratic rule must function through a human machine of delegated authority, a pyramid of graded officialdom, each layer subservient to those above and overbearing to those below. Unless there are brakes of genuinely democratic control and the corrective of a hard-and-fast legality to which everyone, even the anointed of the Lord, is subjected the machine of power becomes an engine of oppression. Where there is only one employer, namely, the State, meekness is the first law of economic survival. Where the same group of officials wields the terrible power of secret arrests and punishments, disfranchisement, hiring and firing, assignment of ration categories and living space – only an imbecile or someone with a perverted taste for martyrdom will fail to kow-tow to them.'[1]

If concentration of power in a single organisation – the State – is not to produce the evils of despotism in an extreme form, it is essential that power within that organisation should be widely distributed, and that subordinate groups should have a large measure of autonomy. Without democracy, devolution, and immunity from extra-legal punishment, the coalescence of economic and political power is nothing but a new and appalling instrument of tyranny. In Russia, a peasant on a collective farm who takes any portion of the grain that he has himself grown is liable to the death penalty. This law was made at a time when millions of peasants were dying of hunger and attendant diseases, owing to the famine which the government deliberately refrained from alleviating.[2]

[1] *Assignment in Utopia*, p. 195.
[2] Ibid., p. 492.

III

I come now to the propaganda conditions for the taming of power. It is obvious that publicity for grievances must be possible; agitation must be free provided it does not incite to breaches of the law; there must be ways of impeaching officials who exceed or abuse their powers. The government of the day must not be in a position to secure its own permanence by intimidation, falsification of the register of electors, or any similar method. There must be no penalty, official or unofficial, for any well-grounded criticism of prominent men. Much of this, at present, is secured by party government in democratic countries, which causes the politicians in power to be objects of hostile criticism by nearly half the nation. This makes it impossible for them to commit many crimes to which they might otherwise be prone.

All this is more important when the State has a monopoly of economic power than it is under capitalism, since the power of the State will be vastly augmented. Take a concrete case: that of women employed in the public service. At present they have a grievance, because their rates of pay are lower than those of men; they have legitimate ways of making their grievance known, and it would not be safe to penalise them for making use of these ways. There is no reason whatever for supposing that the present inequality would necessarily cease with the adoption of Socialism, but the means of agitating about it would cease, unless express provision were made for just such cases. Newspapers and printing presses would all belong to the government, and would print only what the government ordered. Can it be assumed as certain that the government would print attacks on its own policy? If not, there would be no means of political agitation by means of print. Public meetings would be just as difficult, since the halls would all belong to the government. Consequently, unless careful provision were made for the express purpose of safeguarding political liberty, no method would exist of making grievances known, and the government, when once elected, would be as omnipotent as Hitler, and could easily arrange for its own re-election to the end of time. Democracy might survive as a form, but would have no more reality than the forms of popular government that lingered on under the Roman Empire.

To suppose that irresponsible power, just because it is called Socialist or Communist, will be freed miraculously from the bad qualities of all arbitrary power in the past, is mere childish nursery psychology: the wicked prince is ousted by the good prince, and all is well. If a prince is to be trusted, it must be not because he is 'good', but because it is against his interest to be 'bad'. To insure that this shall be the case is to make power innocuous; but it cannot be rendered innocuous by transforming men whom we believe to be 'good' into irresponsible despots.

The BBC is a State institution which shows what is possible in the way of combining freedom of propaganda with government monopoly. At such a time as that of the General Strike, it must be admitted, it ceases to be impartial; but at ordinary times it represents different points of view, as nearly as may be, in proportion to their numerical strength. In a Socialist State, similar arrangements for impartiality would have to be made in regard to the hiring of halls for meetings and the printing of controversial literature. It might be found desirable, instead of having different newspapers representing different points of view, to have only one, with different pages allocated to different parties. This would have the advantage that readers would see all opinions, and would tend to be less one-sided than those who, at present, never see in a newspaper anything with which they disagree.

There are certain regions, such as art and science, and (so far as public order allows) party politics, where uniformity is not necessary or even desirable. These are the legitimate sphere of competition, and it is important that public feeling should be such as to bear differences on such matters without exasperation. Democracy, if it is to succeed and endure, demands a tolerant spirit, not too much hate, and not too much love of violence. But this brings us to the psychological conditions for the taming of power.

IV

The psychological conditions for the taming of power are in some ways the most difficult. In connection with the psychology of power we saw that fear, rage, and all kinds of violent collective excitement, tend to make men blindly follow a leader, who, in most cases, takes advantage of their trust to establish himself as a tyrant. It is therefore important, if democracy is to be preserved, both to avoid the circumstances that produce general excitement, and to educate in such a way that the population shall be little prone to moods of this sort. Where a spirit of ferocious dogmatism prevails, any opinion with which men disagree is liable to provoke a breach of the peace. Schoolboys are apt to ill-treat a boy whose opinions are in any way odd, and many grown men have not got beyond the mental age of schoolboys. A diffused liberal sentiment, tinged with scepticism, makes social cooperation much less difficult, and liberty correspondingly more possible.

Revivalist enthusiasm, such as that of the Nazis, rouses admiration in many through the energy and apparent self-abnegation that it generates. Collective excitement, involving indifference to pain and even to death, is historically not uncommon. Where it exists, liberty is impossible. The enthusiasts can only be restrained by force, and if they are not restrained they will use force against others. I remember a Bolshevik whom I met in Peking in 1920, who marched up and down the room exclaiming with complete truth: 'If vee do not keel zem, zey vill keel us!' The existence of this mood on one side of course generates the same mood on the other side; the consequence is a fight to a finish, in which everything is subordinated to victory. During the fight, the government acquires despotic power for military reasons; at the end, if victorious, it uses its power first to crush what remains of the enemy, and then to secure the continuance of its dictatorship over its own supporters. The result is something quite different from what was fought for by the enthusiasts. Enthusiasm, while it can achieve certain results, can hardly ever achieve those that it desires. To admire collective enthusiasm is reckless and irresponsible, for its fruits are fierceness, war, death, and slavery.

War is the chief promoter of despotism, and the greatest obstacle to the establishment of a system in which irresponsible power is avoided as far as possible. The prevention of war is therefore an essential part of our problem – I should say, the most essential. I believe that, if once the world were freed from the fear of war, under no matter what form of government or what economic system, it would in time find ways of curbing the ferocity of its rulers. On the other hand, all war, but especially modern war, promotes dictatorship by causing the timid to seek a leader and by converting the bolder spirits from a society into a pack.

The risk of war causes a certain kind of mass psychology, and reciprocally this kind, where it exists, increases the risk of war, as well as the likelihood of despotism. We have therefore to consider the kind of education which will make societies least prone to collective hysteria, and most capable of successfully practising democracy.

Democracy, if it is to succeed, needs a wide diffusion of two qualities which seem, at first sight, to tend in opposite directions. On the one hand, men must have a certain degree of self-reliance and a certain willingness to back their own judgement; there must be political propaganda in opposite directions, in which many people take part. But on the other hand men must be willing to submit to the decision of the majority when it goes against them. Either of these conditions may fail: the population may be too submissive, and may follow a vigorous leader into dictatorship; or each party may be too self-assertive, with the result that the nation falls into anarchy.

What education has to do in this matter may be considered under two heads: first, in relation to character and the emotions; secondly, in relation to instruction. Let us begin with the former.

If democracy is to be workable, the population must be as far as possible free from hatred and destructiveness, and also from fear and subservience. These feelings may be caused by political or economic circumstances, but what I want to consider is the part that education plays in making men more or less prone to them.

Some parents and some schools begin with the attempt to teach children complete obedience, an attempt which is almost bound to produce either a slave or a rebel, neither of which is what is wanted in a democracy. As to the effects of a severely disciplinary education, the view that I hold is held by all the dictators of Europe. After the war, almost all the countries of Europe had a number of free schools, without too much discipline or too much show of respect for the teachers; but one by one the military autocracies, including the Soviet Republic, have suppressed all freedom in schools and have gone back to the old drill, and to the practice of treating the teacher as a miniature Führer or Duce. The dictators, we may infer, all regard a certain degree of freedom in school as the proper training for democracy, and autocracy in school is the natural prelude to autocracy in the State.

Every man and woman in a democracy should be neither a slave nor a rebel, but a citizen, that is, a person who has, and allows to others, a due proportion, but no more, of the government mentality. Where democracy does not exist, the governmental mentality is that of masters towards dependants; but where there is democracy it is that of equal cooperation, which involves the assertion of one's own opinion up to a certain point, but no further.

This brings us to a source of trouble to many democrats, namely what is called 'principle'. Most talk about principle, self-sacrifice, heroic devotion to a cause, and so on, should be scanned somewhat sceptically. A little psycho-analysis will often show that what goes by these fine names is really something quite different, such as pride, or hatred, or desire for revenge, that has become idealised and collectivised and personified as a noble form of idealism. The warlike patriot, who is willing and even anxious to fight for his country, may reasonably be suspected of a certain pleasure in killing. A kindly population, a population who in their childhood had received kindness and been made happy, and who in youth had found the world a friendly place, would not develop that particular sort of idealism called patriotism, or class-war, or what not, which consists in joining together to kill people in large numbers. I think the tendency to cruel forms of idealism is increased by unhappiness in childhood, and would be lessened if early education were emotionally what it ought to be. Fanaticism is a defect which is partly emotional, partly intellectual; it needs to be combated by the kind of happiness that makes men kindly, and the kind of intelligence that produces a scientific habit of mind.

The temper required to make a success of democracy is, in the practical life, exactly what the scientific temper is in the intellectual life; it is a half-way house between scepticism and dogmatism. Truth, it holds, is neither completely attainable nor completely unattainable; it is attainable to a certain degree, and that only with difficulty.

Autocracy, in its modern forms, is always combined with a creed: that of Hitler, that of Mussolini, or that of Stalin. Wherever there is autocracy, a set of beliefs is instilled into the minds of the young before they are capable of thinking, and these beliefs are taught so constantly and so persistently that it is hoped the pupils will never afterwards be able to escape from the hypnotic effect of their early lessons. The beliefs are instilled, not by giving any reason for supposing them true, but by parrot-like repetition, by mass hysteria and mass suggestion. When two opposite creeds have been taught in this fashion, they produce two armies which clash, not two parties that can discuss. Each hypnotised automaton feels that everything most sacred is bound up with the victory of his side, everything most horrible is exemplified by the other side. Such fanatical factions cannot meet in Parliament and say 'let us see which side has the majority'; that would be altogether too pedestrian, since each side stands for a sacred cause. This sort of dogmatism must be prevented if dictatorships are to be avoided, and measures for preventing it ought to form an essential part of education.

If I had control of education, I should expose children to the most vehement and eloquent advocates on all sides of every topical question, who should speak to the schools from the BBC. The teacher should afterwards invite the children to summarise the arguments used, and should gently insinuate the view that eloquence is inversely proportional to solid reason. To acquire immunity to eloquence is of the utmost importance to the citizens of a democracy.

Modern propagandists have learnt from advertisers, who led the way in the technique of producing irrational belief. Education should be designed to counteract the natural credulity and the natural incredulity of the uneducated: the habit of believing an emphatic statement without reasons, and of disbelieving an unemphatic statement even when accompanied by the best of reasons. I should begin in the infant school, with two classes of sweets between which the children should choose: one very nice, recommended by a coldly accurate statement as to its ingredients; the other very nasty, recommended by the utmost skill of the best advertisers. A little later I should give them a choice of two places for a country holiday: a nice place recommended by a contour map, and an ugly place recommended by magnificent posters.

The teaching of history ought to be conducted in a similar spirit. There have been in the past eminent orators and writers who defended, with an appearance of great wisdom, positions which no one now holds: the reality of witchcraft, the beneficence of slavery, and so on. I should cause the young to know such masters of eloquence, and to appreciate at once their rhetoric and their wrong-headedness. Gradually I should pass on to current questions. As a sort of *bonne bouche* to their history, I should read to them what is said about Spain (or whatever at the moment is most controversial) first by the *Daily Mail*, and then by the *Daily Worker*; and I should then ask them to infer what really happened. For undoubtedly few things are more useful to a citizen of a democracy than skill in detecting, by reading newspapers, what it was that took place. For this purpose, it would be instructive to compare the newspapers at crucial moments during the Great War with what subsequently appeared in the official history. And when the madness of war hysteria, as shown in the newspapers of the time, strikes your pupils as incredible, you should warn them that all of them, unless they are very careful to cultivate a balanced and cautious judgement, may fall overnight into a similar madness at the first touch of government incitement to terror and blood lust.

I do not wish, however, to preach a purely negative emotional attitude; I am not suggesting that all strong feeling should be subjected to destructive analysis. I am advocating this attitude only in relation to those emotions which are the basis of collective hysteria, for it is collective hysteria that facilitates wars and dictatorships. But wisdom is not *merely* intellectual: intellect may guide and direct, but does not generate the force that leads to action. The force must be derived from the emotions. Emotions that have desirable social consequences are not so easily generated as hate and rage and fear. In their creation, much depends upon early childhood; much, also, upon economic circumstances. Something, however, can be done, in the course of ordinary education, to provide the nourishment upon which the better emotions can grow, and to bring about the realisation of what may give value to human life.

This has been, in the past, one of the purposes of religion. The Churches, however, have also had other purposes, and their dogmatic basis causes difficulties. For those to whom traditional religion is no longer possible, there are other ways. Some find what they need in music, some in poetry. For some others, astronomy serves the same purpose. When we reflect upon the size and antiquity of the stellar universe, the controversies on this rather insignificant planet lose some of their importance, and the acerbity of our disputes seems a trifle ridiculous. And when we are liberated by this negative emotion, we are able to realise more fully, through music or poetry, through history or science, through beauty or through pain, that the really valuable things in human life are individual, not such things as happen on a battlefield or in the clash of politics or in the regimented march of masses of men towards an externally imposed goal. The organised life of the community is necessary, but it is necessary as mechanism, not something to be valued on its own account. What is of most value in human life is more analogous to what all the great religious teachers have spoken of. Those who believe in the Corporate State maintain that our highest activities are collective, whereas I should maintain that we all reach our best in different ways, and that the emotional unity of a crowd can only be achieved on a lower level.

This is the essential difference between the liberal outlook and that of the totalitarian State, that the former regards the welfare of the State as residing ultimately in the welfare of the individual, while the latter regards the State as the end and individuals merely as indispensable ingredients, whose welfare must be subordinated to a mystical totality which is a cloak for the interest of the rulers. Ancient Rome had something of the doctrine of State-worship, but Christianity fought the Emperors and ultimately won. Liberalism, in valuing the individual, is carrying on the Christian tradition; its opponents are reviving certain pre-Christian doctrines. From the first, the idolators of the State have regarded education as the key to success. This appears, for example, in Fichte's *Addresses to the German Nation*, which deals at length with education. What Fichte desires is set forth in the following passage:

'If any one were to say: "How could any one demand more of an education than that it should show the pupil the right and strongly recommend it to him; whether he follows these recommendations is his own affair, and if he does not do it, his own fault; he has free will, which no education can take from him": I should answer, in order to characterise more sharply the education I contemplate, that just in this recognition of and counting on the free will of the pupil lies the first error of education hitherto and the distinct acknowledgement of its impotence and emptiness. For inasmuch as it admits that, after all its strongest operation, the will remains free, that is oscillating undecidedly between good and bad, it admits that it neither can nor wishes to mould the will, or, since will is the essential root of man, man himself; and that it holds this to be altogether impossible. The new education, on the contrary, would have to consist in a complete annihilation of the freedom of the will in the territory that it undertook to deal with.'

His reason for desiring to create 'good' men is not that they are in themselves better than 'bad' men; his reason is that 'only in such (good men) can the German nation persist, but through bad men it will necessarily coalesce with foreign countries'.

All this may be taken as expressing the exact antithesis of what the liberal educator will wish to achieve. So far from 'annihilating the freedom of the will', he will aim at strengthening individual judgement; he will instil what he can of the scientific attitude towards the pursuit of knowledge; he will try to make beliefs tentative and responsive to evidence; he will not pose before his pupils as omniscient, nor will he yield to the love of power on the pretence that he is pursuing some absolute good. Love of power is the chief danger of the educator, as of the politician; the man who can be trusted in education must care for his pupils on their own account, not merely as potential soldiers in an army of propagandists for a cause. Fichte and the powerful men who have inherited his ideals, when they see children, think: 'Here is material that I can manipulate, that I can teach to behave like a machine in furtherance of my purposes; for the moment I may be impeded by joy of life, spontaneity, the impulse to play, the desire to live for purposes springing from within, not imposed from without; but all this, after the years of schooling that I shall impose, will be dead; fancy, imagination, art, and the power of thought shall have been destroyed by obedience; the death of joy will have bred receptiveness to fanaticism; and in the end I shall find my human material as passive as stone from a quarry or coal from a mine. In the battles to which I shall lead them, some will die, some will live; those who die will die exultantly, as heroes, those who live will live on as my slaves, with that deep mental slavery to which my schools will have accustomed them.' All this, to any person with natural affection for the young, is horrible; just as we teach children to avoid being destroyed by motor cars if they can, so we should teach them to avoid being destroyed by cruel fanatics, and to this end we should seek to produce independence of mind, somewhat sceptical and wholly scientific, and to preserve, as far as possible, the instinctive joy of life that is natural to healthy children. This is the task of a liberal education: to give a sense of the value of things other than domination, to help to create wise citizens of a free community, and through the combination of citizenship with liberty in individual creativeness to enable men to give to human life that splendour which some few have shown that it can achieve.